Reminiscences
of Manchester

AND SOME OF ITS LOCAL SURROUNDINGS FROM THE YEAR 1840

BY

Louis M Hayes

Originally published by Sherratt & Hughes - 1905
Reprinted by Empire Publications - 2009

First published in 1905
This edition published 2009

This book is copyright under the Berne Convention. All rights are reserved. Apart from any fair dealing for the purpose of private study, research, criticism or review, as permitted under the Copyright Act, 1956, no part of this publication may be reproduced, stored in a retrieval system, or transmitted, in any form or by any means, electronic, electrical, chemical, mechanical, optical, photocopying, recording or otherwise, without the prior permission of the copyright owner. Enquiries should be sent to the publishers at the undermentioned address:

EMPIRE PUBLICATIONS
1 Newton Street, Manchester M1 1HW
© Empire Publications 2009

ISBN 1 901 746 55 0 - 9781901746556

Cover design and layout: Ashley Shaw

Printed in Great Britain by
D.B.P., Milton Keynes, Bucks.

*These Pages
are lovingly dedicated
to the memory
of
my dear Wife*

PREFACE

WHEN first jotting down from time to time these "Reminiscences", it was with the idea, that they might have some interest for my family circle. On this account there is therefore, a personal element running through them, which, had they been originally intended for publication would have been best left out. But to eliminate the personal matter would have involved a remodelling of the whole; so when friends to whom they were also submitted, considered that irrespective of this, these "Reminiscences" contained matter which might be of general interest, I decided to publish them in their present form.

I am aware that these jottings can lay claim to no literary merit, and my excuse for letting them go forth is that their interest may in some measure counterbalance their defects.

LOUIS M HAYES

Manchester 1905

LIST OF CONTENTS

PREFACE ix
CHAPTER I.— Introductory 5
CHAPTER II.— Faulkner Street — Dr. Dalton — Street Cries —
Chimney Climbing Children. 7
CHAPTER III.— Street Amusements and Attractions in the Old Days.
.... 11
CHAPTER IV.— Street Vendors, and their wares — Professional
Beggars — The Old Postman — The Old Woman and her Keys. 15
CHAPTER V.— On Fires (No. 1). General and Particular.
Theatre Royal, Fountain Street, May, 1844. On Fires (No. 2).
John Rylands and Sons — Robert Neill and Sons
— The Manchester Fire Brigade — Thomas Rose. 17
CHAPTER VI.— Dr. Comber's School — The Manchester Quakers. 24
CHAPTER VII.— The Mechanic's Institution. 27
CHAPTER VIII.— The Manchester Athenaeum —
Van Amburgh's Circus — Franconi's Hippodrome................ 29
CHAPTER IX.— Manchester Streets 60 years ago — Candles. 33
CHAPTER X.— Some Personal Reminiscences in connection with
St. George's, St. Jude's, and St. James's Churches. 36
CHAPTER XI.— Knott Mill Fair (No. 1) formerly called Acres Fair. 39
CHAPTER XII.— Knott Mill Fair (No. 2) — Cheap John. 43
CHAPTER XIII.— Knott Mill Fair (No. 3) — The Quack Doctor. ... 47
CHAPTER XIV.— Country Life — Old Broughton Lane —
Lodge's Nursery Gardens — Bleackley's Farm. 50
CHAPTER XV.— Cricket — The Athenaeum, and some of its
Members — Broughton Club — John Karl —
Joseph Makinson. 54
CHAPTER XVI.— The Broughton Priory — Philip Gould —
The Old River Irwell. 60
CHAPTER XVII.— William Murray, the Horsedealer —
Peace Eggers — Rushcart Bearers — Christmas Carols. 64
CHAPTER XVIII.— Broughton continued — Mr. Jackson's School
— Some of its Scholars: William Hy. Houldsworth, William
Mather. 67
CHAPTER XIX.— Broughton Schools continued — Dr. Beard's,
Mr. Makinson's, Mr. Figgins's, Mr. Dixon's — Tuck Shops. ... 73
CHAPTER XX.— Bury New Road Blackfield Lane —
Prestwich Clough. 76

CHAPTER XXI.— The Old 'Bus Office, Higher Broughton — "Joe," the Prestwich 'Bus Guard — John Stuart, Thomas Barge, Alderman Willert, Mr. Leppoc, Mr. Sale. 82
CHAPTER XXII.— Cabbage Island and the Great Cheetham Street Brickfields — The Boulder Stone in Creat Clowes Street — The Grove Inn and its Gardens. 87
CHAPTER XXIII.— Broughton continued — Bury New Road — Fairy Lane — The Old Toffee Shop — The Little Welsh Chapel — The Old Tollbar, Strangeways. 90
CHAPTER XXIV.— Cheetwood Lane. 94
CHAPTER XXV.— Strangeways Hall — The Jewish Colony. 100
CHAPTER XXVI.— The Assize Courts. 105
CHAPTER XXVII.— The Cathedral — Ben Lang's — Old Deansgate — John Heywood. 113
CHAPTER XXVIII.— Bridge Street — The Shambles — The Queen's Theatre — The Coldbeaters, Whaites's — The Taylor Tragedy — Execution of Allen, Gould and Larkin. 129
CHAPTER XXIX.— Lower King Street — The Star Hotel — Business Recollections. 134
CHAPTER XXX.— John Dalton Street. 138
CHAPTER XXXI.— Princess Street. 140
CHAPTER XXXII.— Bond Street — Portland Street. 144
CHAPTER XXXIII.— St. Ann's Square. 150
CHAPTER XXXIV.— The Old Manchester Arcade. 159
CHAPTER XXXV.— King Street — Brown Street. 166
CHAPTER XXXVI.— Market Street — Piccadilly — London Road Station. 174
CHAPTER XXXVII.— Manchester Coach, Cab, Omnibus and Tram Traffic, past and present. 178
CHAPTER XXXVIII.— Ardwick Green and its Surroundings. 184
CHAPTER XXXIX.— Plymouth Grove — Lime Grove — Greenheys Lane. 189
CHAPTER XL.— The Manchester Art Treasures Exhibition, 1857. 196
CHAPTER XLI.— The Great Flood of 1866. 205
CHAPTER XLII.— Our Manchester Moors. 209
CHAPTER XLIII.— The Late Queen's First Visit to Manchester. ... 218
CHAPTER XLIV.— The 5th of November — St. Valentine's Day. ... 223
CHAPTER XLV.— Mental Epidemics — Table Turning — Spirit Rapping — Clairvoyance — Dark Sceances — The 15 Puzzle — The Comic Song Craze — Other National Periodical Weaknesses. 228
CHAPTER XLVI.— Stage Recollections — A Few Introductory Remarks.......... 236
CHAPTER XLVII.— Stage Recollections, continued. 244
CHAPTER XLVIII.— Stage Recollections, continued. 254
CHAPTER XLIX.— Stage Recollections, continued. 263
CHAPTER XL.— Stage Recollections, continued. 269

CHAPTER LI.— Stage Recollections, continued. 276
CHAPTER LII.— The Growth of Music in Manchester during the last fifty years — Charles Hallé — The Monday Evening Concerts — Catherine Hayes — Sims Reeves — Henry Russell — Mons. Julien. 282
CHAPTER LIII.— Old Manchester Faces. 289
CHAPTER LIV.— The Manchester Chess Club. March 12th, 1897. 317
CHAPTER LV.— Some of the Churches and Chapels of Manchester and Salford, and their past Ministers — St. Simon's and the Rev. Ephraim Harper — St. Alban's and the Rev. J. E. Sedgwick. 327
CHAPTER LVI.— Canon McGrath — Canon Bardsley — Canon Hugh Stowell — Doctor Parker. 333
CHAPTER LVII.— Trinity Presbyterian Church and the Rev. William McCaw — Chorlton Road Chapel and the Rev. J. L. Macfadyen — Union Chapel and the Rev. Alexander MacLaren — The Rev. Arthur Mursell — St. Alban's and the Rev. Knox —Little. 339
CHAPTER LVIII.— The Wesleyan Body and H. R. Harrison — Dr. McKerrow and Lloyd St. Chapel — Dr. Cuthrie, of Edinburgh — The late Bishop Fraser. 345

ABOUT THE AUTHOR

LOUIS MILROY HAYES, son of commission agent, Richard Hayes, was born in Temple Street, Cholton-on-Medlock in 1836. Hayes was one of 13 children.

According to his obituary in the *Manchester Evening News* of 29th April 1912, "Mr Hayes was one of the oldest oil merchants in the city and long had resided in Higher Broughton. In 1905 he published a volume of 'Reminiscences of Manchester' in which his recollections of social and commercial Manchester during an extended period were narrated in a most memorable and interesting manner"

Contemporary Reviews of Reminiscences of Manchester

Published 1905 - Sherratt & Hughes - 27 St Ann's St, Manchester - 6 shillings - 5d. postage

Manchester City News - 15th July 1905

MOST MEN WHO have lived to three-score years and ten have a somewhat hazy remembrance of what their native town looked half a century ago. Mr Hayes is fortunate both in having a good memory and in having taken copious notes throughout his life on anything that seemed to his interest.

He jotted down these 'Reminiscences' with the idea that they might be of interest to his own family. To the wider public they have, therefore, the advantage which comes from a lack of pretentiousness. Mr Hayes modestly disclaims literary merit but his book has the literary merit of directness and simplicity. It is really all the better for being without affectation or art. It is brightly and racily written, fabulously illustrated and there is scarcely a dull page in it.

Without doubt Manchester folk, both young and old, will heartily welcome these reminiscences of the past. Mr Hayes' book is full of quaint and picturesque things but in many ways we may be glad that times have changed. We should say that the Manchester of today is a much more healthy and comfortable place to live in than the Manchester of fifty years ago described so graphically in these pages.

Manchester Guardian - 17th July 1905

MR HAYES HAS produced a book of gossip about Victorian Manchester, which can be read with pleasure.

The bygone glories of Knott Mill Fair left a vivid impression on his youthful mind. His recollection of past theatrical and musical notabilities are full of interest. His book contains much pleasant gossip and information that will help towards an accurate idea of the Manchester of our fathers.

GLASGOW HERALD - 13TH JULY 1905

THIS IS A book that ought to be appreciated by all who know and are interested in Manchester. Mr Hayes has much to record in the way of civic, commercial, political and philanthropic progress. He does so in a manner that is pleasant from its straightforward simplicity and if the personal comment is rather pronounced, that is a matter which may well be excused in circumstances by those local readers for whom the book is specially intended.

THE SPECTATOR - 29TH JUNE 1905

ANYONE WHO CAN recollect Manchester as it was 60 years ago has much to tell us. Most of the personages mentioned in Mr Hayes' pages have or had a local reputation. It is not often that we find Mr Hayes wanting: he has widely extended tastes and he has evidently been in the habit of keeping his eyes open. Among the curiosities of his book is the nature of the 'Manchester Moors'. It is interesting to know that golf was played on Kersal Moor as long as half a century ago.

THE SCOTSMAN - 29TH JUNE 1905

THIS IS A talkative, cheerful and interesting book of memories of Manchester during the past half century and more. The book touches in one way or another, on all the aspects of life of the busy, thriving city. An attractive book for Manchester men, it should also be read with enjoyment by any reader with a special interest in English social history. The volume is graced with many appropriate photographical pictures.

CHESTER COURANT - 5TH JULY 1905

CITIZENS OF MANCHESTER and Lancashire men in

general will welcome this contribution to local literature. The author, Mr Louis M Hayes, disclaims any pretensions to literary merit and so far as rhetorical style goes, he makes no apparent effort, but the book as a whole is a contribution to local literature. It is written in a loose, easy gossipy manner. In his description of its street scenes, social manners and customs of olden days, the author appeals to a wider audience that that of Manchester, for everbody will delight in the accounts of the old chimney-climbing boys, the quaint street vendors, professional mendicants, the Cheap Johns and the quack physicians who used to be in evidence at Knott Mill Fair. Mr Hayes is to be congratulated on the success of his labours. The addition of copious illustrations - well executed, is a great advantage.

CHAPTER I

Introductory.

WHEN Charles Dickens in his tale of "The Haunted Man," brought the book to its close with these words:

"Lord keep my memory green,"

he gave expression to one of those prayers which finds an echo in the breast of almost every human being. And with most of us I think, the longer we live the more fully we recognise the spirit and significance which lie hidden in these few simple words. For is it not a fact that when we commence to look back through a long vista of years, the bright and the happy incidents of our lives come trooping back to us, whilst on the other hand, the troubles, the anxieties and the disappointments, which were so terribly real when they were with us, have altogether faded away? Or should some of them still remain with us, they are so mellowed and softened by Time's healing hand, that all the sting and bitterness has passed out of them. And so it happens that as a rule only the bright and sunny portions of our past lives come back to us with any permanent distinctness; and it is the memory of these that we love to keep green.

It is then in such a spirit as this that my thoughts revert back to dear old Manchester; and although it is impossible to forget its inky streams, its sad and dingy-looking streets, its soot-begrimed buildings, its uninviting slums, and courts, and alleys, I am not ashamed to say that I am proud of my native town, and that in spite of all its drawbacks, it will, from early associations, always be endeared to me.

And first let me say in introducing these reminiscences to my readers, that having been jotted down in an irregular and disjointed fashion from time to time, they are quite devoid of literary merit, but yet notwithstanding this, I am in hopes that from a local standpoint, they may not be found altogether uninteresting.

The changes which have taken place in and about Manchester since I first drew breath in a house in Temple Street, on the banks of the river Medlock, have been many and great. The advance, whether it be civic, commercial, political or philanthropic, has been steady, rapid and material. Our local men have been no idlers in this hive of industry, but have by energy, determination and perseverance, made for their City a reputation of which we have reason to be proud, and which is worldwide in its character.

I wonder if any of my readers have lately paid a visit to Temple Street, Chorlton-on-Medlock. The spot is now, alas, neither attractive nor cheerful, and yet as I remember it over sixty years ago, the dwelling-houses had pleasant grassy slopes down to the water-side. And the water, well, at anyrate it was water, not ink; perhaps not either the sweetest or the purest, but absolutely pellucid as compared with its present condition. The houses had their long stretches of back gardens facing towards the river, the beds profusely bordered with oyster shells, which must, I presume, have been the fashion in those days. The doors to these gardens were provided with small square openings, sufficiently high and large to permit of the admission of a person's head, and so in this way orders could be given and received without having to open the larger door. My reason for remembering these apertures is, that there was a butcher's boy who came for his orders, and when he found me playing in the garden, he amused himself by making at me the most horrible grimaces, which used to send me howling into the house.

By the way, how is it that generally butcher's boys are, and have been more or less aggressive in their nature? They have certain characteristics which distinguish them from other boys. They have red chubby faces and are anything but shy. They are apt to bully other boys who are not as big as themselves, whilst a street disturbance or an upset of any kind, will usually find them interested spectators. They distinctly favour fast trotting ponies whilst executing their orders, driving them sharply and suddenly round street corners, and they delight to come upon you just when you least expect them, and this they do in a bold, "why don't you get out of the way" sort of style. There are few things that timid folk dread more than a typical butcher's boy, with his determined little pony coming clattering noisily along the road, with very little modesty of demeanour, and with still less consideration for those with whom he may come into contact. What an ideal butcher's boy dearly loves is a race with some rival, then he is on his metal, and he may be seen tearing along at full tilt, scattering the cocks and hens in all directions, and only truly happy when he has distanced his competitor regardless of consequences.

I regret I am not able to give about C.-on-M. and its neighbourhood, any valuable statistics, but at the ripe age of four one does not take many detailed notes of passing events. Still, although somewhat misty, my impressions of that time were certainly pleasant, and those days come back to me bright, happy and sunny. We owned a huge dog named "Fly," but why "Fly" I know not, unless in contra-distinction to his size, as he would have made two or three of most dogs about, yet although massive he was gentle enough, and he and I were excellent friends.

Our family was large, the children thirteen to the dozen, which, with the father and mother, gave a total of fifteen. When gathered for meals we almost required counting, and having been gifted by Nature with good appetites and digestions, we did our duty nobly, which I have no doubt the bread bill testified.

CHAPTER II

Faulkner Street — Dr. Dalton — Street Cries — Chimney Climbing Children.

I was about four years of age when the family of which I was the most youthful member, removed to Faulkner Street, then I think, entirely consisting of private dwelling-houses. To me it was simply an indistinct merging of one house into another, assuming a more definite shape in my mind by a death in the family. I was too young to realise its true sadness, but I can remember the stillness, and the blinds all down, and my curiosity getting the better of me and peeping through the side of the blind, to see the hearse with black, waving plumes. Then I drew back startled, and saw the tear-stained faces, and I realised in a dull kind of way that death was there.

Dr. Dalton[1] lived in Faulkner Street, where he died, and we lived exactly opposite. His funeral, which was a public one, was the largest that had ever taken place in Manchester. I can call to mind the people passing to and fro as he lay there, but what more especially impressed itself on my mind in connection with it, was the sight of a leaden pipe which, attached to the coffin, had its exit outside the window. Of course I had many opportunities of seeing the great John Dalton, but to me he was a very ordinary-looking individual with a white cravat. I am

---

1. John Dalton FRS (Fellow of the Royal Society) (1766-1844), founded modern atomic theory. He joined the Manchester Literary and Philosophical Society in 1800 and in 1807 published his landmark Atomic Theory. Dalton became president of the Lit & Phil in 1817 until his death. He was ranked 32nd most influential figure in histroy (behind The Prophet Muhammed) by Michael H Hart in his book "The 100".

afraid that at this time of life I attached more importance to the muffin-man, who certainly made more noise in the world (my world) as he came daily along the street on his rounds, with his bell tinkling to let buyers know he was there, and with a clean white napkin laid over his muffins and crumpets to keep them warm.

By the way, street hawking, as it existed fifty years ago, has practically become a thing of the past. One quite misses the old familiar cry of "Shrimps! fresh Shrimps! fine fresh Shrimps!" or the gutteral tones of the cockleman, as his voice, hoarse with shouting, would be heard calling out: "Cawkills alive! alive! alive." I almost think I had a dread of this particular man, for he came when it was dark with a dingy-looking barrow. He was certainly not clean and far from good looking, whilst his voice was a remnant of bygone days. His vocal chords being sadly out of condition, the sounds which escaped from him were weird in the extreme; sometimes bass, sometimes treble, terminating at times in a low stage whisper.

There was also to me, something mysterious about the old watchman who went his nightly rounds, a long while after I had retired to rest, and he at times awoke me by calling out the hour, with an occasional intimation as to whether the night was fine, wet or stormy. To some, such information may have been acceptable, whilst others, probably, would have preferred to take the night on trust, and sleep.

Another interesting couple were the sweep and his little boy, and their plaintive cry of: "weep, wee-ep," could be heard a long way off. In those days the boy was the brush and had to creep up the chimney to bring the soot down. A feeling of uncomfortable fascination possessed me as I used to watch the little fellow having his head covered with a sooty nightcap, and then pushed up the dirty chimney. The grate was then covered with sacking, and all you heard was the knock, knock of the boy's little brush, with an occasional admonition from his master shouted from the other side of the sacking. Then the boy would struggle down again apparently none the worse for the journey, and doff his dirty black nightcap, looking very much like a little statue worked in black, except for some very white teeth, two red lips, and the clear whites of two eyes. The boys seemed to think very little of what they had to do, but as one realises the cruel life to which these children were apprenticed, the wonder is that such a system was ever tolerated. Even in my young mind the whole performance inspired me with a feeling of interested dread, coupled with a desire that I might not be spirited away and transformed into a climbing boy. And yet when these small black sprites reached terra-firma again, they would be as lively as grigs, and would make very short work of a huge slice of bread and butter which I would have ready for them when they re-appeared out of the chimney. It astonished me to see how regardless they were of the fact, that after handling the bread and butter, it was soon nearly as black as themselves. Perhaps the soot gave a special relish to their food.

CHAPTER III

Street Amusements and Attractions in the Old Days.

THERE is no doubt that more especially for young people the streets had many attractions in bygone days. Punch and Judy, for example, was quite a stock entertainment, and could always command a good audience amongst both old and young. There was also the family group who seemed to live on stilts, and occupants of the upper stories were apt to be startled by the sudden appearance of a face at the window, unable to realise for a moment how it came there. The man with his organ was a regular visitor, nearly always accompanied by his clever little monkey, often dressed in military attire, who would go through his evolutions and handle a gun or a sword in first-rate style. There was also the "Buy a broom" girl, a dark-skinned gipsy, with black glossy hair, who dressed in the gayest of colours, and danced and sang her quaint little songs; whilst her little white wooden broom, with its brush of closely-curled spiral shavings, had always a ready sale, more especially when the onlookers were appealed to by a gaily-dressed foreigner adorned with a wealth of massive jewellery.

The Hurdy-gurdy, a cross between a 'cello and a primitive barrel organ, was manipulated by an Italian boy with bronzed features, tyrolese hat, jacket, gay sash, and leggings and gaiters to match. The instrument of musical torture is now happily a thing of the past, but without doubt what the Hurdy-gurdy lacked in melody, was made up for by the merry gambols and the voluble jargon of its performer, who gave a pleasant colour and brightness to Manchester's dingy streets.

Whenever the acrobat and conjuror combined, appeared upon the scene, a crowd quickly gathered, and the feats performed were always watched with absorbing interest. More particularly the cup and ball trick, which consisted in throwing up high into the air a heavy iron ball, and catching it in a metal cup, placed for the purpose, just at the nape of the neck. As the ball descended it looked as if it would crash into the performer's head, but although his back was turned to the ball, it never missed its goal but came down with a heavy thud, into its tin socket. This man usually concluded his performance by a promise, with a proviso. It was to balance his donkey on the top of a ladder, whilst one upright of the ladder rested on his chin.

The proviso was: "Now ladies and gentlemen, tuppence more and up goes the donkey!" This exclamation came after he had apparently drained his audience dry, and so he usually moved on before the extra "tuppence" was to the fore. In this event the youthful portion of his audience followed on, in his wake, hoping for better success at his next stoppage.

Of course, now-a-days, young people are generally to be found taking these amusements, comfortably seated in some theatre or circus, or the performers are specially ordered up to their private houses. Then, however, we were content to enjoy them looking out of a window, or standing in the street. There was then no scarcity of street minstrels, vocal and instrumental. One of the latter, whom I well remember, was a decrepit old singer with a remarkably red nose and a broken-winded clarinet, who shuffled along in an absent-minded manner, regardless of time or weather. In fact I almost think he selected the particularly wet and dismal days for his peregrinations, in order that his bedraggled appearance might call forth more active sympathy on his behalf.

There was also a well organised family group of vocalists, who as they came along the street, were sufficiently numerous to spread themselves comfortably across the roadway. The father would be usually seen dragging two ragged little urchins along, whilst the mother beside him would have a baby in her arms, and another mite would be hanging on to the skirts of her dress. Then there would be a girl of about sixteen with excellent lungs, and a voice so piercingly shrill, that it went through you like a knife. At one moment the mother would be singing deep contralto, at the next she would wander into a cracked soprano, very much the worse for wear.

The father usually affected a deep bass, but when he failed to reach the required depth, he obligingly varied it with a thin falsetto, also much the worse for wear. It was really quite a work of art the way in which the elder ones of the party sidled along in a sort of stage glide, of about three paces at a time, when they would all come to a stop, in order that the listeners might have more leisure to enjoy their vocal efforts. Then the father would air that lovely top note of his, glancing up furtively at the windows as he did so, accompanied by an appealing look and a shiver. That shiver was his special *"pièce de résistance,"* which was meant to touch the hearts and more especially to open the purses of each and all. As to the singing the tune and the words appeared to be a very minor consideration, the heights and the hollows were what they aimed at, and providing that these were sufficiently loud and pronounced to attract attention, their object was attained.

One of the ballads most favoured by the vocal "dismals" commenced as follows:

A baby was sleeping,
Its mother was weeping,
Whilst her husb i and was far,
O'er the wild raging sea.
The tide it was swelling,
Round the fisherman's dwelling,
When she cried Dermot dear,
Oh! come back to me.

I am afraid the general effect produced by this class of ballad singing was irritation of the nerves, and listeners willingly gave something to get them to "move on." And yet, at the same time, it was comical to see this man to whom I more especially refer, in his intensely shabby, genteel attire, combining a dilapidated frock coat and a greasy-looking silk hat, in the latter of which he caught the coppers which were thrown to him, each contributor being favoured with a sickly smile of thanks as he passed on from street to street.

CHAPTER IV

Street Vendors and their wares – Professional Beggars – The Old Postman – The Old Woman and her Keys.

IN the good old days street life had many other interesting phases, which are now altogether absent. There was, for instance, the brazier and tinman who came along with his little fire and bellows, and who would solder and repair your pots, pans and tinware on the "while you wait" principle. He was a handy little man in many ways, and the youngsters who happened to be about were always interested spectators of any work he might have in hand. Then the rag-and-bone man was an individual whose approach I welcomed, for his barrow was always gaily decorated with coloured paper flags, fastened to long thin laths. These small flags revolved like a windmill as you ran them along before you, and were a great attraction to the children. It was an astonishment to me how dirty-looking old rags and bones could possibly be a profitable exchange for these bright-looking wares, but it was evident the rag-and-bone man knew more than I did. Amongst other passers there was the vendor of water-cress, and when he or she came along we realised more distinctly that summer was nigh. There was also the woman who carried a small hosier's shop in her basket. She had laces, cottons, hairpins, and ribbons temptingly displayed, hooks and eyes, thimbles, buttons, and so on. I preferred her cotton balls as they served wherewith to fly my kites.

There was quite an array of professional beggars who periodically came their rounds. There was the blind man with his dog, the latter with a tin mug tied round his neck, and from the rattle of which the beggar could tell when anyone had dropped in a copper. The animal, to all appearances, was a gloomy, sulky-looking specimen, and my impression was that he rather bullied his master, for he dragged him along at the end of his chain in a very determined, ill-tempered kind of style, as much as to say: "Now then, hurry up old man, I really can't waste my time with you here all day," and he would illustrate the mood he was in by another vicious pull at his chain.

There was one beggar who came along with only one leg, and another who had no legs at all. The latter had himself fastened on to a square board with a small wheel at each corner, on which he was able to work himself over the ground both quickly and easily. He had wooden pattens attached to his hands, and with the help of these and the wheels, he managed to get along quite comfortably. There was another unfortunate creature, a man with a diseased arm, who was always most anxious to show you how bad it was, and was quite hurt if you objected. I did get a sight of it once, and this was more than sufficient for me.

There was a poor demented old woman who also frequented the streets in those days. She used to be neatly dressed with a white apron and old poke bonnet, and she always carried about a large door-key which dangled ostentatiously from one of her fingers. From her remarks she evidently had the impression that she was the custodian of the bottomless pit, and from the strength of her language the Pope and she were on anything but good terms. The very mention of his name would rouse her to fury, and knowing this the people who followed her played upon her weakness. Of course the more she was jeered at and teased the more angry she became, and if anyone came in reach of the door-key she made them feel it.

CHAPTER V

On Fires (No. 1). General and Particular.
Theatre Royal, Fountain Street, May, 1844

I am afraid the young people of the present generation have sadly degenerated in the amount of interest displayed by them in regard to fires. That is to say they are altogether too blasé to tumble quickly out of bed at the first sound of a fire alarm, and rush off regardless of appearances, to any point of the compass so as to arrive as nearly first as possible at the scene of the conflagration. When I was young the sound of a fire-bell was like music to my ear, and its effect almost magical. I dressed in no time and was there in less, and I am afraid, too, the motives which prompted such speed were not of the highest order. In fact, I must confess to a very distinct feeling of disappointment, if after arrival on the spot, I found the fire had been subdued, and so could not participate in the excitement. I had received what might have been termed my baptism of fire at the early age of seven, having then been an eye-witness of the great fire which occurred in 1844, in a large pile of buildings fronting to York Street and George Street, when damage to the extent of about £140,000 was incurred. Living in Faulkner Street the back of our house looked directly on to this block of buildings, so that we enjoyed what might have been termed a dress-circle view of this huge conflagration. It was a time of intense excitement, and I am afraid that I bore my baptism of fire none too bravely, showing then no outside indications of blossoming into a Salamander in after years. In fact, it must be confessed, that as anything like a hero I was a miserable failure. When I saw the flames bursting out of the roof of the buildings, my courage, if I ever possessed any, oozed out of my finger ends, and I cried out in terror.

At the same time there was a fascination which kept my eyes fixed on those tongues of fire leaping high up into the air. It seemed to me as if our house was also doomed, and to soothe my fears I was taken from the back to the front of the house, but in my fright it appeared to me as if the other side of Faulkner Street was also ablaze, whereas it was but the reflection of the flames in the windows of the houses opposite. My first thought, therefore, was how to escape, so I at once rushed down the stairs, taking as I did so the clothes I found lying about in my anxiety to save something; and as these belonged to members of the family who had not yet risen, some temporary inconvenience was caused. At this time it seemed to dawn upon the household that it might be better to transfer me to some place of safety where I could take a more rational view of things, so I was taken to some friends in George Street with whom I remained until all danger was over. For some time the firemen were doubtful as to whether our house could be saved; however, acting on their instructions, blankets soaked in water were fastened over the blistering woodwork of the windows, and thus prevented the fire spreading to Faulkner Street. At one period, however, the danger was so great, that they ordered the furniture to be moved out; this was done, our friends and neighbours assisting, everyone taking what they liked and carrying it where they pleased. We had no idea where the half of our household effects had disappeared to, but somehow when all risk was over, they seemed to mysteriously float back to us from all quarters, and by evening the house was refurnished once more and it was said that our net loss was a broken wineglass.

It is a curious, almost melancholy experience to wonder over the ruins of a large fire. I can remember doing so when the Theatre Royal, in Fountain Street, was burned down to the ground on the 7th of May, 1844. In rambling over its charred remains I no doubt hoped to light upon some treasure, for to a young mind there is something weird and mysterious in all that lies hidden behind the stage curtain of a theatre. You are however, soon undeceived. What appeared to you before as massive rich and spacious, you discover on examination to be often cramped, tawdry and mean and as you chance across a scrap of a flaring dress, a remnant of tin armour, or a stage jewel, you realise that "All is not gold that glitters."

During the course of my life I have been the eye-witness of many a stirring scene at one fire or another, and after all it is a grand sight to see the huge flames leaping up high into the air, with a loud crackling noise as they burst through the windows and roof of some doomed building, devouring its contents with a greedy hissing roar. What a beautiful sight it is when the roof is falling in to see those myriads of sparks shoot upwards into the sky. Then as floor after floor falls into the huge burning cauldron, the walls and become red hot, until you are driven back by the intense heat, and obliged to hide your eyes and cover your mouth to protect you from the choking dense smoke. You see the firemen working at some point of danger, clearly defined by the glare of the flames, until they are compelled to beat a hasty retreat, and all hope of saving the building has gone. Such a scene is thrilling and exciting, and is not easily forgotten, even after a lapse of many years.

*

On Fires (No. 2). John Rylands and Sons – Robert Neill and Sons – The Manchester Fire Brigade – Thomas Rose.

TO describe a tithe of the fires in which I have more or less participated would not be an easy matter, but the mention of one or two may not be without interest. There was the one which took place at John Rylands and Sons, High Street, on the 1st of March, 1854. It was not only large, but it was more especially dangerous from the fact that it occurred at a spot where it was separated from large and numerous adjacent buildings, by only exceptionally narrow streets on all sides. The firemen fought with great determination and bravery against the flames, and succeeded in preventing the fire spreading to a large number of other warehouses. I was returning with some members of my family from an evening party, when, on issuing from the house, which was in Cooper Street, we saw the sky reflecting the flames, and hurried away at once to the scene of the conflagration. It was a grand sight and it was wonderful how such a large crowd had so quickly gathered, notwithstanding the lateness of the hour at which the fire had broken out.

Another fire of note at which I was present occurred at the works and offices of Robert Neill and Sons, Sherbourne Street, Strangeways. Owing to the huge stacks of timber stored in and on the premises, the blaze was magnificent and presented the appearance of an immense furnace of flame, which might have satisfied even the heart of a Nero. What helped to heighten the grandeur of the spectacle was that the flames spread across the bridge to the other side of the river, and it happened in this way. The roadway over the bridge had been newly asphalted and was set ablaze by the burning embers falling upon it, giving the whole scene the semblance of a pyrotechnic display. It is astonishing how some people lose their heads at a fire. At this one, I remember, that the portions of the offices which were furthest removed from the flames, and in no immediate danger, were besieged by a number of early arrivals on the scene, who thought the beat way to help was to rush upstairs into the various rooms, open the windows and commence pitching down everything that they could lay their hands on. Tables, chairs, plans, drawings, all came higgledy-piggledy down into the street, and as these offfices were in the end saved from the flames, it will be seen that the hurried and mistaken zeal of these amateur salvage brokers, resulted in much more damage and confusion than if they had stayed at home and lain peacefully in their beds. Of course when the regular firemen got possession this irregular work was quickly put an end to.

By the way, it is wonderful to see the number of babies

who attend fires. Their mothers take the fire craze as badly as most people, and so as they often cannot leave their little ones at home, they take them along with them rather than miss the excitement. These small specimens of humanity are usually in great glee, and may be seen clapping their hands as if the whole entertainment had been especially provided for their amusement.

Whilst on this subject of fires I would like to say a word or two with regard to the splendid work that has been done by the Manchester Fire Brigade. Even fifty years ago they were a body of efficient, brave men, well-drilled, well-officered, and equal to any emergency. They were no doubt especially fortunate in having, first William Rose, and then his son Thomas for their chief superintendent. The father I do not remember, but Thomas Rose in his prime was a splendid man for the position he occupied. He was both tall and handsome, and although altogether too bulky to pass for an Adonis, yet still he carried the weight which was allotted to him with an ease and elasticity of step which seemed to defy fatigue. He looked the very beau-ideal of a fireman, as he came dashing along the streets on one of his engines, armed cap-a-pie for some struggle with his arch enemy. At times in the urgency of a call he might be seen hurriedly buckling on his belt; round his not too slender waist as the engine which bore him flew past to its destination. He shared every danger with his men, and it was an interesting sight to see him directing their efforts from some giddy height, and shouting to them with his powerful voice. Quick and resourceful he seemed to grasp the whole situation as he arrived on the scene, and always appeared to realise where best to direct the energies of his men. Having once made up his mind what to do he carried out his plans with wonderful rapidity and determination.

The old Town's Yard used to stand on a portion of the ground now occupied by the new Town Hall. It was a good open space surrounded by the necessary buildings required by the Brigade. Here the men were most carefully drilled

THE OLD TOWN'S YARD (DEMOLISHED 1866)

Site of the present Town Hall, Manchester

by Thomas Rose, and they went through their interesting evolutions in the centre of this yard, and at times the gates were allowed to be open when people could watch what was going on. He even went to the trouble of building a sham wooden house at times, which would be set on fire, so as to practise his men with the life-saving apparatus.

For many years Thomas Rose was one of the most notable personages in our Manchester life, and he had the respect of all who knew him. As he had always to be on the spot in case of any sudden call to duty, he usually spent his evenings in the dress-circle of the Theatre Royal, where he could be found when wanted. And when you saw someone come in and whisper to him, you always knew there was a fire, and the question you had then to consider was which had the greater attraction – the play or the fire.

It was a great loss to Manchester when Thomas Rose resigned his position of Superintendent of the Fire Brigade, but he continued to take an active part in the Municipal affairs of the City. Then he unfortunately fell into bad health, attacked by a wasting disease which played havoc with his splendid constitution and robust, manly form, until at last he became the very ghost of his former self. When you happened to meet him as he came creeping along, or driving past in his victoria, you could not help turning sorrowfully away, as you remembered what he had been, and saw what he then was.

Manchester may, and will have, many Fire Superintendents, but I do not think we shall have again a man who occupied amongst us such a unique position in the Brigade as did Thomas Rose, for he was a man who not only took a pride in the duties he was called upon to perform, but he was one who had also the true interests of our City at heart.

CHAPTER VI

Dr. Comber's School – The Manchester Quakers

DOCTOR COMBER, the Quaker, and his school, formed one of my pleasantest recollections before the time came when I personally was found "creeping like snail unwillingly to school." The school stood next to the Quaker's Chapel in Mount Street, but it has now entirely disappeared, the Comedy, now the Gaiety, Theatre occupying the bulk of the ground on which it stood. As some of my brothers and sisters attended "Charley" Comber's school, as it was familiarly called, I, being a youngster, had the run of the playgrounds, which were partly underneath the classrooms, and thus sheltered in a measure from the rain. It was a mixed school of boys and girls, but of course they were taught in separate rooms, and the Doctor occupied a high stool at a desk in a recess, which oversighted both chambers, and where he could keep a watchful eye on all that was going on. Well, no, perhaps not on all, for when one girl would come up to the Doctor to ask him some question, it was not an unusual thing for a boy to be seized with a desire to also consult him. And so when this happened I fancy even the Doctor's eyes did not see everything; eyes can speak as well as tongues, even those of quiet-looking little Quaker girls and boys. When I was young I believe I was an innocent-looking small boy, and that at times I acted as one of Cupid's postmen, and did not object to carry notes between one side of the school and the other, having the entry to both the boys' and the girls' playgrounds. I suppose it was wrong to do so, but I do not remember that I troubled myself on this score, more especially as I have no doubt the senders of these missives did not forget the little postman.

Doctor Comber being a Quaker, it was, of course, the

natural thing for all the Quakers to send their children there. He was a kindly man as schoolmasters go, and had the respect of those whom he taught, but boys and girls are pretty much alike – even Quakers,– and I could point today to some white-haired gentlemen in Manchester, old scholars, who could relate many an amusing and interesting incident which happened in this old school in Mount Street. At times the good old Doctor would have to go out, leaving the school in charge of some junior Master. If he were not a favourite an evil spirit seemed to seize upon the boys' side of the school and they would defy his authority. I remember hearing of one boy who, after defying the Junior, and being chased round the desks and forms, rushed down the stairs into the coalhole, whence he returned with a huge cob of coal which he threatened to throw at the head of the Master if he dared to touch him. But, as we read in some of the books for children, it was a very naughty boy who behaved like this, and I have no doubt he suffered for his misdeeds.

Thursday morning being the day on which the Quakers attended Chapel, this was constituted the half-holiday, and a very pretty and interesting sight it was to see them gathering for worship, in their quaint but becoming attire. The men in their broad-brimmed drab or black beaver hats, grey or mulberry-coloured coats, light waistcoats, ample white neckcloths, frilled shirts and knee breeches. The women came in plain, sober-coloured, but rich silk dresses, their long, pointed shawls, and coalscuttle bonnets. Everything they wore, if simple, was good, and it was quite an attractive sight to see them filing into Chapel, arm in arm, husband and wife, with their children led by the hand, placid and serene; an old-time picture, which I fear would now look sadly out of place in the present hurry and bustle of our Manchester streets, and yet sixty years ago the Quakers of Manchester were a large and important community, and without doubt exercised a beneficial influence upon us both commercially and socially. Engaged in the various branches of trade, they were noted for their integrity of purpose, and for their straightforward dealing in the conduct of their affairs. Socially they were simple and kindly in their bearing; and their home life was characterised by the charm of genial warm-hearted hospitality. In my early years I was thrown much into their society, and feel I was the better for it. They were always ready to do a kindness to anyone, and were charitable in every sense of the word.

Amongst the names of Quaker families I can call to mind, there are the Robinsons, the Labreys, the Frys, the Broadfields, the Woodheads, the Rookes, the Whitlows and the Kings, and even their mention recalls very many pleasant recollections, for they remind me of bright, happy days with which these names and those of others are interwoven, and it is therefore with a feeling of sadness I realise that these old associations are altogether a thing of the past.

CHAPTER VII

The Mechanic's Institution

THE old Mechanic's Institution, founded 1825 (now merged into, and re-christened the Technical School, in Princess Street), used to be in Cooper Street, in the building opposite the side of the present Town Hall. It was a place started for the improvement, intellectually and socially, of the working and middle-classes; subscription 5s. per quarter. Exhibitions and entertainments of an educational and interesting character were from time to time held in it, and as we lived near at hand it was a kind of rendezvous for the young people of the families round about. I remember there was an Exhibition held there of Home and Foreign products and curiosities, and being exhibitors the family had a season ticket, enabling me to go to it whenever I wished, and I wished very often, as did also my young friends. I have a strong conviction that the officials would often have preferred our room to our company, as we practically turned the building into a playground, and rambled over the whole place as if it belonged to us. We were nearly always somewhere where we had no right to be, and in one kind of mischief or another. I have the impression that those officials did not love us over much, and would probably have jumped at the opportunity of selling us into slavery like Joseph of old, and so getting quit of us. But we trotted about perfectly happy and contented, and ready for every new piece of excitement which happened to come in our way, or even out of it. There was a Centrifugal, or "Loop the Loop" Railway, as it is now called, which was very much patronised by those who had a weakness for being sent spinning round and round like a human pinwheel. I must say it was always somewhat of a relief to see the cars reach the terminus platform in safety. Accidents were not numerous, but I understand some gentleman named Mr. Dean did break an arm whilst travelling in this railway.

Another object of interest was the Galvanic Battery, which gave you all kinds of shocks, strong or mild as desired. One time when boasting to my companion that I could take the strongest indicator point shock, I illustrated my ability to do so by taking hold of the handles with both hands after pushing the needle to full strength. When doing so I had been careful to see that the battery had been disconnected. I pretended by my grimaces to be having a tremendous shock, when one of the party slipped quietly beneath the table and made the connection, and then I found my hands glued to the handles whilst I was in an agony and kicking out in all directions. Fortunately somebody soon took pity on me and I was released, and I expect the boy who played me the trick had another kind of shock afterwards.

Lectures were given from time to time in the large hall or theatre, varied by magic-lantern exhibitions. One evening whilst waiting for the views to be thrown on to the screen, a companion dared me to stand in front of the sheet just as the light was thrown upon it, so without pausing to consider, I jumped up and in a moment was in full view of the audience, whilst I obliged the company with my ugliest face. Having thus disgraced the family I was taken in hand and I have little doubt I made more grimaces in consequence, before I was permitted to retire to bed for the night. It so often happens that what appears at first sight as a capital joke, turns out to be no joke at all. This is a moral reflection intended for the young, more especially for those who wish to be funny.

CHAPTER VIII

The Manchester Athenaeum – Van Amburgh's Circus Franconi's Hippodrome

THE MANCHESTER ATHENAEUM, facing what was then called Bond Street, was opened in the year 1889, and was a great boon to the inhabitants of Manchester, as a centre for the development of the intellectual and physical aspirations of the people, for which, up to this time, there had been no material opening. On October 2nd, 1848, a bazaar was held in the Free Trade Hall, in aid of its funds, and a Soiree on October 3rd, over which Charles Dickens presided, and which was attended by eminent literary men. There was another Soiree held the following year at which Benjamin Disraeli was present amongst others, which helped to make the work its members were doing more widely known. There was an excellent Literary and Discussion Society, and a large hall where readings and entertainments were given. Amongst these there used to be an annual Assault-at-Arms, where interesting exhibitions of Fencing, Singlestick, Sword Exercises and Boxing were given. At my age these were what appealed more directly to me, and especially as an elder brother of mine was a very capable exponent of Fencing and of the Art of Self-Defence, in addition to being an active member of the Literary Society.

Many enjoyable evenings were spent when these Assaults-at-Arms were held, at which there were also exhibitions of gymnastics given, and at which members displayed their clever and at times amusing capabilities. I am glad to see that Fencing, which for many years had gone out of fashion, is now once more engaging the attention of both ladies and gentlemen, for there is no doubt it is both a healthy and graceful exercise.

The names which are associated in my mind with the early years of the Athenaeum, are Kearney, Badger, Robert Leake (afterwards M.P. and lately dead), A. K. Dyson, Samuel Pope, Peter Berlyn, Malcolm Ross, Richard Burge, and Samuel Ogden. There are others but I cannot just remember their names as I write, but there were many active members of the Athenaeum who worked hard to make it the success it was in those early days of its existence, and to whom the thanks of Manchester are due; for at this period of its life Manchester required an outlet for the exercise of the physical and mental energies of the people, and this want was supplied by the Manchester Athenaeum.

Close to where the Athenaeum stood there was Van Amburgh's Circus, at the corner of Cooper Street and Dickinson Street, and which is now occupied by packers and shippers. This man, Van Amburgh, was quite a celebrity in his way, not only on account of his well-appointed circus, his horses and troupe of performers, but principally on account of the feat he accomplished each night of thrusting his head into a lion's mouth. I can recollect his wrenching apart the jaws of the beast in order to enable him to insert his head, the lion evidently submitting to the operation with anything but a good grace. It was a foolhardy thing to do, and later on, I believe, this man, Van Amburgh, lost his life whilst performing this feat. This desire to risk death by some dangerous exhibition, seems to be a growing evil both amongst men and women, and it appears to me that laws should be passed, prohibiting performances where life is at stake.

Although Van Amburgh's show was a good one, it was not comparable with Franconi's Hippodrome which followed it, and was quite the most brilliant thing of the kind that had ever come to Manchester. He had a magnificent stud of horses, daring riders, and most amusing clowns. He quite took the City by storm, and the performances were crowded nightly. What with the

MR M. F. WALLETT

The celebrated Clown and Jester, appearing before Her Most Gracious Majesty the Queen, His Royal Highness Prince Albert, the Duchess of Kent, and Royal Family at Windsor Castle, July 11th 1844.

gay mountings, the rich dresses, and the high character of the entertainment as a whole, the audiences were most enthusiastic. His principal clown was Wallett, or as he was called "The renowned Shakespearean Jester." He was really a man of exceptional ability, giving a sort of dignity to the profession of a Clown which it had never enjoyed before his time. He had the honour of being allowed to style himself "The Queen's Jester," and was specially presented to Her Majesty at Court in the year 1842. He was a splendid elocutionist, some of his recitations being remarkably clever. He would commence, perhaps, with some outburst of tragic eloquence, and then when he had the complete command of his audience he would finish up with some quaint or nonsensical climax. He was a tall, handsome, well-made man, with an endless variety of costumes of the richest materials and which fitted like a glove. He could almost command his own figures from managers wherever he went, and the bare announcement that "Wallett is coming" ensured the success of the tour of any Circus Company. He was, in fact, the tail that wagged the dog. Still "Fortune is a fickle jade," and so she proved herself even in the case of the Queen's Jester. Whether his success was too much for him I do not know, but there were visible signs of deterioration as time went on, his popularity waned, and the name of "Wallett" on the bills ceased to have the old charm for the public. I saw him at this time, and was sorry to witness the decay of the man who had once been such a favourite. His efforts to amuse were but a ghost-like echo of those gifts which had previously charmed and delighted, whilst his wasted form and faded attire gave an additional sadness to the picture.

CHAPTER IX

Manchester Streets 60 years ago – Candles.

It was no easy matter to get about the streets in the old days, for they were both dark and dingy, and very little light came from the houses when night came, as the closed wooden shutters, either inside or outside, gave no help in this way to the passer by. The lamps were few and far between in the streets, and the light from them anything but brilliant. The pathways were narrow and the roadway paved with cobble stones, very much like petrified kidneys, so that when you were in a conveyance you were jolted about from side to side, "rattling your bones over the stones." There was not much rest for the sick or suffering when a coach came along, for what with the cobble stones and the springless, lumbering coaches (there were no hansoms then), the loud worrying noise was incessant. Watchmen, too, paraded the various streets during the night, of which there were 180 in the year 1888, and of day policemen 41 – rather a difference in numbers when compared with today. Surely Manchester folk must have been very quiet and orderly, when they only required 41 policemen to look after them. The night watchmen, with their bull's-eye lanterns, might be seen flashing the light on to the "locks, bolts and bars" of the houses and buildings, to see that all was secure. Occasionally they would suddenly throw the light on to some passer-by, in order to see if he were a fit and proper person to be at large. On one occasion a relative of mine, fond of his joke asked the "guardian of the night" for a light for his pipe. The man was civil enough to open his lantern and give him one. After leisurely lighting his pipe, he took the lantern and turned it full upon the man's face, saying: "Here take your lantern and be off. Of course it's not your fault, but if I had known how ugly you were I would not have asked you for a light." I never heard what was the watchman's reply, but it was no doubt to the point.

In those days stumps of various kinds, iron, wood, or stone, were erected at the street corners for the protection of pedestrians from lurries and vehicles as they came lumbering round the corners. Street boys manifested a great affection for these stumps; they were handy for leapfrog as the boys came scampering along on their errands of business or pleasure. They exercised a sort of fascination on a boy, which seemed to compel him to put down his basket or parcel on the curbstone (for the inspection of any stray, passing dog, of an enquiring nature), whilst he took a leap, and then catching up his parcel he would hurry on to the next stump. Of course where a number of boys collected together they would have a fine old time, and business and baskets were left to take care of themselves, until perhaps a "bobby," as he was then called, appeared on the scene, when there would be a general skedaddle. To do away with this nuisance spikes were let into the top of the stumps, but eventually they were improved out of existence. In Cannon Street these stumps were made from old cannon, which, I suppose, gave it its name. I wonder if any of my readers recollect the stumps which led into St. Ann's Square, the passage into which was widened in 1842, as I seem to have a faint remembrance of them?

Although it appears that as far back as 1824 a further Act was passed relating to the lighting of Manchester gas, in the year 1880 – 1881 the profits for the whole year only amounted then to under £7,000. It was therefore very gradually that its use in dwellings became general, so at night "Ring for the candles" was quite a household word; and then would appear two long candles in silver sticks, with tray and snuffers, when those who wished to make particular use of the lights gathered in cosily round the table, leaving the remainder of the room, if not in darkness, at anyrate in a somewhat dim, religious light.

Then, too, it was not everyone who could snuff a candle effectively. A clumsy hand would often snuff out the light, or would leave what was called a "little man" in it and so causing the candle to drip; or else it might not snuffed sufficiently close and the light would be dull. When gas became more general in its use, a favourite trick was for someone to go to the top of the house, and blow down one of the gas jets, when suddenly the whole house would be in complete darkness. Having done "the deed of darkness" it was advisable for the culprit to lie low, as if discovered ructions were sure to follow.

At bedtime a candle was left with children, just sufficiently long for them to get to bed by, and woe betide those who were not ready when the servant came for the candle, as if they were lazy they had at the last to tumble in anyway. It was a necessary precaution not to leave the light, as I can call to mind one night when I placed the candle so close to the window curtain that it suddenly took fire. Fortunately someone came in, and immediately opening the window, threw out the burning material, and so prevented further damage being done. Probably the last thing a child would do before letting the candle would be to look under the bed to see that there was no burglar or bogey there; for, unfortunately, servants in those days were disposed to cram children with all kinds of uncanny stories, which left a deep impression on young minds, making them nervous and frightened when left to themselves in the dark. Some servants would do this simply for the pleasure they derived from the dread they inspired, others as a threat to obtain obedience to their orders. Education has now, thank goodness, done away with nearly all the mischief caused by playing upon the fears and fancies of the young.

CHAPTER X

Some Personal Reminiscences in connection with St. George's, St. Jude's, and St. James's Churches.

At the mature age of ten, recollections of my Church life, are somewhat faint and fragmentary. The Church with which, as a family, we were connected, and where is the old family grave, was St. George's, Hulme. It is, as anyone can see who pays it a visit, a very handsome structure with massive square tower, and tall, graceful pinnacles, standing in the centre of a large, though now disused graveyard. Inside it is large and roomy, with commodious galleries, where the military used to attend and were a great attraction to me as I watched them in, their gay, scarlet uniforms. At the time of which I am speaking St. George's Church was the most fashionable one in the town, and this part of Hulme was supposed to be in the country, forming the centre of a well-to-do residential population. In the body of the Church the old fashioned, large, square, family pews were numerous, and being owned by the wealthy people of the town, they were handsomely furnished, and gave an air of comfort and ease to the Church.

Now there is a sad change in all this. It is a melancholy sight in worshipping there to see the wilderness of empty pews surrounding you on all sides, and to think of the crowds that gathered there in the old days. But what is true of this Church applies almost equally to all the City churches, some of which have been demolished, and it is only question of time as to others. When living in Faulkner Street, we worshipped partly at St. Jude's, the minister of which, a Mr. O'Leary, was a personal friend and an excellent man, and with the son of whom, Arthur, I was afterwards a schoolmate at Mr. Jackson's school in Broughton. An incident comes back to me in connection with this Church, which had to me, as a child, the elements of a little tragedy. One peaceful Sunday morning, as we were walking along to service, I saw a poor dog run over by a passing cab. Sixty years have passed and gone since then, but the whole scene is present to my mind, as if it had happened lately. There was the sudden rush of the dog, its fall beneath the wheels of the lumbering coach, its piteous yelp, as for a moment it struggled to its feet, staggered a few paces, and then fell dead before me. The last appealing look of that dumb creature, as with a last gasp it fell on its side, will always remain with me.

How certain days are mentally associated with certain individuals in our past recollections! They seem as it were to hang together; and it was so with my Sundays at this period of my existence. We had a family visitor, an Irishman, with a pronounced brogue. He was altogether built on a large scale, he had a big head, a big nose, big feet, and big hands. He had also a large mouth, with a very keyboard of prominent white teeth, which seemed to come out and look at you. His whiskers were long, black, and plentiful, and he had a caressing way of stroking them as he smiled upon you. He wore large collars, which, pointed and assertive, seemed to grow out of the thick folds of a black satin stock. This gentleman favoured voluminous white waistcoats, and the impression left as you looked at him was, that what was not nose and teeth was waistcoat. He posed as a friend of the family, and after completing his Sunday toilet, which I imagine from the result achieved must have been an elaborate afair, he would drop in upon us, usually just as he knew we should be sitting down to dinner, and there he would stand with his back to the fire, legs apart, and with his hands beneath his coat tails, conversing affably, whilst he watched the various courses as they came to table. He had a loud, pompous voice, and when he spoke he had a way of breathing with short snorts through his nose, like the first efforts of an engine when moving out of a station. Then his visit and inspection ended, he would take his leave, with no very particular expression of regret on the part of the family.

St. James's Church we only attended as being near at hand and convenient to get to when the weather was unfavourable, and it had no features of interest or attraction for a young mind. It was not a handsome Church either inside or out, and my early impressions of it are, I think, what would be pretty much the same as the feeling of anyone who visits the Church at the present time – uninteresting mediocrity.

CHAPTER XI

Knott Mill Fair (No. 1) formerly called Acres Fair.

It was in the year 1828 that Acres Fair was removed from St. Ann's Square, where it used to be held, to Campfield, where it afterwards became familiarly known as Knott Mill Fair, and where it formed for a generation or so a very distinctive and essential feature of Manchester life. It was held once a year, on the open space of ground to the rear of St. Matthew's Church, and as the time came round it caused a flutter of excitement amongst children and young people generally, as it was one of the treats of the year which was looked forward to with every anticipation of enjoyment. And what a scene of noise and bustle it was as you passed along Deansgate to the Fair proper. The street was plentifully lined with stalls, laden with all manner of temptations for the young. Apples, oranges, nuts, cocoanuts, toffee, and gingerbreads, of all shapes and varieties, met your longing gaze on all sides. There were gingerbread men and toffee built up in huge pyramids, and in all the colours of the rainbow. At night the stalls were illuminated by cans of flaring naphtha, the smoke of which was apt to get into your eyes, whilst the smell was as pungent as could be desired, or even more so. But this was merely the introduction to Fairyland, as the real Fair only commenced as you turned out of Deansgate into Campfield, where the stalls and booths were almost bursting out with toys of every possible description, all of them brilliantly laden with new paint. To this day I can mentally detect the pleasant smell of the new paint, which gave a sort of Knott Mill aroma to the toys themselves. Here the crowds of youthful purchasers formed their undrilled forces into a series of unpremeditated German Bands, causing a concentration of discord which it was delightful to listen to. You would hear the sound of the drum, whistle, fiddle, accordion, jew's harp, and all manner of squeaking things in the shape of dogs, cats, beasts, birds and reptiles, the whole making a strange medley of sound, which if not musical, had without doubt a charm of its own for young minds. And so you would pass through the avenues of booths with an ever increasing toy-hunger upon you which could never be satisfied. Then you would be hurried along so that the temptations surrounding you might not be too much for you, when suddenly you would find yourself round the corner and in the full whirl of the Fair.

What a delightful racket there is, as you gaze around at the sea of faces and listen to the bands of the various shows, trying to drown each other in their efforts to attract the people to their various entertainments. The noise at first is certainly a little bewildering, but you gradually get accustomed to it. You begin to distinguish the voices of the showmen shouting hoarsely, the thumping energetically on big drums, or the sudden shrill blast of a long brass trumpet, nearly cracking the drum of your ear in its piercing determination to be heard. Mingled with this there is the clanging of cymbals, the firing of guns, the cracking of whips, and the distant roars of the wild animals, in the then, far-famed Wombwell's Menagerie.

And then, when by squeezing and struggling, you have succeeded in getting close in front of one of the shows, you probably find a man gesticulating wildly and shouting to the crowd, in a voice considerably the worse for wear: "Be in time, be in time, just a-goin' to begin," urging you, as if your very life depended upon it, to hurry up before the last chance of witnessing the wonderful performance inside had been snatched away from you by some more fortunate individual. To tempt you still further, a couple of the actors in full costume come outside and perhaps engage in a broadsword combat, looking very fierce the while. Then, as a climax, the heroine appears heavily laden with massive jewellery, supported by the

"Heavy Father" and the Comic Man. After perambulating the narrow strip in front of the show, they all suddenly disappear behind and below. This has the desired effect and so you hurry up the ladder, or steps, as the case may be, and rush down into a kind of damp and dismal looking well, where the blood-curdling play of "Ada, the Betrayed," or the "Murder in the Old Smithy," is to be performed. The title is fetching, and if it be your first experience you are filled with suppressed excitement.

However, this has time to cool, as you and the place is anything but crowded, and the company of actors go up outside again for another forage. Eventually an audience is secured and the tragedy begins. The curtain rises to a strong flavour of naphtha, wet sawdust and oranges. The action of the play, if somewhat mixed, is certainly rapid, and before you know where you are, the villain has been stabbed to the heart, the heroine and her massive jewels have been rescued by the daring hero, the heavy man follows with his blessing, and after a joke from the comic man, which ought to be funny and isn't, you find the whole thing is over. You are then quickly bundled out by some mysterious exit in the canvas, and you find yourself in a dismal little side passage, from which you are thankful to emerge into the light again. Having visited a number of these shows, you probably arrive at the conclusion that, on the whole, what you saw outside of them, and didn't pay for, was greatly superior to what you saw inside and did.

The variety shows at Knott Mill were pretty much the same as are to be found at any of these Fairs. There is, of course, at these, the Fat Woman, the Living Skeleton, the Dwarf and the Giant, the learned Pig, the performing dogs, cats, fleas or birds, the Conjuror's booth and the Wax Works. The last named is always ready to oblige you with the figure of the very latest murderer, with a representation of the deed itself as actually committed, with all its horrors. This has a great fascination for the people, and the exhibition is sure to be crowded.

Of course, Knott Mill was not without the Swings and "Merry-go-rounds," but the steam organ and propeller was not then in existence.

CHAPTER XII

Knott Mill Fair (No. 2) – Cheap John.

ANY description of Knott Mill Fair without an account of its Cheap John, would almost be like "Hamlet" minus "the moody Dane." He was always quite a character in his particular way, and was sure of an interested and highly amused gathering round his caravan, for he was a man of ready wit and excellent humour. It has always been more or less of an astonishment to me how "Cheap John" manages to earn a living, for he does part with his wares at such ridiculous prices, and when I first heard him holding forth I really felt sorry for the man, and angry with those callous creatures who seemed so ready to take advantage of him. He told us all so frankly that he was simply being ruined, and I was quite ready to believe him when I saw the prices he took. But it is every man to his trade, and I have lived to learn that "Master Jack" is as good as his master, and perhaps sometimes even a little better.

You would hear his jocular, deep-chested voice calling his customers together. "Hallo! Hallo! Hallo! Here I am; here you are; here we are; here they are! Ah, there's grammar for you. Bless your little hearts, I'm a regular Lindley Murray, if you only knew. If you'll just step round the corner after I've cleared this 'ere caravan I'll give you fits in grammar, Greek, Chinese, double Dutch (or double Gloster), and the use of the globes, all free, gratis and for nuffin'. In the meantime I've a small matter of about five tons of every thing you can possibly want to your dying day, and which I'm prepared to positively pitch away. I'll tell you why; the fact is, I'm pursued by a demon, who's always whispering to me, 'Oh, pitch 'em away.' Now it's mortal hard on a poor fellow trying to earn an honest living to be told 'pitch 'em away.' But he says so, and it'll have to be done, regardless. I've always been giving away things ever since I was born. When I was a baby I used to give away my feeding-bottle to other babies, whilst I starved. I gave away my toys, apples, oranges, toffee and liquorice; I've been known to give the measles, scarlet fever and hooping-cough, without asking for anything in return. My mother says – and she wouldn't tell a lie, for we're a truthful family from conviction – well, she says that when I was three years old I was found in the back garden taking off my clothes and giving them to another little boy. Well, giving away can't go on for ever, or else there'll be nothing left; so I've made up my mind that when I've cleared this little lot away to-night, I'm going to give myself away. I'm going to retire into a lunatic asylum or a nunnery; I've not decided which. I incline to the nunnery as being more quiet like, for my motto has always been 'anything for a quiet life.'

"And now a little less talk and more business. What do you want? There's positively nothing I can't oblige you with – from a periwinkle to a row of cottages; toasting-forks, night-caps, warming-pans, flannel petticoats, dutch-ovens, eight-day clocks, floorcloths, wedding rings, feeding bottles, gold watches, goloshes and mixed pickles. Now, here's a pair of velveteen cord trousers; look at the material and the cut of them; made in Paris. Now the price! But stay, before I speak about the price I'm bound by law to ask if you're waxinated. My children are all waxinated. I do it with a red-hot poker; it's handy, and it marks plain, and what we wants in this wale of tears is things marked plain and that'll last for ever. Now, that's the beauty of these cords, they'll last for ever; they are that thick that they'll keep you from getting cold, even in your grave; that's luxury for you. Now what shall l be allowed to say for the pants – a sovereign? Let's say twenty shillings then. No! Now I see a young man there with his sweetheart a 'anging on his arm; he's a longing for them. Young man, at ten shillings they're yours. You won't; well what will you offer? Five shillings! you say;

how dare you? Do you think I stole the cords? Any advance on five shillings – and sixpence; thank you. If my poor wife only knew what was happening she'd break her heart, poor thing. Six shillings; six shillings and sixpence has broken out in two places; now look alive young man, it's your turn. Seven shillings, thank you. Any advance on seven shillings? going, going, gone. Pass the cords to the man with the piebald hair and curly teeth. Sold again, and got the money. Hands up for any more cords at the same price – 1, 2, 3, 4, 5, 6 pairs more, Jim; rush 'em out, and pass on to the next.

"Now this 'ere is a lot as I'm going to offer and no mistake; it's a reg'lar bobby dazzler. It's a special combination lot for the pretty lasses, for I see you're in great form to-night. To begin with, here's a looking-glass; it's a magic glass is this, for the oftener you look at yourself in it the prettier you are. That's the sort of mirror to have a 'angin' up in your room, more especially when you're smarting yourself up to meet dear Harry. Oh, you needn't blush, my dear, for I've done a bit of courting myself, and know all about it; besides Harry's a personal friend of mine, and he tells me he loves you to substraction. Still, what's a looking-glass without a brush and comb; so there's one for you, made of the best pig's bristles and so strong that you can hear the little pig squeaking as you brush your hair; and the beauty of this comb is that when you've finished doing your own hair it's a splendid one for combing your husband's hair with when he stops out at night, or forgets to bring his wages. There are teeth in this comb that'll make his hair curl, I can tell you.

"Then there's a basin and jug, both made of the very best Wedgwood china, and warranted never to break. Will stand all climates and tempers, however. Well, what's the use of a basin and jug if you've got no Windsor soap, so here's a slab of soap, the same as used by Her Gracious Majesty at the Castle; and so strong that it is said (but I am not prepared to vouch for its truth) that the bars of Windsor Castle are made of it. That just shows what kind of soap I'm giving you. As regards its cleansing qualities, it will whiten the very blackest character that never was; what a comfort to have a bit of soap like that knocking about your house. Well, when you've washed you, you naturally want a towel to dry yourself with. Now here's a towel that'll put a polish on your face so dazzling that your friends will take you for a perambulating sunbeam. Come, what may I say for the lot? Eh! what does the young lady say? She wants a pair of stays; well, here's a pair that the longer you wear them the more lovely your figure becomes. Won't that satisfy you? No! Well, I'll include a packet of hairpins, the language of flowers, a pudding roller and a penwiper; what will you say for the whole bag of tricks?"

I need not further detail how, "Cheap John," having thoroughly interested and amused his numerous listeners with his introductory remarks, proceeds to make hay whilst the sun shines, drawing the money out of their pockets with wonderful skill, and having succeeded in getting one or two in the audience to nibble, the bulk of the crowd follow like a flock of sheep.

CHAPTER XIII

Knott Mill Fair (No. 3) – The Quack Doctor.

THERE is just one other individual in connection with Knott Mill Fair, I would like to particularise, and that is the Quack Doctor. Of course he is a totally different type of man to "Cheap John," but at the same time quite as resourceful and clever in his own way. Quack Doctors, in these days, are becoming somewhat scarce, as there is such an abundance of the genuine article, but in the palmy days of Knott Mill Fair, he was a man of some importance. He had usually the appearance of a foreigner, although the possibility was that he might have been a Welshman and his real name Jones. As a rule he was a tall, thin, gaunt-looking individual, with long, oily black hair hanging down his back. His hands were long and bony, and although on the genteel soil, were adorned with massive gold rings of antique design. He wore a white tie also on the soil, black waistcoat and funereal-looking, black frock coat. After his page had claimed attention for him energetically thumping away on a large gong, he would commence in something like the following style:

"Leddus and ghentlemen. You must 'cuse me, but I no speak ze English much goot, but when I shall expose you my name, you shall be glad for I am ze renown Doctaire Polishemoff. I have ze large establishmong in Paris, Wien, London, Timbuctoo, and all ovaire ze world. Now my frens, I can cure anyzing vat trouble you. I can cure ze headache all ovaire ze body. If you hev pain in ze high chest or ze low chest, no mataire, I can make him run away in vot you call vun jiffy. Dis botelle which I hold in my hand is vunderful verr much; you feel leetil bad, dis botelle make you big vell at vunce. You catch dat nasty leetil man, vat you call him, influenz, vun small dose of dis medcin and ze influenz, he fly away like mad. You can no sleep, you take small vineglas, you tumble down and sleep like vat you call vun o'clock; nobody can wake you not at all. If you want to sleep too much, you take only dree drops of dis oder leetil bottel it make you vide awake like any zing. You hev cold in ze head, you robe your nose vid diz small box of ointment, and all at vunce Mister Cold he gallop right avay. You feel hot in de head like fire, den dere is mine peels, mine leetelle peels for ze livaire; ach! dey ish grandt, magnificent, vunderful. Your livaire is stupid, lazy fellow, he do no vork at all, den you svallow just one leetil pill, and go to ped, where you sleep like vun tope. In ze morning you vake, you feel too happy, you laugh, you sing, you kick, you run, you jump just like vun crackman. Bat ia vot make you my livaire peels.

"Perhaps, too, you are trouble vid ze lumps; lumps on ze head, lumps on ze back, lumps on ze feet, lumps everyvere, anyvere. Well, you take dis plastaire and stick him on ze lump, and in twenty-four hours he is gone, nevaire to come again not no more. Shall I tell you what happen vun patient of mine; listen. Dis man he hev hear of me, myself, the great Doctaire Polishemoff. He came to me, he show me vun lump on ze tope of his head, verr large indeed, just like vun football. Ven you look at ze man you tink he hev two heads. Vell, he pye vun of zese plastaires; he stick it on his lump; he lie down and go to sleep quiet, like vun leetelle baby. In ze morning he vake up; he feel for his lump. Ach! it has gone; it has gone avay vile he vas sleep. When he look in ze glass he scream for joy; den he run to me, and he pye from me vun gross of zese plaistaires, to give to all his frens who hev lumps, his heart vas so full of ze large peety for zem. So he keep open his eye, and ven he see in ze streets vun man who hev lumps he run to him, and he slap-bang vun of ze plaistaires on ze lump, which go away like magic, and so ze pore man is made at once verr much happy indeed."

With some such introduction as this the doctor trumpets forth the marvellous efficacy of his various medicines, and finds a ready sale for them, the country-folk being more especially impressed with the account of the miraculous cures effected.

CHAPTER XIV

Country Life – Old Broughton Lane – Lodge's Nursery Gardens – Bleackley's Farm.

IN MANCHESTER, about the year 1840 and onwards, the middle classes began to realise that town life was not very desirable, and families began migrating and settling in the various suburbs. In the summer of 1845 we removed from Faulkner Street to Teneriffe Street, Broughton, and it was very pleasant to get away from the town with all its dingy and uninviting surroundings, and to breathe the pure, fresh, country air. The country began at this time about Sherbourne Street, fields being on both sides of the road, and as you walked along and turned down Broughton Lane it was very sweet and nice, and you realised that you had said good-bye to the town. The lane had its hedgerows thick with hawthorns and wild flowers peeping out from beneath in gay profusion, whilst the gardens about were gay with bloom. A few yards down the lane you came to Lodge's Nursery Gardens, approached by a long, wide pathway, and bordered by a small, running brook. Inside the Nurseries there was an extensive orchard of pear, apple and plum trees. Scattered about were summer-houses and arbours, where people could sit and have their tea with water-cress. In the Springtime it was quite a sight to stand on the higher ground in Bury New Road, and look across towards Lodge's Gardens, at the wide expanse of fruit trees laden with bloom. Now this ground is covered with workshops and ugly looking buildings of all descriptions.

On the other side of Broughton Lane there used to be a Racquet Court, supported principally by the German community. Amongst its members I call to mind, Milner Van Hees and his brother; Rolfson, Stullmann and

Hermes. Near to this, on the same side, stood Slade's School, afterwards occupied by Robert Neill, senior, as a private house; then by the sons, who divided it into two, and later still it became a part of their large business premises, and is so to this day.

Teneriffe Street, when we first lived there, had houses built only on one side of it, and terminated in a cul-de-sac with fields beyond. In front of the houses was a long stretch of meadowland right across to Broughton Lane. Even Great Clowes Street at this time was in its infancy, for I remember when the removal took place one of the lurries laden with furniture stuck fast in the ruts, as Great Clowes Street was then very much of a quagmire in wet weather.

What happy days have I spent in and around our Teneriffe Street home! In the centre of the field in front of us was a pond of water, where we sailed our toy boats, and watched them scudding gaily along its surface on a windy day. The fields which began where the street ended belonged to a butcher named Lambert, whose shop stood a little back from Bury New Road. He and his wife were a tall, handsome-looking couple, and were related to the Lamberts who keep the Old Trafford Hotel. Through the centre of one of these fields coursed a brook which in rainy weather broadened almost into a stream. Beyond this was a steep hill, and at its top another pond, bordered with willows and rushes, and over and around which in the summer-time there were dragonflies, butterflies and all manners of pretty insect life to be seen in abundance. This was one of our happy hunting grounds, and many a time have I sat on the banks of this pond fishing for jacksharps, my rod a willow-switch with a piece of string attached, a bent pin and a worm at the end completing my simple tackle.

The gardens to the houses in Woodland Terrace commenced where the pond terminated. I might mention that Keswick apples grew in those gardens; and I am afraid it was not always the owners who gathered those apples. They looked so tempting growing there, and they were so juicy and had such a wonderful flavour, and youth does not always pause to consider. But apples were apples in those days; it seems to me there are none like them nowadays; or perhaps it is that I am like the Lancashire farmer and the dumplings. John had a special weakness for apple dumplings, and his wife made them for him; but as years went on he began to think they were not as good as they used to be; so one day he said to his wife: "Eh, Mary lass, these dumplings ain't a patch on those as moi mother used to mak when I wur a leetle chap." So Mary put on her mettle, tried her best to please him, but he always harked back to the old tune that his mother's were the best. So one time, when his mother was visiting them, Mary persuaded the old lady to make some of her old-famed apple dumplings. John, not knowing the maker, commenced on them, but after tasting them he turned to his mother, and said: "Eh, mother, these dumplings aint nowt loike those as yau used to mak." "Whoy, tha fulish lad," said his mother, "oi made these myself, and they aint nowt different to what they wur when tha first tackled 'em. Oi'll tell thee what it is, lad, it's thee as has changed and not th' apple dumplings."

The pond of which I have been speaking at one end abutted on to Bury New Road, opposite to which, on the further side of the road, there stood Bleackley's Farm. To the rear of one of those huge, ugly advertisement hoardings, instead of the entrance to the farmyard, you are now, alas, faced by Raring placards asking you to buy Colman's Mustard, Harvey's Sauce, Rickett's Blue, Sunlight Soap, Grape Nuts or somebody's whiskey. This farm was one of the old-fashioned sort, where you could ramble over the orchard or the fruit gardens, watch the haymakers at work, or the girls milking the cows. It was a busy place in its day, and on occasions I have played the part of fruit picker myself, the terms of payment being, "Eat as much as you can, but pocket nothing." When a boy makes a bargain like this he thinks he has the best end of the stick, but the capacity of even the healthiest boy's interior is limited, and I found that I was satisfied long before my work was done. The Bleackleys who kept this farm were part of a large family connection of this name, well known in Prestwich and Broughton for generations past. You could always distinguish them by their height and build, being men of large physique, tall, broad-shouldered and massive.

CHAPTER XV

Cricket – The Athenaeum, and some of its Members – Broughton Club – John Karl – Joseph Makinson.

IN WAS about the year 1845 that the Manchester Athenaeum established a Cricket and Athletic Club in Broughton, on the ground now partly occupied by the Broughton Town Hall, the new Swimming Baths, and the Cobden Liberal Club, etc. Great Clowes Street was its boundary on one side, Camp Street on the other, and Duke Street on the third. On the fourth side there was an intersecting field betwixt it and Broughton Lane. It was an exceptionally pleasant Club with which to be connected, and although I was personally too young at that time to be a member, the family connection with it enabled me to enjoy all the privileges of membership. Cricket was the main purpose for which it was formed, but archery, quoits, fencing, boxing, singlestick, with sword drill and exercise, were provided for those whose predilection lay in any of these directions. The tent contained a good gymnasium, where members' performances delighted the young people, who were always welcomed by their elders and encouraged in the development of all kinds of healthy amusements; and I am satisfied that the influence exercised by the Athenaeum Club in this direction was distinctly beneficial in many ways. As a Cricket Club, pure and simple, it did not stand very high, but nevertheless there was no lack of enthusiasm amongst either young or old. Their great local rivals were found amongst the members of the Broughton Club, and although all my sympathies naturally lay with our own Club, I could not but acknowledge that the laurels of victory usually rested with our rivals. Of those who were members of the Athenaeum in its early years, amongst others I call to mind Joe Rooke (graceful

Joe, as he was called) and his brother George, R. C. and J. J. Stonex, the brothers Garnett, J. H. Fildes, Tom Ord, T. B. Payne, Harry Smith, Matthew Lodge, W. Berry and Lamport (familiarly called Daddy Lamport). The latter, I remember, was unduly stout for his age, and was blessed with a thin, squeaky voice, like an old man's treble, which, I suppose, accounted for his nickname. There were others who sometimes figured in the cricketing eleven, amongst them Sam Pope, the barrister, George Beasley and Will Turner, son of James Aspinall Turner, afterwards member of Parliament for Manchester. On the whole, the best, I think, that could be said about the Athenaeum cricketers was that they could play a good, steady, plodding game, and on occasions would make a stubborn fight for victory. In those days underhand bowling was the rule, in which department of the game the Club was not strong, and some of the members were unenviably noted for bowling "grubs". The tent being at the far end of the field, the scorer had a special bench provided where he was in closer proximity to the players. An old Quaker gentleman, named Whitlow, generally acted as scorer, and, being a man of kindly, genial nature, he was endeared to all who knew him. Mentally, I can see him now sitting behind his little table and scoring-book, a large umbrella shading his face from the sun, and the smoke curling up lazily from a large cherry-stemmed meerschaum pipe. At other times he was to be found playing a very excellent game at quoits, and although he was considerably more than eighteen inches round the waist, he was as active as many a younger and lighter-weighted man.

I have said that there was great rivalry between the Athenaeum and Broughton Clubs, but the man whom we most dreaded on the other side as a batsman was old John Earl. He was one of the finest cricketers of his day, at least in our part of the world. He was an exceptionally handsome man, tall and erect. At the wickets he had a splendid defence, and was a big hitter. He always wore the orthodox white tall hat, and a likeness is to be seen of

JOSEPH MAKINSON, ESQ., J.P.,

Present Stipendary Magistrate for Salford

him in cricketing attire in the Broughton cricket tent at the present time. I suppose John Earl must have been over seventy years of age before he retired altogether from the cricket field, but during the last few years of his cricketing life he had become so feeble that his son, John Henry Earl, used to attend him to the wickets to run for him. Broughton took a pride in their stalwart old gentleman cricketer, and realised that he gave a dignity to the game as he walked out to the wickets with his bat under his arm, and his tall, dark, handsome-looking son walking by his side. As a batsman the son lacked the steadiness and resource of the father, but he could play a dashing game at times, and score sometimes faster than his father. The Broughton Cricket Ground as I first remember it occupied the land on which Albert Park is now laid out, and was not so large as it now is, the tent and general surroundings being very much more primitive in their character than the pavilion on the present site. It was, however, on the old ground that Joe Makinson (the "little wonder", as he used to be called) first showed evidence of his great capabilities as an all-round cricketer. As a batsman, bowler and fielder combined he had no equal at one time amongst amateurs, and in the encounters of Broughton against All England our hopes for success were always largely centred on "little Joe". When he came off we were jubilant, but when he failed our hopes of victory were clouded. The All England matches in the olden time were great events, and formed the principal outdoor festival of the Broughton year; here all the youth and beauty of the neighbourhood gathered and promenaded to the enlivening strains of a military band.

Before parting with the subject of cricket, on which so much has been written, I should like to express my conviction that there is in the world no other game its equal, developing, as I firmly believe it does, some of the best traits in our characters, such as manliness, pluck, self-reliance, endurance and determination. Cricket, to my mind, has done much, perhaps even more than appears on the surface, to unite the peoples of Australia and ourselves into one harmonious whole, these interesting international contests have helped to make us better known to each other, and have increased our mutual self respect. In India, too, cricket has not been without its effect upon our subjects there, and has helped to develop social intercourse and friendliness of feeling between ourselves and our darker brethren in our great Empire over the seas.

Were cricket to lose its hold upon the English people I for one should look upon it as a national calamity, for the game is a real and vital bond of union amongst all classes – the rich and the poor, the old and the young. You will see an old man of seventy seated by a boy of ten, each watching the game with the same keen interest, and discussing with one another the various points of what is passing before them with an earnestness and enthusiasm that is quite delightful to witness, and I know of no other game in existence which has similar characteristics. Long may it continue therefore to be our national game, for I believe it to be the embodiment and outcome of a healing and vigorous national instinct.

LORD'S CRICKET GROUND IN 1841

CHAPTER XVI

The Broughton Priory – Philip Gould – The Old River Irwell.

THE Broughton Priory, or Harrop's Folly as it was at one time called, was, as I first remember it, a very interesting and almost romantic spot. The grounds on which it stood were bounded by Lower Broughton Road, Duncan Street, Great Clowes Street, and a small lane, rejoicing in the name of the Broughton Spout, but afterwards happily rechristened Laurel Grove. This lane skirted, at the time of which I speak, a pretty fancy sheet of water in the Priory grounds, with a tiny little island in its centre, reached by a boat or a raft. It lay at the foot of a hill, which sloped down from the Priory itself through prettily wooded paths and gardens, studded here and there with small pavilions and quaint little summer-houses.

The Priory, with its grounds, was a delightful playground for myself and friends, when we could manage to elude the eyes and ears of the caretakers, who did not altogether approve of our methods. The mansion itself, which stood on the crest of the eminence, was a handsome building with steps and tall Corinthian pillars forming the main entrance. Originally the house had, I believe, been occupied by a Mr. Williams, and its internal arrangements had evidently been both rich and elaborate. You entered a wide entrance hall with corridors running round the ground floor, and leading to the various apartments and entertaining rooms. After ascending a wide, handsome staircase branching out on both sides, you found that the apartments on the first floor were also approached from similar corridors to those on the ground floor. By this arrangement a large open space was left from basement to roof. The roof itself was flat and leaded under foot, except where its was glazed to give light below. Leading to it there was a narrow staircase, where a splendid view was obtained of the surrounding country. When we were able to get on the soft side of the caretaker, we scrambled on to the roof and had generally a good time. Here there was a good view of Fitzgerald's Castle (since demolished) and the old racecourse, which after having migrated to Old Trafford, is once more back again on the old ground. Close to Fitzgerald's Castle was also the course where the steeplechases were held for gentlemen riders. Amongst them I remember Will Turner, son of J. A. Turner, who was at times one of the competitors. The caretaker of the Priory was a man named Abraham Knott, whose wife carried on the business of a washerwoman, and to see the various apartments decorated with newly-washed clothes certainly did not materially add to the dignity of the place. This Mrs. Knott was a very worthy hardworking woman, and although her sharp shrill voice has often brought me back to my senses when I was getting into mischief, she was really a kindly woman in her way. Later on she and her husband owned and occupied the Priory Inn until the time of their deaths some years ago.

There was, I believe, a romance associated with this Priory, which terminating unhappily, caused its builder to allow it to moulder to decay untenanted; but with ordinary care bestowed upon its upkeep, it might still have continued to the present day, a pleasant link with the past to old Broughtonians. Robert Gardiner ("Old Robby" as he was familiarly though somewhat disrespectfully called), an old Manchester worthy, had some interest, I understand, in this property, having purchased it for a maiden sister to live in, but which she never did.

Close to the Priory on the Duncan Street side lived Philip Gould, a well-known, eccentric little gentleman, somewhere about five feet two in height, and who used to ride about on a diminutive pony, even smaller in proportion than he was himself. The pony, a light brown, shaggy-looking little animal with an especially long tail, was as full of life and energy as his master, and the two of them were both characters in their way. It was amusing to see Philip Gould when he wanted the pony, go out to the field where it grazed (which formed a part of the Priory grounds), and bring it in to be saddled. He usually had something tempting in his hat which he held so that the pony could see it, and as soon as it did it would be quickly at his side, then he would jump on to it barebacked and ride it to the stable to be saddled. Having accomplished this, it was still more amusing to see Philip Gould in his tall white beaver hat, astride the pony and with his feet nearly touching the ground riding along the road, perhaps with a large market basket on his arm going to do some shopping. The pony came trotting along, and you could always tell it even before it overtook you, by the noisy patter of its little feet. The two of them always appeared to be in a great hurry, as if they had business on hand that required immediate attention. Philip Gould, notwithstanding his odd little ways, was quite the gentleman and very polite. His hobbies were horses and hunting, and he was an enthusiastic follower of the hounds. He had a son of the same name as himself whom it is said he had christened in topboots and spurs.

The river Irwell, which ran close past the grounds of Fitzgerald's Castle, was not always the inky stream which it is now unfortunately is. I can remember when, although it was not actually a trout stream, we could gather on its banks in my school days and bathe in it with enjoyment. The spot we frequented was opposite the Castle, where there was a stretch of clean, nice yellow sand, in which after our dip we could roll and dry ourselves in the hot summer sun. Fancy doing such a thing now! Close to where we bathed the river took a sudden dip, and those who could not swim were rather afraid of this spot, as here the water was deep, and it went by the name of "The devil's hole." Good swimmers did not mind this hole, but I remember once being carried over it on the back of one of the older boys; in my fright I believe I nearly choked him, so happily for me he did not try this again.

Romantic tales were current in my young days about Fitzgerald's Castle, of subterranean passages leading down to the river, and of a lady who, in the olden time, had been confined within the Castle walls. These gave an air of mystery to the whole place, and therefore made it more interesting and attractive to young people. Now the old Castle and its grounds are cleared away, and with it has vanished also all the romance which attached to it.

To me the Castle and its environment is a very pleasant memory, with its turrets peeping out from amidst the trees and shrubs which surrounded it. Looking up the river Kersal Edge was to be seen prettily wooded, with the river winding along past the Cliff and Scarr Wheel, forming quite a charming panorama. Yes, life went very quickly and happily in those days when the warm blood of youth coursed through the veins, and when "every prospect" pleased. And yet, whilst this was so, we longed for the time when we could leave school and become men and, imagined that with the increase of years would come additional pleasure and happiness. Whereas it is when we are "grown ups" that we first begin to realise that there is a seamy side of life, and that what seemed so much to be desired in prospect, was not in reality what it promised to be. When boyhood's happy days are past we find that we have then to grapple with the stern realities of life; that each one has his own particular battle to fight, and that if we earnestly desire success we must struggle for it with energy and determination, meeting our disappointments which must come to us, like good men and true, remembering that the battle of life terminates only with its close.

CHAPTER XVII

William Murray, the Horsedealer – Peace Eggers – Rushcart Bearers – Christmas Carols.

IN the year 1846 there was a very well-known man who had his stables in Milton Street, Broughton Lane, and this was William Murray, the celebrated horsebreaker and horsedealer. He had an almost world-wide reputation for the splendid horses in which he dealt, and people came from all parts of the country to his establishment to purchase or exchange. The stables were most beautifully kept, and no expense was spared in their upkeep. As you approached them you found Milton Street, in which they were, exquisitely kept, and the pathways marked out in fancy tracings of sand or sawdust, representing various birds and animals. Inside the stables themselves was to be found a collection of the finest hunters and carriage horses. It was at that time one of the sights of Manchester to see William Murray turn out in his brake with a couple of splendid-looking animals, which he handled like a master in the art. He was himself a tall, handsome, even stylish-looking man, as well groomed as his horses. He wore a tall white hat, a spotlessly white neckcloth, with long, white, driving coat, and was booted and gloved to perfection. It was a positive pleasure to see him handle the reins, and to watch his complete control over the most nervous, excitable, or vicious of animals. When he drove through the town people would invariably turn round or stand still to admire his turnout. His perfectly appointed brake, with handsome harness and shining mountings, which sparkled in the sunlight, would often be seen standing at Brooks's Bank, where he transacted his business. The nobility, gentry, and army patronised him very largely, and he was able to command very high prices from his customers, who knew that they received good value for their money, even though his prices were at times somewhat startling to those who came to him for the first time.

Fifty years ago the country lanes and suburbs were, at Easter time, invaded by various troops of boys, called Peace Eggers, and consisting usually of about half-a-dozen to a troop. Their appearance was rendered as martial as it was possible for them to be, when attired in coloured Calico blouses, trousers to match, and decorated with as many gaily-coloured ribbons as they had been able to lay their hands on. They were armed with cross-handled tin swords, very primitive in their workmanship, and thus provided they assumed as fierce and warlike an appearance as they were able to do under the limited circumstances. The drama they enacted was supposed to have something to do with St. George and his enemies, but I was never able to unravel the mystery they represented. There was a combat or two, fought in the usual penny-show style, three cuts above and three cuts below, a thrust and then a verse of doggerel, closing with a death scene where one of the combatants falls to the ground and dies. There were a number of verses accompanying the affecting tragedy, but the only one of them which clings to my memory is the following: –

"Oh George, oh George, what hast thou done?
Thou'st kilt and slain my only son;
My only son, my only heir,
How canst thou look on 'im bleedin' there?"

After this followed a most important item in the entertainment, namely, the collection, after which the troop "moved on."

Then in the Autumn the Morris Dancers came round with their attractive rushcart, a sort of house made of rushes and raised on to a lurry. It was very ingeniously made and hung over with bright metal mugs, teapots, etc, and was drawn along by one or more horses. The men who accompanied it wore some kind of fancy dress, bedecked with gaily-coloured ribbons, and they danced along the road in front of the cart and tum-tummed away on the tambourines which they held in their hands. It was rather grotesque to see big lumbering men trying to be graceful, but it did not appear to strike them in this way, and they were quite satisfied if the coppers came in freely. The whole affair seemed like a sort of travesty of David dancing before the Ark.

Then again, at Christmas, we had the Carol singers, and although even today, at the Yuletide season, there are to be found wandering about some melancholy specimens of this genus, they are now in a very moribund condition. In the old days, however, they were quite an institution, and many of the parties who then came round were of the better class, and were really good part-singers, forming quite a pleasant and integral part of our Christmas Festival. Now this ancient custom has degenerated into a number of ragged urchins banding themselves together, and levying blackmail on the inhabitants of quiet neighbourhoods, by planting themselves on the doorstep of the houses, and yelling out with discordant voices a few of the best-known Christmas hymns. Here, again, the sole object is money, which some will foolishly give them in order to get them away, but this is a mistake, as such a procedure only brings others in their wake. Probably in old-fashioned country places the "waits" are still to be found, who are capable of giving some pleasure to their listeners, but in and about the large centres of industry they have practically disappeared, and thus another agreeable link with the past has been severed.

CHAPTER XVIII

Broughton continued – Mr. Jackson's School – Some of its Scholars: William Hy. Houldsworth, William Mather.

THE school which I first attended in Broughton was situated in Northern Terrace, Great Clowes Street, and was kept by a Mr. Jackson. In the first instance one house was found large enough for its requirements, but about the year 1848 the numbers had so materially increased that another house was added, and so continued until the school was given up. The houses are still pretty much as of old, but there have been many changes in their surroundings. In the lane leading down to the playground, which was at the back, there stood a pump, a necessary adjunct to every few houses before the town's water was laid on. Here we quenched our thirst and our mode of doing so was as follows. A small hole had been bored in the spout, and by holding a hand over its mouth to prevent the egress of the water, it was forced through this small aperture, and very refreshing it was to drink in this way. New scholars and the uninitiated were asked to apply their eye to the hole instead of their mouth, and the effect was not so pleasant. I cannot say that the amount of learning instilled into us was either very deep or varied, but it was probably equal to the standard of most schools at that time. It certainly would not compare favourably with a course of present-day teaching, and regarded in this light I consider we had a fairly easy time of it on the whole.

In appearance Mr. Jackson was a tall, thin, gaunt-looking man with high shoulders, a hard, stern mouth, and thin, compressed lips. He had long, loose-looking, spidery legs, and he had a habit of grinding the two palms of his hands together as if he were grinding corn, whilst at the same time he elevated one shoulder and depressed the

MR. JACKSON'S SCHOOL, GREAT CLOWES STREET, 1848

other. This was accompanied by a nervous contraction of the mouth and a slight protrusion of the tongue. When he entered the schoolroom, shod in list slippers, he moved very noiselessly past our desks, and as he came along he was apt to give you a sort of "all-over-ishness," more especially if you happened to be larking at the time, or if you did not feel that you were quite word perfect in your lessons. On the whole, I consider Mr. Jackson was a conscientious man, and did his duty towards the boys, and although he could hardly be styled a genial man, still he acted fairly and squarely, for though he was strict he was neither harsh nor unjust. And, after all, 100 boys or so, ranging from ten to sixteen, are not born angels, and require a firm hand over them to keep them right.

He had a housekeeper whom we did not absolutely love, perhaps because it was she who dosed us when we were suffering from school headache or other ailments. However, Mr. Jackson must have discovered some attractions in her, as he eventually married her. Talking of school headaches, I remember on one occasion a school companion who sat next to me, made up his mind that he would be ill and ask off for the rest of the day. I remonstrated with him on the score that he had got off on the same plea just lately, and that if anything was to be done on these lines it was my turn. Eventually he gave way, and so getting my desk, and looking as poorly as I could on the spur of the moment, I walked towards Mr. Jackson's desk, just as my friend said in a stage whisper, "Tell him you're speechless." This was too much for me, and I exploded, seeing which Mr. Jackson called out, "Put down Hayes for being out of seat." To add to my discomfiture, a few minutes later my schoolfellow went up, pleaded illness, and got off for the afternoon, giving me a wink and a nudge as he passed me. Moral: Always speak the truth.

We had amongst us as scholars some whose names have since become as "Household words." For instance there was William Henry Houldsworth[2], who was certainly a very attractive example of the school companion. He was perhaps a little my senior in age, but at school a year or so makes a material difference in the eyes of the junior. On this account, therefore, he took me in a measure under the shelter of his protective wing, and saw that I was not unduly bullied by the bigger boys. We had many pleasant times together, as he was of a bright, happy, genial nature, and many is the ramble we have had through the grounds of his home at Oak Hill, which was then a charming country residence, but is now one of the Rescue Homes connected with the City Missions.

Of the Mather family, Colin, William and John provided a liberal contribution to the school. Colin was an especial favourite with all, and was very bright and merry. Unfortunately he died when he was only twenty-three years of age, a loss that was felt by many of those who had been his old schoolmates. He was one of the privileged wags of the school; he was crowned by nature with a crop of short, crisp curls, had a merry eye, and dimples which helped to make a laugh of his most infectious. If there was any innocent mischief brewing you might be sure Colin would have some share in it. Even Mr. Jackson could not resist his sunny disposition. One time when the school had received tickets for some entertainment at half-price, we wisely selected Colin as our spokesman to get permission to go, and he emphasised our plea by saying: "Oh, Sir, please let us go; we can get in for sixpence and get out for nothing." The joke seems old now, but we thought it very good at the time. Perhaps the humour lay in the telling, like the tale about the man whose friend said to him: "John, your coat's very short," to which his friend replied: "It will be long enough before I get another." Some Verdant Green, in repeating the

---

2. *William Henry Houldsworth (1834-1917), 1st Baronet, was a mill owner and Conservative MP for Manchester North-West (1883-1906). He built Houldsworth Mill, Reddish (1865) then the largest cotton mill in the world. It survives as a Grade II listed building. Freeman of Manchester 1905.*

anecdote gave it as follows: "John, your coat's very short," to which he replied: "Well, it will be a long time before I get another." And nobody laughed as he anticipated, and he could not tell why.

William Mather[3] is still happily with us (he was called Rufus at school), carrying along with him, as the years roll on, a full share of the energy and earnestness which characterised him even as a schoolboy. For a long period Manchester and Salford have had very many proofs both in and out of Parliament of his ability and indefatigable energy as a worker in support of all schemes either of local or National importance. Whilst, at the same time, he has been a wise but generous supporter of our numerous philanthropic institutions.

Amongst a number of others who attended Mr. Jackson's School, I may mention the following: David and John Stuart, sons of John Stuart the Banker, who, before his death, built and endowed the Presbyterian Church in Singleton Road, Kersal; William Sale, son of William Sale, the solicitor; Richard and John Hobson, the former afterwards becoming a Liverpool merchant, the latter an Analytical Chemist of some note, but long since dead; James and Hunter Spence; William Wright, afterwards of the firm of Wood and Wright, calico printers; Charles, Edwin and Herbert Grundy, sons of the well-known auctioneer, and all now dead; Charles Darbyshire, and a number of others, whose names would now have no significance for my readers at this time.

The sons of W. D. Whitehead, William Henry, and Charles, were also my schoolfellows, the last named first came when he was adorned with long, brown ringlets falling down almost to his waist, and very sweet and nice he looked, the very joy of a mother's heart. But, unfortunately for him, ordinary school boys do not regard long corkscrew curls with the same favour as a mother,

---

3. Sir William Mather (1838-1920) - British industrialist and Liberal MP for Salford (1885-6), Gorton (1889-95), Rossendale (1900-04)

so his charms were a constant worry and trouble to him, and although he did not, like Absalom, come to an untimely end through being hanged by his locks from a tree, still ever and anon the Philistines were upon him, and eventually he pleaded that he might, like Samson, be shorn of his locks, and shorn he was accordingly, from which time he had peace from his tormentors.

CHAPTER XIX

Broughton Schools continued – Dr. Beard's, Mr. Makinson's, Mr. Figgins's, Mr. Dixon's – Tuck Shops.

OF the many schools which were to be found in Broughton previous to 1860, the following may be mentioned. There was Dr. Beard's, which was held in the house at present occupied by Dr. Kinghorn, at the corner of Great Cheetham Street and Bury New Road, and where a number of my companions attended. Dr. Beard was a very clever man and an excellent schoolmaster, and he was also the minister at the Unitarian Chapel in New Bridge Street, where he had a very fair congregation, the Unitarians being at that time a more numerous body than they are at the present day. After the doctor gave up the school he went to live at a house at the bottom of Broughton Lane, near Lower Broughton Road, and his bright, genial face, sturdy figure, and staid white cravat, were often to be seen in the locality, and he had a pleasant word for all with whom he came into contact. His son James, of Beard, Agate and Co, is still with us.

Mr. Makinson's School was in Hilton Street, and the building where it was is still in existence. Here Tom, John, Charles, Will, and Joseph Makinson all went to school, but Tom the eldest, also attended Owens College when it was in Quay Street. These were all sons of Mr. Makinson, the solicitor, who lived in Wilton Terrace, Bury New Road. There was a sort of acknowledged standing feud between Mr. Jackson's School and Mr. Makinson's, but it was really not of a very deadly nature. We were always both of us very pot valiant whenever one side outnumbered the other, but we never came to much actual business. However, there was one of Makinson's boys, Matt Hedley by name, who was considered their champion in the pugilistic line; he was then a high-shouldered, bullet-headed young fellow, with red hair, who always looked as if he were spoiling for a fight with someone. When you met him he had his fists doubled up as if to be ready for the fray, and my impression is that Makinson's School made the most of their reputation for fighting on the strength of this one boy. Like Goliath of old he would come out and defy us, but with the character he held amongst us, we were none of us over anxious to accept the numerous challenges which he flung at us. We had no objection to fling an occasional stone after the manner of David, but when we did so we took good care to be well out of his reach. When he was on the warpath he reminded one of a small bantam cock, flapping his wings and urging us to come on. In after years we grew up to be good friends, and strange to say, as if his old nature in a measure clung to him, he became (as a pleasant hobby) a great bird fancier and breeder of gamecocks, whilst as a Judge at Poultry Shows his opinion was held in high esteem.

There was another school kept by a Mr. Figgins, near the bend of the river, at the foot of the Cliff, but I knew it more by name than reputation. Here the Rutter boys attended, the sons of the late coroner, and the boys of the Smith family, who lived at Broughton Rank, at the junction of Lower Broughton Road and Great Clowes Street. There were a number of boys of the Smiths, but they are all now dead.

Another Broughton school, of which I must speak, was the one kept by a Mr. Dixon, at the corner of Grove Street and Bury New Road. In this instance Mr. Dixon had almost a school ready to his hand, for he had a family of about a dozen boys, of all ages and sizes. Mr. Dixon himself was a short, thick-set man, with legs which rounded outwards, and strange to say most of his boys had the same characteristics, and you could generally distinguish them as they came along the road, on account of these distinctive features. Two of his sons, John and William, I think, afterwards attended Owens College in Quay Street. The old house where the school was held is still in existence, but tacked on to the front of it, in the garden that was, there is now a provision shop, where pork and sausages may be bought, and so its educational glory has passed away from it never to return.

Not very long ago, I remember, one time when walking from Blackpool to Fleetwood, that nearing Fleetwood as the clocks struck twelve, a crowd of boys came trooping out from school, dancing, shouting and yelling like a band of wild Indians, and as they did so they brought back the same period in my own school life, when we used to act like a lot of mad things, and in our excitement fling our caps into the air, and our books anywhere. Boys are pretty much the same now as then, there is a certain amount of bottled-up steam which has to be let off, and it is bound to find a vent in one direction or another.

In the old days Tuck Shops had not become an established institution, but at the same time there was always some place where boys could be relieved of their superfluous cash, in exchange for something to eat. School boys do not very much mind what it is they get, so long as it is something to eat. They love eating, no matter whether they are hungry or not. Opposite to Mr. Jackson's school there was a grocer's shop kept by a man named Ambrose Atkins, whom we naturally patronised to the best of our ability financially and physically, although there were limits in both directions. Atkins did not keep all the toothsome sweets which can be so easily procured at the present day, but still with acid and raspberry drops, sugar almonds, barley sugar and sugar candy, peppermints and treacle toffee, we were quite able to make our stock of money disappear quickly. I remember there was an economical edible in which we indulged, a mixture of raw meal and moist sugar, which if not exactly luscious was cheap and filling. I have little doubt Ambrose Atkins voted us nuisances many a time in the day, but our combined custom was a matter of consideration, and for the sake of the grist we brought to his mill, he put up with our many foibles.

CHAPTER XX

Bury New Road Blackfield Lane – Prestwich Clough.

HAVE you any objection to take a ramble along with me through Kersal and on to Prestwich Church and Clough as I knew it nearly half a century ago; for when I think back it is hard to realise all the changes that have taken place there during that time?

At the Bury New Road end of Northumberland Street, partly on the ground now occupied by Hanover Square, the Zoological Gardens were to be found, with the birds, wild beasts and reptiles which had taken up their abode there. It is so long since that the only animal I can remember in the collection was a polar bear. It occupied a large pit in the grounds, in the centre of which was a tall pole up which it climbed and took stock of its visitors. It evidently had a desire to be on closer terms of acquaintanceship with myself and others, but the impression left is that the look in its eye was hardly a friendly one, so I preferred seeing it hug its pole rather than myself. In some indistinct way I think the scene reminded me of Daniel and the lions' den. These gardens, which were opened in May, 1838, were not a financial success, and were closed some years later. Mr. Jennison, of Belle Vue, I think, bought most of the animals.

A little further on, on the opposite side of the main road, you came to a grey stuccoed square house, with a castellated roof. It is, I believe, one of the oldest houses in the locality, and was, I understand, before my time a house of entertainment and refreshment for man and beast. In the old days before Bury New Road was made, people walked across from Cheetham Hill, down Broom Lane to this house, as their country walk from town. It has now been all remodelled, or, to speak more correctly, rebuilt – in fact, made waterproof; by one in the trade.

Blackfield Lane, which is now paved, drained, flagged, and walled in, has lost all its old charm, and is of the streets, streety. As I first remember it, it was truly and essentially a delightful country lane. It lay deeply embedded in pure, pale, yellow sand of that exceptionally fine kind which runs through your fingers however you may try to hold it. Even our canaries approved of it, and this is where we came to gather it for the cages.

I have played in that lane by the hour and have lain basking in the summer sun, when even the sand about me has been baking hot to the touch with the heat of its rays. Where, oh where has that old-fashioned sun gone to that used to come streaming down and baking into you and everything about you, with its searching rays? Such days bring to my recollection some of the older Linnell's paintings, and the wonderful power he possessed of making you feel how true he was to nature. One of his pictures is very present with me, and is called, I think, "A dusty road on a summer's day." It is a country lane, with a flock of sheep moving lazily along; you can feel that the air is laden with heat, and that everything in the painting is so charged with it that at last it almost makes you hot by reflection, and lazy and dusty only to look at it. Just as I have felt in that same dear old Blackfield Lane in the days that have gone.

This was the lane that led to "Kairsee Moor Races," as the Lancashire folk called them, and it was the natural approach to the Moor before Bury New Road was made. As you entered the lane, Miss Bradford's house stood at the corner on the left, and on the right on the high ground was Dr. Radford's house. From his grounds there was a deep, sandy drop in the lane, and so deep and so loose was the sand that it would find its way over the top of your shoes or boots, obliging you to empty them out to be comfortable after a run down. The descent was broken by a number of fine trees which raised their graceful heads amidst the sea of sand. Some of these are still in existence, and one of them, a grand old ash, is to be found in the grounds of Osborne House. I have quite an affection for that tree, and feel as if it were a part of my life. I played round it when I was a little fellow, and I like it to be there still, and bring back old memories. I think there is in some particular way an affinity between man and trees, and the words of the old song come back to me with a depth of meaning which was absent from them when I first sang them.

"Woodman, spare that tree,
Touch not a single bough;
In youth it sheltered me,
And I'll protect it now."

I do not think I was ever at the races on the Moor, but I have rambled over the course when its old lines were quite distinct. It ran in front of the Kersal Hotel, which has lately been replaced by a new one. Then it swept round the north side of the Moor, the present practice ground for horses being a part of the course. From thence it ran through a portion of the Kersal Churchyard, past the police station, across the road, curling round by the backs of the houses fronting Bury New Road and Vine Street. After this it took a straight course in front, of the grand stand which stood between the Kersal Cricket Ground and the hotel.

Before the grand stand sank into hopeless decay it was used for some time as the Sunday Schools attached to Kersal Church. What a happy contradiction of circumstances, that the place which had doubtless been a very hotbed of gambling and intemperance should afterwards become the religious training ground of the young and innocent!

Descending the Moor Road, towards Agecroft, by turning to the left when reaching the foot of the hill you come to Kersal Cell, the old home of Miss Atherton. On the left of this road before coming to the Cell there is another quaint English homestead. It is now a farm-house, but this and the Cell are very interesting specimens of the English country house of a century ago.

To those who have not seen them they are well worth a visit. The Cell is getting somewhat dilapidated in appearance, but the farmhouse is evidently still well cared for. They have both of them such an old world look about them that you cannot help thinking of who and what sort of people their first occupants were. Situated as they were in the very heart of the country, they speak of a mode and of conditions of life in every way different to our own. In the front of the farmhouse the ladies' old mounting steps are still visible, though strengthened and built up with new material.

Coming to Agecroft Bridge, which lies to the right of Moor Road, you find it a comparatively new structure, and it is not the original one that I remember. It runs parallel with the conduit pipe bridge which conveys the Thirlmere water to the Prestwich reservoir for distribution through Manchester and Salford.

Passing through Drinkwater's Park and then a bleachwork, you reach Prestwich Clough. Even now it is a pleasant walk enough, but as I first knew it it was simply a charming country ramble. It was then well wooded, with a stream of clear sparkling water running through it from end to end. Here we could come for our picnics, wandering about through the woods and fields, and gathering all manner of wild flowers in abundance. To those who know where to look for them wild hyacinths can still be found, but they do not now last long, for there are many more hands to pluck them.

As I write an incident comes back to me in connection with a Prestwich holiday ramble, and which made its impression upon me at the time. I, with some half-dozen kindred spirits, organised an expedition for the purpose of providing ourselves with shinny sticks (the game is called hockey now). Each member of the gang having provided himself with a serviceable weapon in the shape of a large dinner knife, with which to declare "war to the knife" on the trees and hedges, and thus armed we went on our way rejoicing. However, as we were entering Blackfield

Lane we happened to pounce upon some small boys who were evidently impressed with our warlike appearance and our knives. We, therefore, to let them see the kind of stuff we were made of, and brandishing our knives in the air, performed a kind of war dance around them. Our demonstration, accompanied by a series of unearthly shrieks, so unnerved the poor children that they began to howl. This attracted the attention of some passers by who came to their assistance, and, when they understood the position, they turned upon us and made things pretty lively for the lot of us. Somebody has said somewhere, of somebody, that he got more kicks than halfpence. Well, on the occasion to which I refer, I am quite sure no halfpence came our way, but the kicks (I speak feelingly) did. So after a very feeble effort on the part of some of the gang to look as if they meant business, and with a final flourish of our knives we beat ignominious retreat. Very shortly afterwards the youthful band of desperados might have been seen fleeing for their very lives through Kersal tollbar in search of happier hunting grounds.

There is a little spot about which I should like to say a few words before I bring this chapter to a close. It is at the junction of Singleton and Cheetham Hill Roads. It is the last house, or rather cottage, on the left-hand side before you turn into the road. There is a house there now but it cannot be compared with the beautiful little place it once was. It was then a very bijou kind of Swiss chalet and quite a picture in its way. Everything about it was on the most diminutive scale possible. The cottage itself was altogether lilliputian in its character, and outside in the garden the surroundings were in unison with it. There was a little stream of water running underneath a tiny bridge. The garden was kept in the most perfect order and the Rowers which bloomed on all sides completed very pretty picture.

Mr. Richard Hooke, the artist, who was then a bachelor, lived in it at the time to which I refer. He took the greatest pride in his charming little place, and kept everything about it in the most exquisite order. It was, in fact, a sort of show cottage, and you would rarely pass by without seeing a crowd of people looking over the railings at the landscape in miniature.

If you were a friend you were very sure of a hearty welcome inside, where he would dispense his hospitality with a generous kindly grace. It has been my privilege to claim Mr. Hooke as a personal friend for a very long period of my life. And although illness has laid him aside from his work as an artist, it is still always a real pleasure to get into social contact with such a true-hearted gentleman and companion, and one gifted with such an inexhaustible fund of anecdote and dry humour (appropriately, though perhaps at times somewhat nervously, expressed) the outcome of a well-stored and cultured mind.

CHAPTER XXI

The Old 'Bus Office, Higher Broughton – "Joe," the Prestwich 'Bus Guard – John Stuart, Thomas Barge, Alderman Willert, Mr. Leppoc, Mr. Sale.

THERE is an old spot about which I should like to say a few words, and which I am sure has an especial interest for all those who lived in Kersal and Broughton fifty years ago, and this is the 'Bus Office, which stood on the ground now occupied by the stables of The Manchester Carriage Company. It was a small, modest structure, built of wood, where a few people could shelter on a wet day until their 'Bus drew up to carry them to town. It was built on a bare patch of cindered ground, lying back some distance from the road, but plain and uninteresting as it was compared with the buildings which succeeded it, it had its time and place, and as it were, dovetailed into the daily lives and circumstances of those, who, many of them have now passed over to the great majority.

Here it was that the Prestwich 'Bus made a special stop for passengers, and as the driver drew up in front of the office, he did so with as much of the Old Weller air as could be manufactured out of a prosaic three-horse omnibus and its usual appointments. "Joe," the guard, who before he degenerated into an ordinary tram-guard, was a well-known figure on this Prestwich 'Bus, was young, bright and obliging. He would stand on the step at the back and blow his horn as he came along with great vigour, whilst the driver flourished his whip and handled his horses in quite the old stage-coach style, as if to the manner born. I think Joe felt that he had lost caste when he had to desert his 'Bus for a machine-like tram, which could not get along as it liked, but he was obliged to swallow his pride, and accept the inevitable. Joe was

JOHN STUART ESQ.,
MANCHESTER BANKER

a great politician in his way, and if things did not go kindly for him in that direction, he was apt to be "a little bit crossish i'th grain," and could not altogether refrain from giving expression to his feelings. He fell into bad health some time ago, and died after a somewhat lingering illness. But I like to think of "Joe" as I used to see him, a fresh, ruddy complexioned young man, tootling his horn down Bury New Road, and thus filling in his allotted space in the drama of life, and in the eye of the world.

The terminus for the old Prestwich 'Bus was at the "Old Boar's Head," in Withy Grove, and here, as it drew smartly up, the residue of the passengers alighted; and here, too, almost as regular as the morning came round, the sturdy figure of John Stuart, the banker, or "plain, honest John Stuart," as he was christened by his friend Thomas Barge, might be seen descending the steps and walking along to his place of business in Corporation Street. He nearly always rode on what was termed the "knifeboard" of the 'Bus, for he liked to keep himself as young as possible; and I think, too, that having a simple, frugal mind, he liked to save the extra coppers, however generous he might be in larger matters. He always carried a rug with him, and as soon as he had mounted the 'Bus, he would open it out and share it with his next-door neighbour. If this happened to be a friend he would chat away with him on the various topics of the day, business, political or social. He loved a bit of gossip, but as he was a little deaf you would see him with his hand to his ear, enjoying with an interested expression on his face the latest bit of social chit-chat that happened to be going.

Another regular traveller on the road was Thomas Barge. He was a very thin, proper looking man, and remarkably methodical in all he did. He nearly always wore a pair of black or very sombre-looking gloves, as serious looking as himself, and to the extremities of which his long fingers never seemed capable of travelling, and there was consequently a row of twisted corkscrew ends, something after the style of Aminadab Sleek in the play of "The Serious Family." He had an apparently unconscious habit of taking off his gloves and then immediately putting them on again, the operation being performed again and again for the most trivial of reasons. He was a kindly gentleman of the old school, quaintly polite and especially careful to show every attention to the ladies, and when in the 'Bus he seemed to consider that they were for the time being under his special care and guardianship.

Then there was Alderman Willert, who used to live in a fine house at the corner of Bury New Road and Park Lane. It was pulled down many years ago, and on a portion of the grounds the house occupied by the present Dean Maclure was built. The Alderman was quite a beau in his own particular way. He was always very spruce and debonair, and was never without a large handsome flower in his buttonhole, and in a paper called "The Free Lance," which was published in Manchester at that time, he was christened "Mr. Bloomingrock." It was whispered (hush!) that he wore stays, but be that as it may, he had an air and style, "tout à fait, à la militaire." He also wore a very tight-fitting, black, satin stock, which seemed to make him walk erect, but which gave him a screwed up, uncomfortable sort of appearance. He, too, was a great ladies' man, and had a remarkably quick eye for any pretty faces.

When he entered the 'Bus he would look around, and if possible plant himself in as close proximity as he could, to the most attractive-looking young lady he could see. This done, he would engage her in conversation, and as he had a loud, metallic voice, all his compliments and pretty speeches could be heard all over the 'Bus, which was at times rather embarrassing for their recipients.

Mr. Leppoc, of Messrs. Hermann, Samson and Leppoc, was also a well-known man in Broughton. A German by birth, he had been so long amongst us that all his interests and affections seemed to be centred in the place which he had adopted as his home. He was a large-hearted, kindly man, ready to succour the distressed wherever they might be found. He took a real pleasure in doing good, and a deaf ear was never turned to any one who came to him in trouble. Moreover, he sought out those who, suffering silently and secretly, would not let their misfortunes be known, and when any such were found, he was never content until in some way or another they had been relieved. He lived in a house close to the old Kersal toll bar, and although many years have elapsed since Mr. Leppoc passed away, yet even to this day the small man with the big heart is missed by high and low, rich and poor.

Mr. Sale, the solicitor, who does not remember him,

with his clear, sharp, searching eyes, and the iron-grey whiskers at which he was, from habit, constantly pulling? Not very talkative except when he was so disposed, he took a great interest in all that was passing around him. At the time of which I am speaking he was generally considered one of the most astute and ablest lawyers in Manchester, and had probably the largest practice. He was a man who could quickly grasp the salient points of a case, and define a wise and equitable solution. As a rule he avoided Court issues, if this could be done without in any way sacrificing the interests of his clients. What he aimed at was a fair and reasonable settlement of the matter in dispute, but after having once put on his armour he would fight out the case with ability and determination.

There is a portrait of Mr. Sale hanging in the dining room of the Clarendon Club in Mosley Street, of which Club he was president, and I do not think that a better or more speaking likeness could have been obtained of him. You could almost imagine that the man was there in person before you, ready to listen to what you have to say to him. He was a man whose strong individuality of character impressed itself upon all those with whom he came into contact. I look back to my friendship with him with true pleasure, and must always regret that such an intercourse has ceased.

CHAPTER XXII

Cabbage Island and the Great Cheetham Street Brickfields – The Boulder Stone in Great Clowes Street – The Grove Inn and its Gardens.

Some mention of other changes which have taken place in Broughton since 1845 may not be without interest, more especially for its older inhabitants, and so I give a short account of the most noticeable. Where St. James's Church now stands, there used to be a large pond with a small island in its centre, which went by the somewhat unpoetical name of Cabbage Island, so called from the fact that somebody who lived near at hand did originally grow a few feeble-looking cabbages on this spot, getting across to his possessions by means of a raft. At that period of my existence I belonged to a tribe of ubiquitous mortals, which, if it did not literally go about seeking for its prey, was certainly not averse to laying hold of anything that came in its way, and which could in any material sense minister to its pleasure or profit. It was, therefore, good sport for our party to get sailing about on this pond on the raft, until admonished by its owner, when, of course, we took to flight, but were always ready again to brave the dangers of the deep when the enemy was out of sight.

This spot, too, was one of our favourite places for skating in the winter, and it was rather a pretty sight to see the pond skirted by lanterns and candles, whilst we enjoyed ourselves skimming over the ice, the merry voices of the youthful skaters being heard in all directions. Now there no longer remains a vestige of either pond or island, and the whole thing seems like a dream, as you look at the crowds of houses, shops and buildings, which cover the ground where once they were.

This pond was situated in a very wilderness of

brickfields, which naturally did not add, conspicuously to the beauty of the landscape. Not, however, that I am aware that this particular fact made any impression upon me at the time. But the eye could hardly dwell with much sense of gratification on avenues and walls of unbaked bricks interspersed with huge unsightly-looking brickfields, where what vegetation there might be was rank and uninviting to a degree. However, even the making of bricks is an interesting occupation to watch, and many a time have I gazed in wonder and admiration at the rapidity with which the men would turn them out. They always seemed to be able to gauge to a nicety the size of the slab of wet clay required to fill the box, and then with a quick dab and the scrape of a wooden knife, out fell a perfect brick; whilst a small nipper kind of boy would carry the bricks away on a wooden board to be piled for drying. The impression left on my mind was that the clothes and faces of the men and boys, were perhaps more thickly coated with clay than appeared absolutely necessary. Possibly they, like sweeps and bakers, are inclined to a somewhat lavish display of their various trades insignia.

There was another object of interest in this locality and this was the large boulder stone which was originally to be found on a spot called Stony Knolls (and which probably accounted for the name given to this place). The stone rested securely on the gravel bed at the junction of Great Clowes Street and Murray Street, long since covered with house property. The boulder was considered such a fine specimen of its kind, that it was eventually removed to Peel Park, where duly labelled, it remains still an object of interest. This stone being a distinctive object as it stood there alone in its glory, was often the rendezvous and playground for the young people of the neighbourhood, forming a sort of rallying point in our various games. I think I may say with truth that it has largely helped me to wear out my suits and drag off my buttons as I and my companions jumped and sprawled upon it.

The Grove Inn (which was lately the terminus of the

Manchester Electric Tram system, and is the boundary line between Manchester and Salford), is in outward appearance pretty much as I remember it for the last fifty-seven years, but its immediate surroundings have changed considerably. On the ground now occupied by the two houses below the Inn, and further on by other business premises, and the Congregational Chapel, there was a tea garden and bowling green connected with the Grove Inn. To encourage people to come from Manchester to these gardens, the landlord used to have periodical displays of fireworks. They were nothing very grand, but to a young mind the very mention of fireworks in those days had a particular fascination, and as I lived close at hand I was naturally drawn in the direction of these gardens on firework nights. As I was not in those days always the lucky possessor of sixpence to pay for admission, I sometimes endeavoured to see them free of charge by climbing the wall which encircled the gardens. There I was happy unless I happened to be disturbed and caught, in which case I probably saw fireworks of another kind; some people have such prejudiced views as to the ordinary rights of merely looking over a wall.

CHAPTER XXIII

Broughton continued – Bury New Road – Fairy Lane – The Old Toffee Shop – The Little Welsh Chapel – The Old Tollbar, Strangeways.

FROM the Grove Inn to Sherbourne Street, green fields were to be found on both sides of the road. Fairy, or Lover's Lane, as it was sometimes called, a little below the Congregational Chapel, was once a sweet country walk, which was very tempting to town pedestrians in the summer time; it is now a dirty, sloppy place and anything but inviting, as you glance up at it in passing. On the top of the hill there were a few old-fashioned country houses, in one of which lived a Mr. Cooper, a dancing master, and a man well known in Broughton. He was the father of Edwin, Albert and Fred Cooper, the first named afterwards continuing for a number of years his father's profession, but he and his brothers have been dead for some years. The father was a very dignified old gentleman, and although he lived to be an octogenarian, he was a great advocate for walking, and could put many a young man to the blush by the long distances he could cover in a day.

A little below this lane on the same side, there stood a very diminutive Welsh Chapel, only capable of accommodating a mere handful of worshippers, it was very old-fashioned, primitive and quaint, and might have been dropped down from some little Welsh mountain hamlet, but I presume it served its day and generation.

Next to it was an odd-looking little cobbler's shop, both of which stood back a little from the road, the spot where they once were being now hidden away behind one of the many unsightly advertising hoardings which so disfigure our roads in all directions. In this respect at any rate the "Good Old Times" were certainly best.

Nearly opposite to the little Welsh Chapel there abutted on to the road, "a long time ago," a little shop, perhaps the oddest sort of thing to be found in the neighbourhood. It was like an overgrown sentry box, sufficiently large to allow for a doorway and a window, and in the latter was displayed, toffee, apples, nuts, gingerbread and oranges. The toffee was then often sold in long, round sticks, of about the thickness of your finger. It was wrapped round with white, or coloured paper, screwed at the end, and buying in this form you always seemed to have such a lot for your money, a very material consideration to a young mind. The gingerbread was the real old-fashioned gingerbread man – head, arms and legs, all complete. Perhaps the paint that was used to mark his large blue eyes, his red nose and mouth, might as well have been omitted from a stomachic point of view, but boys in the matter of eating do not usually devote themselves largely to the study of hygienic principles.

The shop was attended by a plain, large-boned but respectable old woman, who lived in the hollow below in a cottage that had probably been built generations back, and was apparently all that was left to her of some old farmstead. As time passed on I am afraid stick toffee and gingerbread men must have fallen off in demand, for the old lady ceased to expose these articles for sale, and eventually the shutters to the window of the tiny shop went up, but she continued to live on in the cottage in the field for many years after this. Whenever I used to see her she always seemed to be either filling pails with water from the pump, or else emptying them out. In any case she appeared to keep her place clean and tidy, and to take a pride in doing so, having likely lived there all her life. But there came a day when she and her pails came no more out, and then slowly but surely the cottage in which she had lived and died, sank quietly to decay.

In the same field close to this cottage there stood the skeleton of some old brick building, which had been falling, to pieces even in the old woman's time, until at last it became a mere hillock of old and broken bricks. But even then these were not removed for a long time, and the impression was that this building had some connection with the old lease of the land, and that this accounted for the respect with which this old rubbish heap was treated for so long a time. Talking of the old woman and her pump, it is almost impossible to realise that in those days all water for drinking and culinary purposes had to be drawn and brought from the nearest pump. Of course all houses had rain-water cisterns, but these were only available for cleansing purposes. Just imagine the labour this used to be to domestic servants? For it must be borne in mind that one pump had to do for many households, and the distances from the pump were often long, but this was perhaps not an unmixed evil from the servants' point view, as it gave them an opportunity of having a chat with their friends and sweethearts, and from which cause, I am afraid, the water was often a long time in getting to its destination.

Milkcarts, too, at this time were a luxury in which only the few indulged, and the custom was for the men to pass from house to house with two large cans fastened to iron hooks, and suspended from a shoulder yoke of wood, which fitted close round the neck, like a wooden collar. As they passed along they called out "Meque," or something like it, and then the maid would come out with her bowls to have them filled. What a wonderful economy of labour there is now in these and similar domestic matters, and what a hardship we should find it to have to go back to the old state of things, and yet of which our forefathers seemed to think so little.

From the Grove Inn to Sherbourne Street, and partially as far as Frances Street, where the Boys' Refuge now is, there lay, running parallel with the road, a long belt of hilly ground sloping down gradually to the level of the road. These grassy slopes formed in summer time a very pleasant prospect as you walked along from town, and even to this day you come across some of these green slopes which give an indication of what they once were. Of course one must understand that North, South, East and West, the fields and open spaces which then existed, are now covered over with factories, shops, houses and other erections of various kinds, altering materially and alas unfavourably, the whole aspect of the locality. Even on the river side of Sherbourne Street, and where Muir's Works now stand, I can remember running along the old hedgerows and across the fields, when going to St. Simon's Church in Springfield Lane.

The old Strangeways Tollbar stretched across the road from where Harwood's shop now is to a shop which was built on the site of the old Tollhouse, and which was for sometime occupied by a Jew of the name of Marx, so at that time he marked the spot where it stood. How almost impossible it is to conceive that at one time every conveyance, big or little, horse or donkey, had to stop here and pay toll, and this at a distance of less than half-a-mile from the Cathedral, or "th' owd Church," as the Lancashire folk then called it. And if you arrived at the Bar after twelve at night you had to wake the people up, a dreary sort of business after perhaps coming off a long journey on a winter's night. It is no wonder that the use of strong language was indulged in to a much greater extent a generation back under such trying conditions. Fancy young people of the present day returning home from a dance say about three in the morning, and reaching the tollbar in a heavy fall of snow. First they would have to hammer at the door to rouse the sleeping and unfortunate collector, and to wait until he robed himself to come down to them, then after satisfying his demands they could proceed as far as Kersal Bar, when a repetition of the same thing occurred, whilst tired, sleepy and angry they would be wishing themselves at home. Truly we have much to be thankful for in the fact that we live in a day when tollbars have ceased to trouble us.

CHAPTER XXIV

Cheetwood Lane.

OF all those who daily pass along Strangeways and Waterloo Road, there is probably not one in a thousand who is aware that there is such a place as Cheetwood Lane; and yet it is without doubt one of the most interesting, and at the same time sad-looking relics of the past which can well be imagined. You can enter this lane either from Waterloo Road by passing along the western side of Cheetwood Park, or else by Sherbourne Street. But enter Cheetwood Lane how and where you may, you are no sooner in it (if it be your first visit) than you begin to wonder where you are, as you look around at your strange and almost grotesque surroundings, and you are inclined to exclaim: "Have I lived in Manchester all these years and never taken the trouble to come here before?"

The first thing that strikes you as you gaze around, is the number of old-fashioned, tumble-down houses which are perched about in all directions. They are of all shapes, sizes, and qualities, some of them are up hill, others are down dale. There are houses that have been family residences, with Corinthian pillars in front of the verandas, hodnobbing with primitive little cottages. To judge by appearances you would come to the conclusion that here at anyrate every man was his own architect, and that the object of each was to build something different to his neighbour, and plant what he built in the most out of the way place that he could select. Of course the place has very much changed since I first remember it. Then it was a really sweet, pretty country lane, up and down which it was a pleasure to ramble, and admire the gardens with their flowers and foliage. Now excavations in many directions have demolished much that was attractive, and

VIEW IN CHEETWOOD LANE, 1901

EXCAVATORS AT WORK, CHEETWOOD, 1901

robbed the place of almost all its old charm; but still there is just enough left, even now, to enable you to picture in some measure at least what it once was.

When you get on to the high ground and look around, you realise what an ideal country paradise it must have been say a hundred years ago, and yet you see you are but a stone's throw from Bury New Road, the Assize Courts and the Prison. As you ramble on you feel as if you had been dropped into the middle of some God-forsaken place, which somehow had been omitted to be cleared away in the ordinary course of things. Everything seems so topsy-turvy and has such a woe-begotten look about it, and yet there is withal a fascination about the whole place which somehow impresses you, and instinctively links you with the past, and sets you thinking about many things.

Cheetwood Lane can boast three taverns, the "Wellington Inn," the "Cheetham Arms," and the "Blue Bell," the quaintest of these is the last named, and here it is where the gay and festive beings of the neighbourhood are informed that they can riot in a game of skittles. One can hardly realise people playing skittles in any such odd-looking hostel, and yet the last time I passed the "Blue Bell," I looked over the pailings of the courtyard adjoining the house, and there were the skittles standing erect in the full light of day, and only waiting to be knocked down. So it is evident that even at the present time "beer and skittles" are to be had for the asking at the sign of the "Blue Bell" in Cheetwood. The name of this tavern does not now seem to fit into the place and its surroundings, but sixty or seventy years ago I have little doubt that bluebells and wild hyacinths might have been found there in abundance, for from my earliest remembrance of Cheetwood with its hills and hollows, it ought to have been the very spot for these and many other kinds of wild flowers. And it is very probable that here in the summer time the townsfolk strayed about, indulged in "beer and skittles," and gathered their bunches of bluebells to carry home with them.

POND, CHEETWOOD, 1901.

DUKE OF WELLINGTON INN, CHEETWOOD, 1901

OLD COTTAGE, CHEETWOOD, 1901

THE BLUE BELL INN, CHEETWOOD LANE 1901

One of the oddest-looking houses to be found in Cheetwood Lane is, what is, and has been for some time past, St. Alban's Rectory. Here it was that the Reverend Knox-Little used to "reside," and to whom, I believe, it was very much endeared, as the centre of his labours amongst his flock for many years. It still continues to be the Rectory, but from its general appearance, it does not impress you as being a very luxurious abode, and I should imagine it is no easy matter to keep it in even moderate repair. To live in it in the ordinary way with its dreary surroundings, must require the exercise of an exceptionally cheerful temperament to drive away the blues.

The sketches herewith were taken several years ago, but they give some excellent views of the locality, and are interesting, seeing that Cheetwood at the present time is being practically carted away.

CHAPTER XXV

Strangeways Hall – The Jewish Colony

ON the ground now covered by the Assize Courts, there stood before their erection, the old family mansion called Strangeways Hall which, although it had no special features of attraction, had been, no doubt from its appearance, a comfortable residence. It had a broad frontage of grey stucco, and had probably, in its best days, been surrounded with well-wooded grounds and pleasure gardens. In the front of the house was to be seen the lawn with its flower beds, and shut off from the road, by handsome massive gates, which made an excellent approach to the Hall. These gates were supported by large square stone buttresses, and gave a certain dignity to the whole place. When the Hall was demolished to make room for the Assize Courts, these gates were removed to Peel Park, where they are still to be seen. Where Southall Street now is, there used to be a pond adjoining on to the gardens, which at one time had probably added beauty to the grounds; but as I remember it, it was only a dirty piece of stagnant water, a receptacle for dead dogs, cats, boots and shoes, and stray garbage of all kinds. When, therefore, this pond was improved out of existence and Southall Street replaced it, there was no cause for regret. The last occupant of Strangeways Hall before it was pulled down was a gentleman of the name of Junius Smith.

On the same side of Strangeways, joining on to the other side of what was then the pond, there stood a row of private houses, which had evidently from their appearance and the gardens in front, been residences which might have been considered "out of town." In one of these there lived, half-a-century back, a gentleman of the name of Cook, a well-known Manchester man, formerly a partner in the calendering business of Goodier, Krauss and Company, and afterwards a stock and sharebroker. What most impresses itself upon me as regards this Mr. Cook was, that he was a short, stout, pompous, though at the same good-tempered-looking individual. He was very proud of his tall, handsome wife, who stood head and shoulders above him, and was a well-known and attractive figure at that time on the road. This row of houses degenerated with the locality in which they were placed, and when the Assize Courts were built, they were refronted and made into what is now the Woolsack Hotel. The transformation was made in a somewhat novel manner, the outside walls facing the road being pulled down and the various living rooms exposed to public view, and it was rather quaint to watch the interiors of these houses disappearing gradually, as the present front was being literally patched on to the old framework.

On the other side of the road facing the Courts and where Grierson's the baker now is, there stood a pretty red-brick country residence with garden and trees about it. As it gradually lost its residential character, it developed into a chemist's shop, a branch of Taylor's, then of St. Ann's Square. Now the once pleasant little garden is covered by the storerooms of Hodson and Waddington, but what I write will give an indication how in the period mentioned the country dipped down into close proximity to the town. As another instance of this it may surprise some of my readers to be told that there used to be a field at the corner of Kew Bridge Street and Strangeways, approached by a steep decline from the side of Great Ducie Street, and which ascended as sharply again on the Workhouse side. I can recollect this field being covered with patches of rank grass, and where the field reached the high ground on the side of the Workhouse, there stood a row of private houses, facing Strangeways and reached by a narrow footway leading from Kew Bridge Street. An iron balustrade in front of these houses prevented people on a dark night from tumbling down into the field below.

It seemed an odd sort of spot to build houses, and as you glanced across at them in passing, they gave you the idea of having beep stranded there in a flood, like Noah's Ark up Mount Ararat.

From a pedestrian's point of view there can be no manner of doubt that Strangeways has been rapidly degenerating in every way during the last few years. The old private dwelling-houses with their gardens have gradually been converted into shops, and these unfortunately of a most uninviting character, and where the stock-in-trade is anything but tempting in appearance. No doubt the fact that this portion of the City is practically swarming with Jews, does not encourage our own people to settle amongst them, seeing that their whole mode of life is so different to ours. These Jews are mostly of Russian and Polish extraction, who, having been harried and persecuted in their own Countries have sought an asylum here. One, cannot but be sorry for them and for the hardships they have had to endure before they reached our shores, but at the same time it is difficult to be enthusiastic about them, as they present themselves to us in their daily life. For instance, to watch a crowd of dirty, unkempt creatures, in one of their kosher meat shops in the early morning, is anything but an edifying sight. There you may observe, the oddest-looking assortment of female purchasers surrounding the counters of these uninviting-looking establishments and waiting their turn to be served. It would seem to be quite an understood thing that whilst these women are thus hovering about, that each one should thoroughly examine and handle the selection of meat that is offering, in order to satisfy themselves as to its merits. What the condition of the meat must he after all these handlings it is not difficult to imagine, and a purchase made at one of these shops under such conditions can hardly recommend itself to the ordinary English mind. Most of the married women, whether young or old, are, I believe, obliged by some social law to shave their heads, to show their subjection and fealty to their husbands. What these wives were before their marriage I am unable to say, we will hope they were nice looking, but what they now are anyone can judge for himself who passes daily along Strangeways. To the ordinary beholder they are certainly not very attractive in their dingy brown wigs which cover their bald heads. These wigs seem to be all alike in colour, make and ugliness, and give you from their appearance the impression that they are bought wholesale and manufactured by the ton.

When, however, the Jewish Sabbath comes round there is a wonderful transformation, you see the youths and the maidens arrayed in their very best, parading the streets. The women are to be seen in a blaze of dazzling colours, and the men, as far as they dare, following in their wake. Your attention is perhaps arrested by a vision of ultramarine inexpressibles, surmounted by a light waistcoat and a ponderous gold chain. The coat is cut in the excess of the then prevailing fashion, or, if possible, a little more so. The cloth is usually very shiny in finish, and the pattern – well, one sometimes wonders where makers can be found courageous enough to manufacture such remarkable designs. When you have managed to withdraw your astonished gaze from the clothes, you glance at the form and features of the wearer. The height usually runs to a little over five feet, and the face, well, it varies, and we have not always the same ideal as to the human form divine.

The men come sauntering along in twos and threes, with their shoulders up, and their hands, as a rule, deep down in their pockets; and as you look at the most of them you can see what generations of cruelty, oppression and wrong have accomplished, in striving to stamp out all that is noble, manly or attractive. But I must frankly admit that in spite of what I write, the Jews who live in the Strangeways Colony have greatly improved both physically and otherwise to what they were even a few years back. In many instances their features have lost the marred, hunted look, which they once had; and as you glance down the side streets, where a large crowd of little ones are growing up, you will notice that if they are not actually good-looking, they are at least healthy and vigorous in appearance, whilst some of the little ones are even cleanly too, a charge which cannot always be brought against their parents.

CHAPTER XXVI

The Assize Courts[4].

WHEN, over thirty years ago, Strangeways Hall was razed to the ground, and the present handsome Assize Courts built on its site, with the County Prison on the background, Manchester assumed a legal status in the kingdom which had hitherto been denied her. It had been felt, for some time previous to this, that with the very great development of the city, commercially and otherwise, it had become a necessity that Manchester should be able to hold her own Assizes.

My earliest recollections of the interior of the courts, after watching the course of their building daily on my way to town, was when the Social Science Congress held its meetings there in 1866, Lord Shaftesbury presiding. At one of these meetings which I attended Lord Brougham, who was then a very old man, gave an address. Whilst he was speaking his dental fixtures refused to remain in their appointed place, and fell out. However, he did not appear very much disconcerted, and, quietly replacing them, mumbled indistinctly, "Ladies and gentlemen, our teeth are a trouble to us from the time we are born to the time of our death," and then proceeded with his address. I must confess that these Assize Courts had a great attraction for me, and I still think that there is nothing more interesting, and even enjoyable, than listening to some "cause célèbre" in which able counsel are engaged. The Crown Court I have as a rule carefully avoided, as the issues tried in it are usually painful or distressing; but in the Civil Court I have always been glad to avail myself of

---

4 - *Manchester Assize Courts. Designed by Alfred Waterhouse built 1859 demolished 1950s following extensive WWII bomb damage.*

the opportunity of being present when the development of some case has allowed the leading and shining lights of the old Northern Circuit to display their forensic capabilities. Next to the stage there is, I think, no body of men where the idiosyncrasy of the individual is more readily distinguishable than amongst the members of the Bar; and to a quiet observer there is nothing more interesting than to note the various personal characteristics which seem to attach themselves more distinctly to those who belong to this particular profession.

Perhaps a few remarks on these members of the old Northern Circuit of a past generation – some of whom have passed away – may not be without interest. The figure which seems to bulk most prominently on my mental vision in the early days of the Manchester Assize Courts is that of Edward James, Q.C.[5], elected in 1865 after a few days canvass as member for Manchester. If I happened to drop into the Nisi Prius Court and found him engaged in the case I was more than satisfied. He was perhaps not the most amiable Q.C. in the world, and at times he would get to angry words even with the judges. But he had a wonderfully acute legal mind, and when he got thoroughly roused in the cross-examination of some witness it was interesting, but at the same time almost painful, to listen to him as he tortured his victim by extracting from him the evidence he wanted. I remember on one special occasion, when the witness was evidently trying to deceive the Court, he turned the wretched man's evidence so completely inside out that when he had finished with him he came out of the box so limp and crestfallen that you could hardly help feeling sorry for him. Woe betide the witness who tried to bandy words with James or endeavoured to make a joke at his expense! He would have a very bad time of it whilst under examination. In fact, a very distinct impression was left upon my mind that there was no man whose cross-examination I would

---

5 - *Edward James (barrister) (1807-1867) MP for Manchester (1865-67)*

have avoided as readily as his.

He was a powerful advocate, and he had the gift of presenting his case to a jury in an exceptionally clear and forcible manner. He was not a man who tried to win over a jury to his side; he tried to convince them. His irritability of manner prevented him being as great a favourite as he might otherwise have been, more especially with the judges, who were apt to resent his brusque, determined style.

Another very able man on this Circuit, and one who was a great favourite on account of his genial presence and disposition, was Sam Pope, K.C., the news of whose death I have just heard. He had a splendid connection, particularly amongst the temperance party, whose advocate he was. His practice during late years was confined to London, as, owing to his enormous bulk, he was not able to move about as he once did. My first recollection of him dates back fifty years, when he used to be a member of the Athenæum Cricket Club, and I recall his large, manly form as he walked, bat in hand, to the cricket crease, or with sword waving above his head going through his exercise with other members of the club. He was then young and full of health and vigour, and although he was always of large physique, he had not developed the amount of adipose tissue which in later years became such a burden to him.

It was always a pleasure to see his full, round, bright, cheery, dimpled face in court, and although he did not worry his witnesses in cross-examination as James often did, he was still quite capable of ferreting out all he wanted to know, though he arrived at his goal through a more agreeable channel.

After the death of James, John Holker came more prominently into the front rank, and soon became a general favourite on the circuit. He had certain peculiarities which causes him to remain more distinctly with me mentally than is the case with many others. When he was on his feet he invariably held a crystal ball, which he gently rubbed and passed from hand to hand behind his back. This crystal, which was egg shaped, was especially active when he had the cross-examination of a witness in hand, and I think he must have had the impression that it inspired him. But, whether or not, I am sure he would have felt completely lost if anyone had deprived him of his talisman. When he had asked a question he closed his lips and moved his head to one side, with a glance in the direction of the jurybox of a confidential nature, as much as to say, "Now I've given him a poser, just you listen to his answer."

I do not remember to have ever seen him ruffled in temper, and when he got on his feet it was with a thoroughly satisfied air, as if he felt it was his innings and that he was going to have a good time of it. He always looked like winning whether he did or not, and when a case did go against him he marked his brief and gathered up his papers, to all appearance just as satisfied as if he had won instead of having lost.

He was eminently wise and judicious in his arguments with the judges, and he never allowed his witnesses to travel too quickly for the pen of his lordship; he invariably gave a quiet upward glance to see if the judge were ready before he proceeded. He spoke in an easy conversational style, which was pleasant to listen to; and his sort of "I quite agree with all you've been saying" manner often threw an adverse witness off his guard, and enabled him to get in the easiest and most innocent looking way what a less conciliatory manner might have failed to extract.

Then he had the happy knack of making his own witnesses feel quite at home with him at once, and so was able to get their evidence from them in the clearest and best form for the strengthening of his case both with judge and jury. There was a smooth, persuasive way about all he said and did, and at the same time a freedom from irritability and excitement, which had a good effect upon the jury. And in listening to him you were inclined to say to yourself, "Well now, here's a man who evidently wants to get at the simple facts of the case." This might be so, but at the same time I fear his motives were not so innocent as they appeared on the surface. There lurked in what he did the wisdom of the serpent beneath the soft feathers of the dove. After all, there is no denying the fact that the Bar is a wonderful stage for the exercise of the actor's most finished and delicate talent.

When Russell[6], our late Lord Chief Justice, was in full swing on the Northern Circuit, he had a busy time of it, and anyone who had secured him for any case in which he was interested, always felt that the battle was half won with Russell on his side. He had a wonderfully clear logical mind, and was remarkably gifted in getting quickly at the salient points of any case he had in hand. This must have been exceptionally so with him, to have enabled him to grapple so successfully with all the work that was thrust upon him. He had a brusque, determined manner, and even his own clients came in for a fair share of this as well as the opposing side. He always liked a full consultation with his client before going on with the case. I remember a friend who had secured him as his counsel, and when he was summoned for consultation, my friend said he felt more like a culprit than a plaintiff. He was bullied, harried, and cross-questioned, as to why he did this and why he did not do the other, until he felt as if he were the guilty party and was very sorry for himself. However, when he heard Russell argue the matter in court, he felt he had the whole case at his finger ends, and that he was making the very best use of all the information he had worried out of him when in consultation.

He came into court in a quick, hurried manner, and immediately became busy amongst his papers, showing unmistakably that the sooner the business of the court began, the better he would be pleased. He vas very ready to pull up the opposing counsel when he was travelling

---

6 - Charles Russell, Baron Russell of Killowen - (1832-1900) - advocate of Irish Home Rule, successfully defending Parnell at his Commission trial of 1888. Lord Chief Justice 1894-1900.

over wrong ground. Nothing escaped him in regard to sight or hearing, and when the opportunity presented itself of risking a point in his favour he was not slow to take advantage of it, and was at once on his feet. When he strongly disapproved of some argument on the other side, it was not difficult to see by the set look in his face, and the arm thrown protestingly over the back of the bench, what he thought of it. He was a very fearless man in court, and he did not scruple to disagree or argue with the judge himself if he considered himself in the right.

Who does not remember Sowler, another Q.C., as, short of stature, he might be seen at Assize times hurrying along to the courts with his brief bag in his hand? He was a quaint little man in appearance, and if not brilliant in his profession, he was at least a sound, safe man to have on your side, whilst socially he was a favourite with the Bar.

Then there was J. H. P. Leresche, an excellent lawyer and a good man for counsel's opinion. He was one who always tried to look at life from the bright and cheery side. He liked his little joke in court and out of it, and wherever and whenever you met him he was merry and light-hearted, his laugh being infectious.

There are many others of whom I could speak. Dr. Pankhurst, the vocal Esau and Jacob, bass and tenor in combination. The ever and always beaming and radiant Ambrose, Addison, Cottingham, Tor, Edwards, whose promising career was cut short by mental decay. Makinson, now the Salford Stipendiary, Washington Heywood, who only enjoyed for a short period his promotion to the judgeship now held by Judge Parry, Jordan, afterwards Judge Jordan, who when I first knew him was a reporter on the staff of the "Examiner and Times." Then there was Ernest Jones, Bigham, Mannisty, and many others. Some are still with us, some have changed their fields of labour, whilst others have passed over to the great majority. Compared with a generation past the personnel of the Bar of the Northern Circuit has greatly changed, and many names which were once so familiar in our ears have ceased to exist. Still, it is pleasant to think of those who were the legal props and pillars of the Assize Courts in the days gone by, to recall their features and the personal characteristics which distinguished them.

There are, of course, some special and distinctive peculiarities which seem to pertain to the Bar as a whole, respecting which I might add a few words. And, first of all, how is it that so many of the members of the Bar are addicted to wearing glasses? Is it because their sight as a general thing is bad, or has what was once a small vanity developed into a very general characteristic of the profession? Be this as it may, there is no manner of doubt that very effective by-play can be made with a solitary eye-glass or a pair of pince-nez. I can call to mind one barrister who, when he glanced at his brief, always glued a piece of round rimless glass into his eye. I suppose the action must have helped his vision, or he would not have done it; but this was not the impression conveyed to the onlooker. Then, when counsel is on his feet, it seems a help towards the birth of a new idea, in examining a witness or addressing the jury, to place suddenly the pince-nez on to the bridge of the nose, and commence a rapid stampede through the folios of his brief, finding his place just as he is ready with another point in his case, or with another question for the witness. When a barrister is not trifling with his pince-nez, he feels he must have something to play with; it may be an envelope, a quill pen, a piece of pink tape, or perhaps some article which has come before the court during the course of the trial. As a rule, however, counsel is never really quite at ease, unless he has something in his hand to emphasise and give more direct point to his remarks. When the case allows of the introduction of a model of some sort, to which he can point with a long stick or wand, then counsel is thoroughly happy. He rambles about over that model like a child with a new toy. He pokes it here and he pokes it there, until there is not a crevice or corner with which the jury is not familiar.

When counsel is anxious to get on a confidential footing with the jury, he will often put his foot on the bench beside him, lean one arm on his knee, clasping his two hands together, whilst he pleads with the jury on this point or that. But when he wants to prove what a villain the man on the other side has been, he stands erect, full of virtuous indignation, while he metaphorically shatters his victim into a thousand fragments. During the process he every now and again pulls his gown up fiercely on to his shoulder, and gathers his hands together underneath its folds. Then he will summon up once more, in imagination, the man whom he has been denouncing in such unmeasured terms, and place him in the witness box whilst he points at him the finger of scorn. Gradually he cools down as previously he had warmed up, and, after the delivery of his peroration, he suddenly sits down, with the air of a man who has really nothing further to do with the case, that it has lost all interest for him, and that it is now altogether a matter for judge and jury.

CHAPTER XXVII

The Cathedral – Ben Lang's – Old Deansgate – John Heywood.

THE Cathedral, or the "Old Church," as it was called before Manchester could boast of a Bishop, was black with soot and age as I first recall it to mind, and so begrimed was it with the accumulated deposit of many generations, that it gave it quite a velvety appearance. Old age, too, had begun to tell upon the tower, to such an extent that the pinnacles were pronounced unsafe and had to be removed, and in their place there was erected upon the top of the tower, a square balustrade made of heavy beams of black painted wood. This addition was certainly not ornamental in its character, in fact it was ugly to a degree. It reminded you of the framework of a scaffold, wanting but the block, the headsman and the victim, to make the resemblance complete. The object in erecting this wooden structure was to lend additional safety to the rest of the tower, by keeping the old worn blocks of stones in position. However, at last the tower itself was declared to be unsafe and had to come down, when the present one, which is, I believe, an exact copy of the other, was erected in its place. As long as I can remember the Old Church, in one form or another, the edifice has been in the hands of architects, builders and masons, for no sooner had one portion of the structure been removed, that it seemed necessary to pull down another, and so the work of renovation has gone on almost continuously. Lately a West Porch has been added which, although it does not meet with universal admiration, does give a general effect of completeness and finish to the Cathedral and its surroundings. No doubt there are some of us who remember "Old Manchester" in the Exhibition of 1887, where the Church was approached

THE RIVER IRWELL FROM BLACKFRIARS BRIDGE, 1859

on the North side by natural formations in the old red sandstone on the crest of which the Old Church stood. I seem to have some recollection of this approach, or is it some old print that recalls this fact to my mind? In the old edifice there was in the centre the small tower, by which it is said that Guy Fawkes escaped from the hands of his pursuers, and which had always a special interest for me on this account. As I used to glance up at it in my young days it was more particularly associated in my mind with Harrison Ainsworth's romantic history of Guy Fawkes with its thrilling incidents of local colouring.

After passing the Cathedral we are practically in the precincts of the business centre of the City, and the changes which have taken place in this locality are so great and widespread, that there is really nothing left to remind you of what it once was. There was no statue of Oliver Cromwell[7] to arrest your attention, and where the Grosvenor Hotel now stands, there was to be found Ben Lang's Music Hall, which was liberally supported by the working-classes. I was never in the place myself, but to judge of those I saw going in and coming out, as I passed along, there would probably be a strong flavour of corduroy and tobacco at these entertainments. It must have been pretty warm, too, inside, as it was usually found expedient to keep the windows open, and for this reason one could often hear the chorus or refrain of the last Music

---

7. *A statue of Cromwell by Matthew Noble was erected in Manchester (1875) outside the cathedral, a gift to the city by Mrs Abel Heywood in memory of her first husband. It was the first such large-scale public statue of Cromwell erected in England. The statue was unpopular with local Conservatives and the large Irish population. When Queen Victoria was invited to open the new Manchester Town Hall, she is alleged to have consented on condition that the statue of Cromwell be removed. The statue remained, Victoria declined and the Town Hall was opened by the Lord Mayor. During the 1980s the statue was relocated outside Wythenshawe Hall, which had been occupied by Cromwell and his troops during the Civil War.*

Hall ditty, coming wafted along to you on the breeze.

From this place also you could take steamer down to Pomona Gardens, which was likewise a much sought-after place of entertainment at this time. You had to get on to these steamers by a long flight of narrow steps, and in the firework season at Pomona, large numbers of people used to avail themselves of this mode of getting to the gardens. The steamers were not very gay or festive looking, but they served their purpose, and people in those days were not so particular about appearances, provided they got to their destination.

On the 31st of July, 1868, a dreadful accident occurred at Ben Lang's. During a performance an alarm of fire was given, and in endeavouring to get out of the building, twenty-three people were crushed to death and many more injured. On leaving Ben Lang's after the entertainment, those who felt inclined could indulge in an *al fresco* supper outside, of trotters and tripe, flavoured with a dash of vinegar which trickled through the holes in the cork of a ginger-beer bottle. These tripe stalls were then quite numerous throughout the town, and as they were on wheels they could easily be moved about from place to place. They were illuminated by a flaming naphtha lamp, which would no doubt help to give an extra flavour to the delicacies exposed for sale. Perhaps the eating of sheep's trotters is somewhat cannibalistic in appearance, seeing that knives and forks are dispensed with. After all, I fancy it required a certain amount of courage to stand up in the street with a trotter in one hand and a ginger-beer bottle in the other, surrounded by an interested audience, watching the progress of your repast; whilst at the same time the hungry ones would be looking at you with envious eyes, and regretting no doubt their inability to take a more personal part in the entertainment.

Potato cans also were to be found at many of the street corners, and it was at times amusing to watch a purchaser of a hot potato, trying to hold it, and passing it from hand to hand to escape being burned. Or you might see him

SOUTHERN ARCH OF HANGING BRIDGE
(inside Mynshull's House) erected 1422; photo 1901

turning over an extra hot piece in his mouth, in order to try and get at its coolest side, and looking anything but at ease in the process.

In Cateaton Street, where Mynshull's House now stands (built, I think, some ten years ago), there was a shop in the occupation of Bromiley and Sons, the tea merchants. Underneath this shop there lay hidden a portion of the old Hanging Ditch, and further portions of the same were more clearly brought to light when Victoria Street, at this point, was lately widened. A section of this ancient erection is seen in the accompanying photograph.

Turning round the corner from Ben Lang's you entered Deansgate, "as it used to was," and as you did so there was nothing in the surroundings to give you the impression of an earthly paradise, the buildings and shops on both sides being old and dingy to a degree. On the right there was a cook-shop and eating-house, where the windows were always filled with an abundance of savory pies in large fins, cut in squares, and huge legs of underdone roast pork, absolutely bursting out with stuffing of sage and onions. Everything in the shop looked greasy and swimming in rich gravy, and the very odour of the viands was almost sufficient for a first course.

As you walked along there were numerous hovels for carts and lurries, and passages leading to various warehouses abutting on to the river side. When you entered one of these hovels you found yourself in a courtyard surrounded by a number of tumbledown, old-fashioned-looking places of business, without a ghost of attractiveness about them. At night time these courts were but dimly lighted, if at all, perhaps a small flickering lamp or gasjet at the doorway just so as to make darkness visible. So dismal and uninviting were these places at times, that you might be excused for indulging in the feeling that they were not altogether safe, and you would hardly have felt surprised to find someone pouncing out upon you from one of the many dark corners which surrounded you. The lookout from the windows of these warehouses and offices was hardly more inviting, for you saw beneath you the flow of the black, dirty river, crawling sluggishly along; and you realised what the fate of anyone would be who fell into its poisonous waters. And yet here in places such as these it was, that many of our leading business-men passed the best, or would it not be more correct, from a health point of view, to say the worst part of their lives?

The present generation have much to be thankful for, when they are able to compare the well-built, airy, thoroughly ventilated offices and warehouses of today, with the miserable places in which their forefathers had to spend their business days; and it must also be remembered that the length of an ordinary working-day did not consist of the proverbial eight hours of which we hear so much at present, but began early and finished, well – when it was done, which meant anytime up to 12 o'clock at night, and sometimes later. "And theirs was not to reason why, theirs was but to do and –," well, look as pleased as you could under the circumstances, just as if you rather enjoyed getting home to the bosom of your family in the early hours of the morning.

The employees in shipping houses especially had a very hard time of it, where, when steamers were closing, lurries would wait for goods until perhaps 3 or 4 o'clock in the morning, the packing presses going all the time. Then, too, it must be remembered, there was no Saturday half-holiday to make up for the long nights, but there was a steady, continuous drudge from Monday morning until Saturday night. It goes without saying that this condition of things could not possibly be healthy, mentally, morally or physically for the community at large, but more especially for young people such a business training was positively pernicious. We may therefore all be thankful that such a wonderful transformation has taken place in regard to these matters, and that the arrangements of present-day business life have so materially improved in every respect.

OLD HOUSE, SMITHY DOOR, MANCHESTER 1875

On the other side of Deansgate, on a portion of the ground now covered by the Victoria Hotel, there stood the old Victoria Market. As I first call it to mind, it was a very primitive sort of place, just open wooden stalls with narrow passages between, where fruit and vegetables were offered for sale, and not too well protected from wind and weather. However, later on many improvements were carried out, the stalls being remodelled, and the whole roofed in and glazed Victoria Market did not abut directly on to Deansgate, an intervening block of dilapidated property extended from the entrance to Deansgate as far as St. Mary's Gate, and the backs of it looked on to the market. Most of this surrounding property was, so to speak, "on its last legs;" but, notwithstanding this, there were many quaint and interesting bits to be found peeping out here and there, with ancient black-timbered buildings, which were probably a century or two old. (See photograph.) Amongst the stallholders was a Mrs. Clark, who had established a reputation for herself on account of the superior quality of the fruit she sold, and her daughter afterwards married Mr. Copeland.

But, to my mind, the most interesting figure in Victoria Market was the man who stood at the extreme north end of the market with his tray of toffee piled in little pyramidal blocks of various colours. I can see him today quietly standing there, with his large tray and a leathern band round his neck supporting it, in addition to a wooden support underneath. Here he would stand the day through, chipping off his small pieces of toffee with his hammer, and retailing it in little paper packets at a penny each. The man, the tray and the toffee were all scrupulously clean, with a white apron hanging down in front of him. He had a ready market for his confections, for they were of the very best, and his very appearance inspired confidence in his wares. The individual to whom I refer was the original Mr. Parker, who laid the foundation of his later success in this simple way. As he progressed in his business his tray developed into a small stall, and then into the pretty little triangular glass house, which just filled in the extreme corner of Victoria Market, the old spot where he had made his first successful start. Here he commenced the sale of general confectionery, and very excellent it all was, as I can personally testify. As to his cheesecakes they beggared description, and in my youthful days I did them full justice, to the extent of my means. His little glass house was the very pink of neatness and cleanliness, whilst its contents could not fail to tempt the eye and the appetite of the passer-by. I am sure it must have been one of the mottos of Mr. Parker's life that whatever he traded in it should be of the best, and on this basis he soon established a name for himself which he never lost. Now the old gentleman has passed away, but the sons, and sons' sons, have greatly developed the business which he commenced in so modest a fashion, and to see how businesses like these should be managed one has only to enter either of their establishments in St. Ann's Square or St. Mary's Gate, and the answer is to be found in the crowds which are to be found there. I am sure old Mr. Parker must have often looked back with just pride and pleasure to his early beginnings, and he had no doubt the satisfaction of realising the truth of the words "Whatsoever thy hand findeth to do, do it with thy might."

There was another well-known character to be seen in the old days in the streets of Manchester, who earned his living with a tray; in his case, however, he began and ended with a tray. This was the old Chelsea bun man, and quite an "original" in his own particular way. I think it would be no exaggeration to say that he was as well known in Market Street and Piccadilly as the Infirmary clock, and as regular and systematic. He was a very short, thick-set man with a peculiar gait, and with a voice perhaps as unlike an ordinary human being's as can well be imagined. The Chelsea buns, which he sold hot, were kept so by a small fire underneath his tray, which he carried before him. He helped you to a bun with a fork,

THE VICTORIA FISH MARKET, VICTORIA STREET 1860

with which he refilled the warm corner vacated by your purchase.

As he passed you, you would hear his sepulchral voice, with its extraordinary whirr, apparently rising from somewhere in the direction of his boots, and almost startling to those who heard it for the first time. The words he gave voice to were not many, but very effective on account of their grotesque delivery: "Yellsee buns; thank-ee, sir." To those who never heard the man it would be impossible by explanation to give the faintest idea of the quaint effects he could produce with his voice. The variations from bass to treble were as sudden as they were mysterious; you could never tell what vagary he would oblige you with before his sentence was complete. You could hear the rumblings in his chest, but what they would be when they came to the surface you could not tell until you heard them. It was currently reported that he had sold his body to some doctor who was anxious to make a post-mortem examination of his chest for scientific purposes, but l cannot say if this were really the case.

Talking of Victoria Market, I remember a rather amusing incident which took place at Mrs. Clark's stall. A Greek gentleman, whom I knew, had but lately arrived in Manchester, and was unable to speak or understand English. Unless he happened to have a Greek friend with him to interpret his requirements he had to explain himself as well as he could by signs. One day as he passed the fruit stalls alone, he saw some large luscious-looking peaches, for which his mouth watered. I believe his English vocabulary consisted of two words, "how much," so, pointing to the peaches, he asked "How much?" The woman who was serving told him the price, but unfortunately he could not make out what she said, so seeing this she then held up two fingers, hoping he would understand her dumb show. This explanation by signs seemed quite satisfactory to my Greek friend, so he stood at the stall and disposed of three of the finest peaches he could select. After his repast he offered the

THE VINTNERS' ARMS, SMITHY DOOR, MANCHESTER 1875

woman sixpence in payment, which she very indignantly refused, eventually the two of them coming to very high words, each in their own language, whilst my Greek friend kept holding up his two fingers as she had done, to show that the price was twopence each peach. Then, happily, another Greek who was passing came to the rescue, to whom the woman explained that the peaches were two shillings each, and that he must pay her for them. I believe the matter was eventually settled by Mrs. Clark accepting some moderate reduction in price. Although my friend was still dissatisfied, on two points at least he was a wiser man, first he was a distinctly better judge of the exquisite flavour of a perfect English peach, whilst secondly, he had had brought home to him in an unmistakable manner, the price at which a taste for these English luxuries could be indulged.

When Deansgate was widened and improved large blocks of old shops and buildings were cleared away, and amongst these vanished the original shop occupied by John Heywood, the stationer, bookseller and printer. It stood close to Hardman Street, on the opposite side to both the shops to which he afterwards removed, the first at the corner of Brazennose Street, and also to the present buildings. To those who remember the premises first occupied by John Heywood, the increase of the business to its present dimensions is almost romantic. Three generations of John Heywoods have passed away since I used to visit the old place some fifty years ago; but during all that time I have witnessed a steady and even rapid development of the business, until now the inside of Heywood's establishment is almost like a little town; not to speak of the manufacturing branches in other parts of the city. As shops went in those days, the old one was well enough, although somewhat gloomy and untidy. But what always struck you as you entered the premises was the busy stir about you in all directions, and the feeling that the place was too small for its trade. It must, therefore, have been a great relief to the pressure when the business

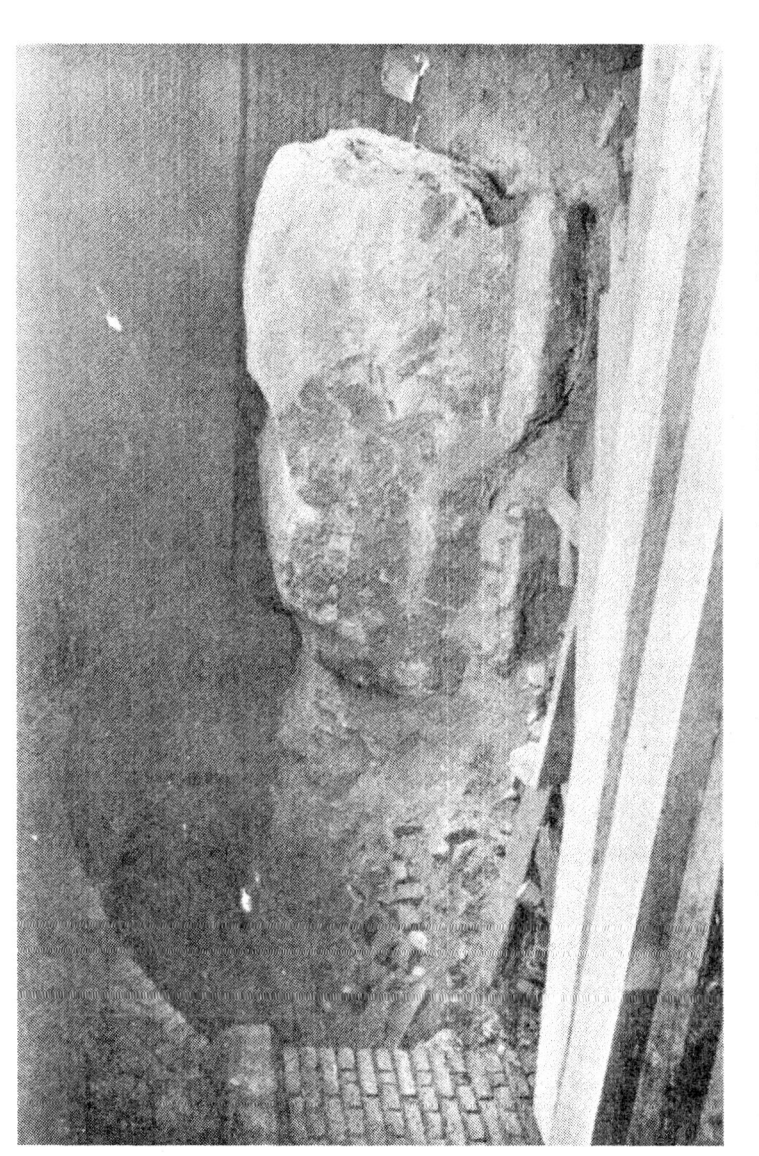

POETION OF ROMAN WALL AT CASTLEFIELD, KNOTT MILL

Built AD 83 to protect the roman station

was removed to larger premises at the corner of Deansgate and Brazennose Street. Yet even here, although the place was roomy, the various departments were so scattered and undefined that you required to be thoroughly conversant with them before you could clearly localise your wants. The second John Heywood was a splendid man of business, and I think it must have been greatly owing to his sagacity, foresight and determination, that such wonderful success crowned his efforts. He reminded me very much of Wannamaker, of Philadelphia, both being men of great resource, and remarkably practical. If you interviewed them they were equally ready to listen to, and to discuss any matter you wished to bring before them, but this done you felt instinctively that they had no further time for you, and that the interview was at an end. When I visit the present establishment from time to time, it is a pleasure to see some of the old faces that I was accustomed to see in the days of yore.

At the Peter Street corner of Deansgate, when the Great Northern Railway Company were excavating, a portion of the old Roman wall was discovered, as may be seen in the interesting photograph herewith.

CHAPTER XXVIII

Bridge Street – The Shambles – The Queen's Theatre – The Coldbeaters, Whaites's – The Taylor Tragedy – Execution of Allen, Gould and Larkin.

HAVING now traced back my way with my readers from Broughton, through Strangeways, into town again, some of the alterations and incidents, tragic and otherwise, which have taken place in the various localities of the City during the last two generations, may probably be of interest to both young and old. In referring to these, perhaps the easiest plan will be to ramble mentally through some of the streets and recall their past recollections as they float back to my memory.

To commence with, at the corner of Bridge Street, and a small side street to the rear of the present Household Stores, there once stood the old meat shambles, a large, gloomy-looking building, where the dripping carcasses of oxen, sheep and pigs, exposed for sale, presented an appearance of uninviting and realistic unloveliness, and it is difficult to imagine that such a coarse and ugly place of traffic was allowed to remain in such close proximity to the centre of the City.

When the Queen's Theatre shut its doors in Spring Gardens it migrated to Bridge Street, where it transformed the old London music-hall into a theatre. This was afterwards burnt down, and the present building erected on the same spot. Here the Queen's at first continued to cater for the same class of people who patronised them at the old place in Spring Gardens, and where the bill of fare was usually highly melodramatic and sensational. But of late years, under the able direction of its manager, Mr. Flanagan, a number of Shakespearean revivals presenting features of great artistic merit have been produced with much success. Amongst these may be named "Anthony and Cleopatra," "Henry the Fourth," "Macbeth," "The Merry Wives of Windsor," "Much Ado About Nothing," "Romeo and Juliet," etc. But as I remember the Queen's Theatre originally, it relied principally upon what used to be called the "blood and thunder" sort of business for its success; so it is pleasant now to see it the home of the immortal Shakespeare, and still pleasanter to see that the people appreciate the change, and are ready to support the manager in his efforts.

As long as Bridge Street has been known to me it has been associated in my mind with the goldbeaters' industry, and many a time when I was young have I stood looking down interested and surprised at the men working in the cellars beneath. There I would watch them hammering away on their soft blocks at what appeared to be mere specks of metal, until they had converted each piece into a delicate and gossamer-like sheet of gold-leaf, and with which we are all so familiar as we see the sign-writers gilding the letters they have painted. It was wonderful to see the beaters using their mouths as a pair of soft bellows to blow these films into their required position with the help of a blunt smooth strip of wood. To anyone who has not watched a gold-beater at work a visit to see what they can do will be found most interesting and instructive.

At one time the most attractive-looking establishment in the whole of Bridge Street was Whaite's Art Repository, where they kept the very beat selection of artists' materials of every kind, and also a large stock of excellent engravings and water-colour drawings. They had, too, at times, noted paintings on exhibition; in fact, it was quite a place for Manchester people to visit and see anything new that they had to show; but somehow as the years rolled on the place seemed to fall out of the natural avenue of high-class trade, of which they formerly had such a large share; and so eventually it developed into a Christmas toy emporium, where children with their fathers and mothers flocked in almost unmanageable crowds at the close of the year to buy their Christmas presents. To make their show more attractive they turned the cellar portion of their premises into some ice cave or grotto, where is was often difficult to get in, and quite as difficult to get out. However, even this degenerated popularity was not to last, and there came a day when Ichabod had to be written over the portals of its doors, and now you search in vain, in the old locality at least, for any trace of its name or place.

Lower down on the same side of the street, the warehouse which is now in the occupation of Beith, Stevenson and Co, was once the Manchester Police Court, where, instead of today's pleasant hum of commercial life, was heard and detailed the sorrows, crimes and tragedies of our local existence. l call to mind one of the few occasions on which I entered this Court, and this was the morning of the day on which a man named Taylor and his wife murdered their three little children at their home, a shop in Strangeways. The place, afterwards a coffee tavern, is two doors from Sherbourne Street. Having accomplished their fell purpose on their children, Taylor and his wife proceeded to the agents of the property, Mellor and Sons, in Cross Street, against whom they had some supposed grievance as to the way in which they had been treated, and on entering the office of Mr. Evan Mellor they murdered him. As I was walking to business just after the tragedy had occurred, Taylor and his wife, having been arrested, were being taken to the Police Court, and I instinctively followed with the crowd, so I was in the Court when they were placed in the dock. It was a pitiable sight to watch the ghastly faces of the wretched couple as they glanced around them with a look which seemed to separate them from their human surroundings for the time being. They had an absent-minded, dazed expression in their eyes, which clearly betokened some dreadful mental experience, compared with which the Court and all connected with it was as nothing to them. Though it is now forty years ago since I witnessed that scene, I seem to have it before me as vividly in some respects as then, and I trust I may never see that same look upon the face of any human being which I beheld (and more especially upon the countenance of the man Taylor), as he stood facing me in the dock on that summer morning of the 16th of May, 1862, when this wholesale tragedy was enacted.

There is another incident connected with my recollections of Bridge Street, which is perhaps almost as lugubrious in its nature as the one which I have just been relating. In the year 1867, Police-Sergeant Brett was shot dead by armed Fenians, who tried to rescue one of their number when passing along the streets in the police van. Three of these men, Allan, Gould and Larkin, were found guilty and suffered the extreme penalty of the Law at the New Bailey Prison in Salford. Owing to the crowds which it was anticipated would attempt to witness the execution, some of the streets leading to the Prison were intersected with powerful barricades to prevent accidents.

Amongst those so protected was Bridge Street, and it was a dismal experience to walk down this street as I did, on the afternoon before the morning of the execution, and see these melancholy preparations, and the wooden scaffolds being built out from the wall of the prison. How human beings could gather as they used to do in vast crowds to witness the sufferings and death of their fellow-creatures is to me a strange mystery. When I again passed those prison walls after all was over, all trace of what had taken place had, as far as possible, been removed. The bricks had been replaced, leaving, however, black patches of mortar, which stood out distinctly from the old, and whenever from time to time I passed the prison in after days I could never help feeling, as I looked up at those black patches in the wall, that they were associated with the death-struggles of those three unfortunate young men.

Let us be thankful that public executions are now things of the past, and that people are precluded from witnessing such demoralising exhibitions. The wonder is that they were ever permitted by law, or that it could be imagined that the actual sight of such scenes could do anything but harm to those who gathered at them.

Taken on the whole, I cannot fancy that even in its palmiest days, Bridge Street could ever have been considered a bright or attractive thoroughfare. Even as I first remember it, it was dull and uninteresting. The recruiting sergeants who frequented it perhaps gave it a little relief in colour, it being probably a good locality from which to obtain recruits, as a number of doubtful-looking youths were usually to be found hanging about the corners of the streets, with their hands deep down in their pockets waiting, like Mr. Micawber, "for something to turn up." You would often notice these idlers and loafers either emerging from, or disappearing down, the side streets; and from the class of men and women to be found in this neighbourhood you were not greatly tempted to make any unnecessary explorations of the localities which they lived.

CHAPTER XXIX

Lower King Street – The Star Hotel – Business Recollections.

THE Star Hotel, which runs from Deansgate down into Lower King Street, was a house which for generations had occupied a very high position with the country gentry and carriage folk. This was their favourite place of call, and here they stabled their horses and met their friends. It was kept at one time by a Miss Yates, a lady who was highly respected, and occupied a somewhat unique position amongst hotel proprietors. Here you would see some of the best saddle and carriage horses being put up and stabled, and their well-to-do owners alighting on their arrival in town. I had many opportunities of seeing the habitués of the Star Hotel, as when I first went to business at the ripe age of fourteen, the windows of the warehouse in which I commenced my commercial career overlooked the side entrance to the hotel and the rear, where the stables were located.

It was a Greek shipping firm with which I was placed, by name Ionides, Sgouta and Co, my eldest brother having a share in the Manchester branch of the business. Constantine Ionides (who died a few years ago, leaving a valuable collection of works of art to the nation), was the son of the head of the firm in London, and on the death of my brother he took charge of the Manchester end of the business. The warehouse, which is still in existence, was next to Aspell and Fildes, the distillers, and landlords of the property. It is now occupied by Kendal, Milne and Co, who are spreading themselves over this part of the City "like a green bay tree." As I glance up now at the place where I passed so many of my early business days, incidents come trooping back to my mind, some sad, others amusing, and as some of the latter may illustrate the love of practical joking which existed in those days, as compared with the present time, they may not be out of place. For in reading some of Dickens' works now, we are apt to think that the jokes perpetrated by some of his characters could never have taken place, but in these days people did many things which would shock the present generation, both old and young.

Owing to the long intervals intervening in the departure of cargo vessels for abroad the staffs of shipping houses led, in most cases, a very irregular life. When a vessel was loading the whole establishment worked until all hours of the day and night, and often the hand-presses (the luxury of steam-packing being then unknown) would be going as late as three or four in the morning, and the lurries and men waiting in the hovels to complete their loads and take them away. Then after a vessel closed the hands would be comparatively idle, and so at such times the hookers and packers would congregate round the fire and probably indulge in a game of "all fours" to pass the time. When immersed in their game an individual might be seen creeping cautiously along through the piles of grey cloth, and when within easy striking distance he would startle and disturb the party by landing a wet sponge or a ball of sodden brown paper in their midst. On one occasion after a first disturbance of the "all fours" party, one of them put a poker in the fire intending to make it hot for the intruder if he ventured a second time. This he did, and to vary the joke he obliged them with a huge paste-brush filled with sloppy paste, which, being cleverly thrown on to the cross-piece of the mantel-shelf, the contents came spluttering back on to the faces and cards of the players. One man, seizing the poker, rushed after the culprit, but in his anger and haste he unfortunately singed the neck of another of the players, who was heard calling out, "Oh, my neck." The joker, seeing that matters had assumed a serious aspect, took to his heels, pursued by the man and the poker. However, being light of foot, he managed to get into Lower King Street, eventually getting clear away, but he thought it safer to keep out of reach for a time, until the men's tempers and the poker had cooled down.

The man who got his neck burned was an odd, queer-tempered individual, by no means handsome, and troubled with a terrible squint. He was the pattern card-maker, and had his place on the very top floor of the warehouse. The office bell rang into this room, and it was his duty to answer it. The wire of this bell passed through the other rooms, and at times it was a favourite amusement for someone to pull this wire in another room. Down Wright would come the whole length of the long flight of steps, and stand inside the office waiting his instructions. At last my brother would look up and say, "Well, Wright, what is it?" His reply would be, "Please sir, you rang." "Oh, no, I didn't, Wright," would be the answer. Then, realising he had been duped, he would trudge up to the top floor again, vowing vengeance on the culprit if he could only bring it home to him. On his way he had to pass a wooden partition which jutted out on to the stairs. Here there was a small hole where a knot in the wood had been forced out, and he had at times to run the gauntlet of a small squirt, which was very effective and amusing, providing always you did not happen to souse the wrong party. After this little diversion it was well to get away from the spot, mount one of the numerous piles of cloth, and lie as quiet as a mouse until the coast was clear. The culprit did not always get off scot free, in which case, when he was caught, he had to pay the piper, and felt rather sorry for himself.

The packing presses were on the top floor, and another amusement in which we indulged was to collect the small sharp round iron discs which were punched out of the iron hoops for encircling the bales, open the window, and drop them on the heads or backs of any of the horses which might happen to be standing there. Three sharp bits of iron falling from such a height had a most irritating effect on the horses, making them very restive, which their owners could not understand. Of course heads out of sight was a wise precaution when your object had been accomplished, as otherwise more might be heard of the matter.

Things were done in the streets then which would shock us at the present time. I remember the head warehouseman, named Waine, who on occasions when he was out, and met the son of one of our bleachers, would deliberately stand before him and pretend to take a fit, and would only cease when the young fellow, who was rather a dandy in his way, had given him a large plug of tobacco. Fancy a man facing you in the street today waggling his head and waving his hands about like an idiot, and you being expected to take it in good part. Where the Household Stores now stand, there used to be an inn called "The Old Boar's Head," with a music saloon upstairs, and when I would be working late at the office (which might be any time up to midnight), I could hear the singing from across the road as my pen travelled over the paper. They usually kept the windows open, and as some of the singers had lusty voices, especially one man of the name of Gus Grant, there was no difficulty in indulging in a cheap second-hand concert.

The shops in Lower King Street were not much to boast about, but there was Carr's Carriage Repository, which had a good reputation, and at the bottom was Cooper's book shop, with windows facing both to Lower King Street and Bridge Street. Mr. Cooper himself was a mild, almost timid looking individual, thin, pale, and not over-communicative. But he had the reputation of having Chartist tendencies, and issued literature of a very socialistic and pronounced character.

CHAPTER XXX

John Dalton Street.

ALTHOUGH nearly the whole of John Dalton Street has been either built or rebuilt since I first knew it, it is one of those streets which appears to have retained its original characteristics, notwithstanding the many alterations that have taken place in it from time to time. To me there has always been an air of sober sadness hanging about it – a want of life, freshness and energy. It is not, for instance, a street which one would select along which to stroll to while away the passing hour. It lacks individuality and interest, and leaves on the mind a feeling of humdrum mediocrity, so that one almost experiences a sense of relief in passing out of it. Possibly this may only be a personal impression, derived from an acquaintance with John Dalton Street, from its formation. It was, of course, named after our great citizen, John Dalton, and a statue of him is to be found in a niche over a shop at its junction with Deansgate. As a work of art I am afraid this statue of the great chemist has little or no merit, but the one on the Infirmary esplanade is excellent, and was, I think, originally in the vestibule of the Art Gallery in Mosley Street. John Dalton Street was made about 1846–1847, and the dreary blank spaces which were first left after the old property was demolished gave it without doubt a somewhat melancholy and uninviting appearance. In its formation Tasle Street and Sounding Alley were cleared away, and with them many rookeries which were well improved out of existence. Tasle Alley is still to be found in name, but it was a very different place as I remember it first. It had a very unenviable reputation as a resort for bad characters, and as a place to be carefully avoided by respectable people. Sounding Alley only remains dimly on my mind as a long, dark, gloomy covered-in passage, where as you walked along it every footfall and sound came echoing back to you.

From a business point of view, there is no name which has been more closely associated with John Dalton Street than that of Lamb, the cabinet maker, who lately died at the ripe old age of 87. He originally occupied premises on the north side of the street, and afterwards crossed over to much larger premises opposite, which he had built for him. This business has now been absorbed into that of Goodall, Lamb and Heighway, but in the old days Lamb had made a reputation for the quality of his works as a cabinet maker which was unique, and any article coming from his workshops was a guarantee of its excellence, and therefore always at sales commanded high prices.

In this street also the old well-known firm of Aders, Pryer and Co. had their warehouse, and even now the mere sound and look of the name brings back a number of pleasant commercial recollections. It always seems a pity, I think, when some firm which, in the days gone by, had made for itself an enviable reputation should altogether fade out of existence. But so it is in this world, and one has only to glance over a directory of, say, fifty years ago, to notice the host of once familiar names which at one time gave a dignity and importance to our City, but which have now altogether vanished, leaving "not a rack behind."

Later on Waeny, Hill and Co, who formerly had their place of business in Ridgefield, found their way into John Dalton Street. For one of the members of this firm I felt a special regard, as when you approached him on business he always received you with courtesy and consideration, which was not the way in which buyers invariably received sellers; and as at this time I was a young man commencing business on my own account, it was pleasant to be thus received. Some buyers almost prided themselves on their brusque reception of those who came to them for orders, giving one the impression that they considered you came to them on a sort of begging expedition. I can remember one special instance of this, when I called once upon a merchant, clever and capable, but sadly wanting in graciousness of manner. I was young and inexperienced, and he showed me, with unnecessary bluntness how little I knew. His whole bearing towards me was so harsh that at last the "bruised worm turned," and I told him he had no right to treat me thus, however superior his knowledge might be. Strange to say, instead of being annoyed, he took what I said in good part, and from that time forward he was one of my best business friends. There is at the present time, no doubt, a great improvement in the relationships between buyers and sellers, but even yet there are those whose businesses would not suffer if they condescended to be more uniformly courteous in their bearing towards others.

There was in the old days a man named Ashworth, who had his packing place in this street. Perhaps the most remarkable characteristic about him was his great height, and as regards this, he might almost have been classed as one of the giants, so, physically at any rate, was he head and shoulders over anyone else in his trade. It was possible for packers to really make money in those days, whereas in competing for packing for some of the foreign markets today, it is very different, profits are small, and at times it is very much like giving change for a shilling.

It was also in John Dalton Street that C. E. Cawley, the civil engineer, had his offices. He was at one time a well-known and respected citizen of Manchester, and it was he (who in conjunction with Mr, afterwards Sir W. T. Charley) was elected member of Parliament for Salford, at a time of great political excitement.

Here, too, J. H. P. Leresche, the well-known barrister, had his chambers a man universally respected, genial, bright and excellent company. He was a great smoker, and off the bench you rarely came across him without a pipe in his mouth.

CHAPTER XXXI

Princess Street.

THE Princess Street of today, instead of terminating as it formerly did at Cooper Street, continues on along what was then Bond Street and David Street, until it joins Brook Street. The whole character of Princess Street is now so altered that anyone coming back to Manchester after an absence of say sixty years, might well be excused if he failed to identify it with his recollection of what it once was. The building of the Town Hall swept away a large slice extending from Cross Street to Cooper Street. Until just lately one of the old block of shops between Cross Street and Clarence Street on the left-hand side, remained as a kind of relic of the old street. But this has now disappeared and has been replaced by a large, handsome, modern structure. I was sorry when this old portion of past days vanished, as many pleasant memories were associated with it.

One of the oldest shops in the block to which I have just alluded was that of a man named Howarth, a milk dealer and general grocer, in whom I had a sort of direct personal interest, as, when living in Faulkner Street, he used to give me rides in his milkcart when going his rounds, outings which, as a little fellow, I thoroughly appreciated. He afterwards removed to Cross Street at the corner of Bow Lane, where he did a large miscellaneous business as a purveyor, by ministering to the wants and necessities of the young people of limited means employed in warehouses and offices, and who could only indulge in a stand-up lunch on twists and cheese, buns, tarts, milk and ginger-beer. Many is the time I have taken a frugal meal at this establishment, and thoroughly enjoyed it, as what he kept was good, fresh and appetising, and I do not suppose I shall ever partake again of twists and cheese with the same relish; yet the surroundings were neither luxurious nor attractive, for the place itself was small and none too tidy, and the counter narrow and generally crowded. Office boys and junior clerks patronised this shop very largely, but afterwards Howarth started a bad practice of supplying some of these office boys with what they wanted in exchange for postage stamps. It was found out that in many instances these lads stole the stamps from their employers, and Howarth was warned of this fact. However, in spite of this, he continued the system, until at last it became so notorious that he was arrested, tried and sentenced to imprisonment for five years. It was a strange case, and what could have possessed him to act as he did is unaccountable, as he was not a needy man, and was apparently kindly and well-disposed. My impression is that in this matter he acted under the influence of some peculiar mental derangement, as, from my personal knowledge of the man, I cannot believe that he was of a dishonest nature.

In this same old block in Princess Street, Potter and Wood, the solicitors, had their offices, both men being well known in Manchester at the time of which I write. They were members of the Manchester Chess Club, when it was located in St. Mary's Gate, but Bateson Wood more especially was a very ardent admirer and supporter of the game, and it is probable that his name will live longer with us in this connection than as a solicitor. Potter was a largely-built man, with thick, bushy eyebrows of an iron-grey hue. He had a heavy, somewhat awkward gait, and as he looked at you he gave you the impression of being a stern man, but this was not the case. Bateson Wood, on the contrary, was a small, dapper, neatly-dressed man, with dark hair; bright, and quietly chatty, with a quaint little way of rubbing his two hands together as he pondered placidly over some difficult problem on the chess-board. Bateson Wood did not always remain in his offices in Princess Street, but later he migrated to

Brazennose Street.

Close by Potter and Wood's offices, John Newland, the hairdresser, had his shop, and there was no one who had, at one time, a better connection amongst Manchester ladies and gentlemen than this man. He was dark and good looking, with hair perhaps oiled and arranged too much after the style of one of his own window blocks, but in those days most people pomaded their hair, a fashion which has now, happily, almost gone out of date. So conservative were many of the Manchester folk who patronised this shop, that some of them would have as soon thought of leaving Manchester as of changing their barber. A man will change his tailor, his hatter, or even his bootmaker, but very rarely will he change his hairdresser. Death, however, is a necessity in such a case, and when John Newland was called away, he had to take his departure for a new land.

Between Clarence Street and Cooper Street there was a row of what had once been private houses, which were afterwards occupied for business purposes, favoured mostly: by professional men, although Bernard Liebert, amongst others, had his offices and warehouse in one of them. Solicitors and architects flourished here, and in the last of these houses at the corner of Cooper Street, Slater and Heelis, had, and still have, their offices. My early recollections of Mr. Slater, the head of the firm, are of the pleasantest, for he was a man whom to know was to honour and respect. As I glance back mentally, I can see him tall and erect walking briskly along Princess Street to his offices. He belonged to that class of old, trusted family lawyers typified by Dickens's Mr. Tulkinghorn in Bleak House; one who inspired you with confidence, and on whose advice you felt instinctively you could thoroughly rely. Quiet, reserved and gentlemanly, he did not make much noise in the world, but Manchester had learned to regard him as one of her worthy citizens. He had one physical peculiarity, he rarely, if ever, wore an overcoat; and only in the depth of winter was he to be seen with a black and white shepherd's plaid thrown over his shoulders, and hanging loosely down. Occasionally he did acknowledge the extra severity of the weather by having the plaid wrapped across his chest. Then slowly the once erect figure became more and more bent, his visits to the office irregular and fitful, until at last they ceased altogether, and the most he could manage to do was to creep quietly and carefully on the Sundays along to Kersal Church. But even then, feeble as he was, he could not help being the polite old gentleman, and when meeting any lady he would struggle into the roadway so as to give her the footpath, doing so with a natural and inherent gallantry which made you revere the man. Though he has now been many years dead, I still miss his kindly greeting, his earnest face, his bowed form and his brave struggle against the infirmities of old age.

On the right-hand side of Princess Street, where the Town Hall now stands, the buildings had no special or distinctive features, but when they were pulled down, and Bancroft Street and the old Town's Yard disappeared, a number of well-remembered business places and shops vanished with them. Here Thomas Statter, Lord Derby's agent, had his offices. J. Armstrong, the wine and spirit merchant; Charles Heywood, the solicitor (who afterwards had his rooms in Mount Street); Capes and Smith, the pioneers of the present firm Capes, Dunn and Pilcher. Here, too, were the shops of Hunt and Roskell, the noted jewellers; Ransome, the chemist, and a large colony of solicitors.

CHAPTER XXXII

Bond Street – Portland Street.

BOND Street, now Princess Street, extended, as I have remarked, from Cooper Street to Portland Street, had a special interest for me, as it was here I spent some years of my early business career, from the year 1854 to about 1858. On the right-hand side, proceeding in the direction of Portland Street, you came to the offices of John Maclure, the agent for the Guardian Insurance Company, who was succeeded by his son, John William[8], and it was here that I first came into contact with the man who afterwards became such a strong political force in our City, and continued to be so until the day of his death. Those who only knew him in his later years can hardly realise what he was in his younger days; bright, cheery and energetic, with a wealth of animal spirits, he seemed to revel in hard work, and as one of the pioneers of the Conservative cause in Manchester, he did yeoman's service on its behalf. When William Romaine Callender[9] stood first for Manchester, John William Maclure was his henchman, and it was greatly owing to his Herculean exertions that he was so successful in his canvass amongst the working people. A political meeting in those days without John William was never complete; he had a good presence and powerful lungs, and if he did not impress you with his ability, there was a fine unctuousness about all he said, which had a

---

8. Sir John William Maclure (1835-1901) was a key figure in the revival of Conservatism in Manchester. Secretary of the Cotton Famine Relief Fund during the Cotton Famine of the early 1860s he served as MP for Stretford (1886-1901)..

9. William Romaine Callender (1825-1876) - MP for Manchester (1874-76)
and elected to the first Manchester School Board (1870).

wonderful elect in carrying the people along with him. He was not afraid of calling a spade a spade, and the electors liked his sledge-hammer style when dealing with his opponents, applauding all he said to the echo. In fact a political meeting at which John William Maclure appeared was always robust and racy, and he had the happy knack of keeping his audience in a good humour. Then, also, at the time of the Cotton Famine, he was of invaluable assistance to the Committee, by whom he was presented with a sum of £5,000 for his self-denying labours on behalf of the suffering operatives. From his modest beginnings in Bond Street, and from what I then saw of him, I am surprised at his remarkable success in life.

Close to the offices of the Guardian Insurance Company, and where Collyhurst Chambers now are, there was an old, dingy-looking building, which may originally have been a private house, but as I remember it, it was, and probably had been for many years, a shipping warehouse. It was occupied by various nationalities, amongst others, Joseph Nadin and Co, Philip Bauer, Elie Eliasco, Henriques and Blagomeno. These old-fashioned, soot-begrimed places of business are now rapidly passing out of existence, and to see one of them planted down in its old locality would be an interesting object lesson for the present generation. Most of them were entered by rickety, gloomy staircases, often very much the worse for wear, with awkward twists and turns, so as to make the most of the space at command. You would find odd corner offices made out of landings and pantries, and warerooms manufactured out of ancient bedrooms, with rats and mice in abundance.

Such were the ordinary places of business of many of our even wealthy Manchester merchants in days gone by. The building of which I speak, although perhaps not so dilapidated as some I have seen, was no exception to the rule, and had arrived at a ripe old age. The offices of the firm with whom l was, looked out at the front on Bond Street, and straight over the way was the then unpretentious stationer's shop of Henry Dunnill. In those days stationers were not sown broadcast over the town as they now are, so that those who occupied good central positions made rapid progress, and Henry Dunnill was one of these. In the course of time he took a partner, and the firm became Dunnill and Palmer, and still later Palmer and Howe. The business increasing, the premises became too small for them, so, by dint of swallowing up their smaller neighbours, they were enabled to build their two present block of buildings. Mr. Dunnill was a quiet, methodical, almost quaker-like looking individual, but one who thoroughly understood his business, and his partner Palmer was equally reliable. They were fortunate in having with them in their early years, one whom I remember quite as a youth – a Mr. Howe, who developed exceptional business capabilities, and who, by his energy and determination, gave an impetus to their trade, of which the more old-fashioned partners had hardly dreamed. And so under Mr. Howe's fostering care the ordinary stationery business developed into an emporium for foreign literature and art. At the time of which I am writing many of the foreigners settling in Manchester were desirous of becoming naturalised British subjects, and so Palmer and Howe made naturalisation and the passport business a special branch, thus materially helping to get their name more widely known, whilst at the same time adding to the volume and consolidation of their general trade.

Heugh, Balfour and Co, who were at one time very large merchants in the City, had formerly their warehouse on Bond Street; also Sigismund Strauss, another wealthy merchant, whose characteristic features were at one time so familiar to us all. Two of his daughters married the brothers Henriques, whose place of business was, as I have already mentioned, in Bond Street.

On the left-hand side of Bond Street, and turning into Portland Street, we come upon a group of public-houses, so neighbourly to one another that it gives you

OLD BLOCK OF BUILDINGS

Corner of Hart Street and Sackville Street, recently demolished

the impression that this special locality has in the past been consumed with such a never-failing thirst that there was trade enough for them all. You will find here "The Queen's Arms" (formerly "The Three Legs of Man"), "The Circus Tavern," "The Grey Horse," "The Monkey Inn" and "The Beehive." A truly heterogeneous collection of names, but the toper is ever a ready worshipper at all shrines. Of course there are many other taverns close at hand, but at this particular spot they form a sort of drinkers constellation, like the Pleiades amongst the stars.

Whilst on this subject of public-houses, it is a strange fact that wherever you go, you will find that the oldest buildings you come across are almost invariably licensed houses of one kind or another. The gravedigger in "Hamlet" says that graves are the oldest houses, for they last until Doomsday, but I think we might almost say that houses for the sale of drink are certainly next on the list, for even when their outward shells fall into decay they usually appear to flourish internally. Some, if not all, the taverns of which I have been writing, have remained pretty much as they were half a century back, whilst nearly the whole of the other surroundings have disappeared, having been replaced by modern buildings and palatial warehouses of various kinds.

I can quite well remember when the far greater portion of Portland Street consisted of low-roofed houses and shops, dirty, decayed looking and dingy, and altogether devoid of attractiveness. As I walk along it now and look at what is and think of what was, the change is wonderful. Until lately, in the side streets of Portland Street, odd bits were left to remind one of the old state of things, but these have now nearly all vanished, but a photograph of one such spot taken several years back represents the class of property which formerly existed in this locality. It was a block at the junction of Chorlton Street and Hart Street, and I am sorry we have not more sketches or photos of old Manchester, in order that we might realise more clearly from what we have emerged. For instance, Major Street must originally have been residential, and until very lately some of the old family houses were in existence; of course they were sad wrecks of their first estate, but as I glanced at some of them before they were finally demolished, I could not help thinking what histories and mysteries, some grave, some gay, lay hidden away within the walls of those wretched-looking tenements.

CHAPTER XXXIII

St. Ann's Square.

ONE can hardly credit the fact that nearly eighty years ago Acres Fair used to be held in St. Ann's Square, and as you now see ladies and gentlemen promenading quietly and doing their shopping therein, it is difficult to picture that scene of noise, bustle and excitement of which it was once the centre in days gone by. Even in my early years it was very different to what it now is, and it may not be uninteresting to recall the place and the people. The old soot-begrimed Exchange, with its Market Street circular front, and windows on the ground floor, looking into the street, is no more, and is perhaps hardly remembered by some. At that time the entrance through Exchange Street into the Square was much narrower, and the whole of the side opposite to the present Exchange has been rebuilt, in fact it may be said that the whole place has been remodelled in every way. Where The Scottish Union and National Offices now are, the shop of the celebrated jewellers and silversmiths, Hunt and Roskell's, was to be found, after their removal from Princess Street. This firm had established a world-wide reputation for their time-keeping chronometers, they always had one of these displayed in their window, and by it might be seen the leading Manchester merchants and gentlemen regulating their watches as they passed along. Any purchase made from this firm was considered a sufficient guarantee as to its quality and reliability. Whilst on the subject of Manchester jewellers it might be as well to run over a few of those with whom some interesting circumstance is connected.

Almost opposite to where Newall's Buildings stood, at the corner of Cross Street and Market Street, was the shop of Howard, perhaps one of the tiniest-looking jeweller's establishments to be found, considering the excellent quality of the gems which he sold. Here two noted robberies took place, one of them in 1853 at midday, when his eldest daughter was suddenly attacked and overpowered and the place plundered. It created a great sensation at the time, the burglary having been successfully accomplished in the very heart of the City, and at the busiest time of the day. Although small, the shop was always made very attractive with mirrors and crystal jewel cases, and, being well stocked with valuables, the thieves got away with an excellent haul.

Ollivant's shop, which stood at the corner of Exchange Street, where Manfield's shop now is, was also entered and robbed two days after Howard's, and in 1865 Howard's place was again broken into and plundered. In the same year, too, William McFerran's shop was entered, the burglars getting away, it is said, with about £13,000 worth of property. His establishment was in Victoria Street (where W. and F. Terry now are), and to him this loss was a serious blow. Howard's loss was not so heavy, being stated to be about £3,000, but it was bad enough, and these Manchester jewellers could well have spared these unpleasant visitations. These repeated robberies brought about improvements in the locking up of such establishments, holes being bored in the shutters, and lights left burning so that policemen when going their rounds could inspect the shops from the outside to see that all was right.

All these jewellers that I have named were representative men of their class, but I mention these especially on account of the burglaries connected with them. Mr. Howard was in appearance a short, thick-set, determined-looking man, one who could, I fancy, have given a very good account of himself in any physical encounter, and had the thieves attacked him instead of his daughter, the result might have been very different. But no doubt the whole affair was cleverly planned; they waited

MARKET PLACE AND OLD EXCHANGE, MANCHESTER 1859

until Mr. Howard had gone to his dinner, and then came their opportunity. The attack had a serious effect upon the nervous system of Miss Howard, from which she was some time in recovering. Mr. Ollivant was a very different type of man to Mr. Howard, being tall, thin, sallow and fragile-looking, with a quiet, unpretentious manner, but at the same time he was a remarkably keen-witted, clever man of business, and a very excellent judge of a good bargain. He did a large trade as a silversmith, in buying, selling and exchanging, but even when I first knew him he was a comparatively old man, his health had begun to fail, and he had to take things quietly. On this account he took into partnership another jeweller named Botsford, who as a young man had established a good connection in a shop in the Square, the firm then becoming Ollivant and Botsford, which it still continues to be.

How very few of the old names and places of business which were so familiar to the older generation, are to be found at this time in St. Ann's Square. Close to Hunt and Roskell's there used to be Yates, the confectioner's – the Parker, so to speak, of that time. This was the restaurant mostly in favour amongst the fair sex, as Brown's Chop House was in Market Street for the man of business. In the latter you could, if you felt so "dispodged," as Mrs. Gamp used to say, have the extra gratification of selecting your own particular chop or steak as you passed through, or, to add still further to your enjoyment, if it lay in this direction, you could sit near the grid and watch it frizzling away temptingly before your very eyes. Yates's business was afterwards transferred to Corporation Street, but the charm and attraction which were associated with the place so long as it remained in the Square did not follow it to the new premises.

Then there was Cheshire and Parsons, the well-known silk mercers, which is identified in my mind with the person of Mr. Cheshire, a quiet, staid gentleman of the old school, who did not think it requisite to run his business like an express train. Next came the shop of

Isaac Simmons, the jeweller, one of the few places which continues its connection with the old spot, under the style of Arnold and Lewis. At one time the clock outside was surmounted by a ball, which fell from the top of a pole at the exact second of one, each day. In close proximity came the tailoring establishment of H. B. Peacock, who afterwards became associated with the *Examiner and Times*, but whose name was more especially identified with what were called the Monday Evening Concerts, of which he was the pioneer and organiser, and which were very successful for many years. I am afraid there are not many who remember H. B. Peacock in his long-tailed coat and his tall hat with its extra broad brim, which gave him a quaint, semi-Quaker-like appearance, but in his quiet way he displayed great energy in cultivating Manchester's musical talent, at a time when it was very much in need of direction and development, and great thanks are due to him for his perseverance and determination.

Satterfield's, whose place of business now occupies such a large portion of the left-hand side of St. Ann's Square, is another firm which can claim to being one of, if not the oldest of silk mercers in Manchester, and whose name has been associated with its present locality, although within more prescribed limits. They had their place of business on a portion of the present site as long back as 1838, and probably even prior to this. In the old days they enjoyed a very enviable reputation for the superior quality of their goods, and no doubt to this day they can lay claim to the same distinction.

Next door to Satterfield's the then fashionable bootmaker, G. D. Wimpory had his shop. I think I might safely say that he and his wife were the smallest married couple in Manchester, and it was really quite a pleasant sight to watch them arm in arm wending their way home after the day's business. They both wore spectacles, and he, especially, had a peculiar way of staring upwards through his glasses, which added still more to the quaintness of his appearance. Heywood's Bank was at this time the most

ST. ANNS CHURCH, MANCHESTER

Consecrated 1719, photo 1863

important structure in the Square, but, of course, not to compare with the present building which followed later on. It was then carried on by Sir Benjamin Heywood[10], a man who was very highly esteemed both in Manchester and Lancashire. Oliver Heywood[11] was also in the business when it was amalgamated with that of Williams Deacon and Co. It is only a few years ago since he was taken from amongst us, so that in a certain sense he belongs to the present generation. But when I first remember him he was a strong, active, vigorous Christian gentleman, ready to spend and be spent for the general good. He was a man who was thoroughly respected by all classes, and Manchester, justly proud of her good citizen, presented him with the freedom of the City, and his statue worthily occupies a place in Albert Square. He held bravely on with his good work as long as he was physically able to do so, and even when the grip of death seemed to be fastening upon him. One of the last public duties he performed, at which I was present, was the opening of the Bethesda Home for Cripples. It was truly a touching sight to see him on that occasion battling with an affection of the nerves from which he was suffering, as he delivered one of the most pathetic, earnest, practical addresses on Christian work to which I ever listened. He spoke with the solemnity of a man who felt that his course was well-nigh finished, and we realised as we listened to him, that we probably had him amongst us for the last time.

On the right-hand side of the Square there is little to remind us of what it once was. Furniss's Fancy Bazaar, Scarr, Petty and Coulbourn's, Stubb's and Orton's, tailors,

10. *Sir Benjamin Heywood (1793-1865) Propreitor of 'Heywood's Bank'. Founded Manchester Mechanic's institute, MP for Lancashire (1831-2).*

11. *Oliver Heywood (1825-1892) Son of Benjamin Heywood, sponsor of Manchester Mechanics Institute, Chetham's Hospital, Manchester Grammar School and Owens College. First honorary Freeman of the City of Manchester (1888). A Grade II listed statue of Oliver Heywood (unveiled 1894) by Albert Bruce-Joy stands in Albert Square. .*

Holgate's, Rinyon's and Hunter's, Simms and Dinham's, Adshead's, and Ford's, all establishments of repute, have passed away or gone into other hands. Stubb, who was then the fashionable tailor, became a wealthy man, owning a large amount of property in Higher Broughton, just below Murray Street. He was a large, pompous-looking man, who kept his carriage and lived in good style, and who had the reputation of not forgetting to charge for the things you bought from him.

One has almost forgotten that there was such a place as Red Lion Street, as the spot has been altogether changed, and it now goes by the name of Barton Square; but in the old days Thomas Sowler had his bookseller's shop there, but facing into St. Ann's Square; and this place was the nursery of the *Manchester Courier*[12]. At one time the Conservative cause was at a very low ebb in this district, and it was at this time that John Bright[13] said that if he could find a real Conservative working man in Manchester he would put him under a glass case. But when William Romaine Callender came forward to champion the cause, Thomas Sowler, full of energy and determination, lent him all his aid, and with such success that a tide of Conservatism set in, so that it would have taken a very large number of glass cases to have carried out the suggestion of John Bright. Thomas Sowler, realising the possibilities of the occasion, was mainly instrumental in developing the circulation of the *Courier* and *Evening Mail*, until they became the leading

12. *Manchester Courier (1825-1916)*

13. *John Bright (1811-1889) was a prominent Anti-Corn Law MP, an outspoken critic of British foreign policy and an advocate of working class rights and the right to protest. He served Manchester as an MP (1847-57) but lost his place after opposing the Crimean War. He was subsequently elected unopposed in Birmingham and served there as an MP (1857-85). A non-comformist, Bright championed free trade and played a prominent role in forcing through the Second Reform Act (1867) which widened the electoral franchise.*

14. *Manchester Evening Mail (1874 - 1902 & 1914-1915)*

Conservative papers of the district, and a most valuable property. He was a thoroughly practical and capable business man, straightforward and honourable. He was kind-hearted and generous, and was regarded by those who knew him personally with affectionate regard. His was at one time a well-known face on the Manchester Exchange, where he was always able to secure the latest and most valuable commercial intelligence suitable for his papers, and which he was always careful to deal with wisely and discreetly. The times have changed for these papers, as the *Evening Mail* has ceased its existence, and the *Courier* no longer occupies the position it once did.

THE MANCHESTER EXCHANGE, 1859

CHAPTER XXXIV

The Old Manchester Arcade.

IT is thirty years ago since the old Manchester Arcade was demolished to make way for the completion of the present Manchester Exchange. What a crowd of busy life surged in and around that spot! The mere mention of the name of Newall's Buildings sets in motion a flood of political memories. In the old election times, when open voting was the law, this old smoke-begrimed building was a hive of excitement. Here, as each fresh instalment of the state of the poll was posted up, the populace shouted themselves hoarse with delight, if their favourite candidate headed the list. Now all this wild excitement, with the free fights which often accompanied a difference of opinion as to the merits of a candidate, has passed away into the almost forgotten past. The hustings, too, which used to be erected in St. Ann's Square, where the candidates presented themselves officially before the electors, is happily no more. The whole affair was very much of a pantomime, for in the shouting, hissing, and general turmoil, it was hardly possible to hear a word that anyone said. We seldom heard anything the would-be member was saying, but if he was our man we applauded as loudly as if we did, quite satisfied that whatever he said must be right. Then, when our opponent got up and spoke and gesticulated in the same way, we hooted away with the best of them, just as much convinced that whatever he was saying was not worth listening to, and that he was nothing but a villain of the deepest dye. I do not know that I ever saw a candidate pelted with cabbages or rotten eggs. I think to this extent Manchester electors restrained their political bias. But at the same time when the election fever would be at its height, it was astonishing the amount of bad blood that could be displayed.

At such a time you had to be very careful how and where you expressed your political feelings, or you might find yourself with your hat over your eyes, accompanied by remarks of a most unparliamentary character. The ballot box has been a most effective cooler of the political blood, and although we still get pretty warm in feeling at election times, a wonderful improvement has taken place since open voting and the hustings were done away with. I can very well remember listening to John Bright speaking from one of the windows in Newall's Buildings[15] after an election, I think in 1852, and I have his brave, manly face before my mind's eye very distinctly at the present moment. Yes, the associations linked with Newall's Buildings, must be very dear to the heart of the old Radicals of Manchester and Salford.

The old Arcade was at one time one of the very few places where covered walking shelter could be obtained in wet weather. Here ladies and gentlemen could walk up and down and have a little social intercourse in the centre of the city. Now we are better provided with these sheltering Arcades, but there are none too many even at the present day. It seems a pity that in some of the streets, say in King Street, the pathways should not be covered in with glass as is done at Buxton. This would be a great boon to ladies shopping in wet weather, and, indeed, to the community generally.

It is difficult to realise that where the front of the Exchange now is, there stood the calendering warehouse of Goodier, Krauss, and Co. I have often looked through the cellar windows and watched the large rollers revolving and doing their work. As you entered the Arcade from the Ducie Street side, the first shop which attracted your attention was Wheeler's, the newspaper shop, and a busy scene it was when the London papers arrived, to see stout old Wheeler in his shirt sleeves, struggling manfully and

---

15. *Newall's Buildings, St. Ann's Square. Headquarters of the Anti-Corn Law League built by Walter Newall (1780-1863)*

quickly with the huge pile of papers which were before him; getting them folded and sorted into their various lots for distribution through the city. Then the London papers were distributed about one o'clock in the day; now they can be procured early in the morning. *The Times* had then far away the largest circulation of all the London papers, although, I believe, the price was 5d. instead of 3d., as at present.

Opposite to Wheeler's shop Findlater and Mackie had their wine and spirit stores. You could always tell when you were in proximity to their place by the powerful odour of spirits which impregnated the air in all directions. I remember they had two very large tanks in the shape of barrels which could be seen from the outside, and were, if I remember rightly, surrounded at intervals with gaily painted iron hoops. Alderman Ivie Mackie, who was thrice Mayor of Manchester, from 1857 to 1860, was the leading spirit in his business. He was a large, even massive-looking man, with a shuffling sort of gait; but he was a clear-headed, capable man, and one who made an excellent Mayor.

Another occupant of the Arcade in its early years was a Miss Richardson, who kept a library, and whose shop was a great place of meeting for ladies, who made this their rendezvous for social chat. My recollection of the shop is that it was dark and gloomy-looking, but Miss Richardson possessed large treasures in the shape of the writings of Fennimore Cooper, Captain Marryat, Harrison Ainsworth, and G. P. R. James. Oh, how I devoured their novels, and how happy I was when I could sit down undisturbed and read, say, such a tale as "Darnley," or "The Field of the cloth of Gold," "The Last of the Mohicans," "Japhet in Search of a Father," or "Windsor Castle." Those were truly the days of reading with an intense interest. To me at least they will never come again. Then it was positive misery to be dragged away from your book and forced back into the common affairs of life. How the young mind rebelled at the interruption!

Where that library has disappeared to it would be hard to say, but the taste for the class of books to which I refer has gone with the books themselves; and that, too even with the young of today. Then the selection was limited; now there is a very ocean of far better literature from which to pick and choose.

A man named Professor Threader had a hairdresser's shop in the Arcade. He was a character in his way, and having something of the appearance of Napoleon III, he used to try to carry out the likeness as far as nature would allow him. He had a moustache which he twisted and developed in every possible way so as to resemble as nearly as art permitted him the original he was endeavouring to copy. He was a great dandy in his way, and a tremendous gossip. When you went to have your hair cut you could always rely upon hearing the latest piece of news, social or public, whatever it might be. He had a very good connection at one time, but I am afraid he was not a good friend to himself, and eventually he disappeared, and so the Arcade had to dispense with its Napoleon III.

Henry Rawson, the sharebroker, had his offices in the Arcade at one time. What a world of changes the recalling of this name brings back to one's mind! I can remember his dark handsome face and gentlemanly bearing. How earnest and determined he was in all he did! At that time the *Examiner and Times*[16] was a political power, and there was no man who helped more to place it in that position than Henry Rawson. It would have been a sad day for him had he lived to see the decline and eventual collapse of the paper for which he worked so hard.

In this Arcade, too, there was the shop of William Fothergill, the engraver and printer, also that of Nicolson, the confectioner. When the Arcade and the whole block bounded by Ducie Street, Market Street, Cross Street, and Bank Street had to come down to make way for the New Exchange, a number of well-known names disappeared with the old property. There was Fritz Mentha, the jeweller, in Ducie Street, and Spreat, the silversmith.

NEWALL'S BUILDINGS AND OLD MANCHESTER ARCADE

Site of the present exchange

At No. 8, Market Street, there was the toy and cutlery establishment once tenanted by Miss Pipe. The Civet Cat was a similar business, afterwards in the occupation of Charles Henry before he removed to King Street. As a young boy I always used to think the Civet Cat was a very peculiar name for a toy bazaar, and if I do not mistake there was another shop in Market Street which went by the name of the Civet Kitten. In this particular case I am under the impression that the Cat and Kitten were rivals, not friends. Sharp and Scott's, Lee and Kettle's, and Galt's, the stationer's, were also well-known places which were pulled down at the time of the rebuilding of the Exchange.

One has to tax the memory severely to realise the fact that the Magnetic Telegraph Company had its offices in the old Arcade. The word "Magnetic" has now an old-fashioned sound about it, which then was quite home-like in the business world. What a wonderful change has passed over us when we remember that, in the babyhood of electric telegraphing, we used to pay four shillings a message without, as it were, a murmur, whereas now we try to work a message down so as to save even one half-penny, and rather pride ourselves on our ability if we do so! Profits on business transactions were more easily made then than now, and four shillings for a wire and the same for reply was considered of small account. Even for foreign telegraphy the code system of the present day has made the reduction of the use of words almost a science.

The face and figure of that active little business man H. B. Freeborn was well known in the palmy days of the Arcade. He was a short determined-looking little man, who believed both in himself and his business. He realised earlier on than many others the efficiency of persistently advertising his wares, so that, at this long period of time, Freeborn's Hose, Freeborn's Waterproofs, and Freeborn's "Corazza" shirts were uninterkmittingly served up with the daily papers, until you were compelled to realise that

---

16. *Manchester Daily Examiner and Times (1855-1874)*

these items of wear were facts not fancies.

As one gets into the "sere and yellow leaf" one is naturally drawn towards the past, and events which seemed to make but little impression at the time come back with a vividness that at times seems almost wonderful. Though these slight sketches are given, in the first instance, to recall to my older readers facts and faces which have been lying dormant in the lumber-room of our memories for many years, still I think even the young might be interested in knowing how things moved with us thirty or forty years ago.

I have been lately looking through some old Directories, in order to see that my own memory is not at times playing me false in matters I am relating. Talk of romance, here beneath these covers lies a tale of real life, more powerful and stirring than any novel. To an old man looking through the pages of a directory belonging to a place where his life has been spent, and dating back to his youth and manhood, quite a flood of memory comes floating back, as his eye glances down some names or places which in those days long past was so real and personal. The life of many a friend is told in a single line, and yet as you utter the name aloud the very sound of it brings back with it a little world of joy or sorrow, or more probably both. Incidents covered with the cobwebs of forgetfulness start into life again, and places which have now been blotted out of existence appear before you in all their pristine beauty or ugliness as the case may be. If you have lived a fairly long life, and you want to think quietly over the past, just walk along to the Manchester Free Reference Library, take a directory of some forty or fifty years ago, sit down and study it, and you will have ample food for reflection for many a day.

CHAPTER XXXV

King Street – Brown Street.

WHEN Brown Street was opened out into Booth Street, a very great improvement was no doubt effected, but still more was this the case when, instead of allowing the top end of King Street to terminate in an awkward triangular corner without any exit to the right; some large blocks of buildings were cleared away, and Spring Gardens was carried on into Fountain Street, and past Chancery Lane. At that time amongst other buildings at the top of King Street, there stood the Albion Club, forming a sort of cul-de-sac, although there was an exit to the left into Spring Gardens and York Street. This club was a rendezvous for many of the leading men of Manchester, and here, as the luncheon hour approached, you would see the members trooping in through its portals, and amongst them there passed along no better known figure than that of Mr. Sale, the solicitor. This club afterwards developed into the Clarendon Club at the bottom of Mosley Street, of which Mr. Sale became president.

Then, close to this elbow or corner, were to be found the consulting rooms of Dr. Ainsworth, a man who was at one time well known in medical and social circles in and about Manchester. Even when I first remember him he was comparatively an old man, but he still liked to wear his years youthfully, and his hair always assumed the same chocolate-brown hue, as also did his moustache and whiskers. For many years before his death he had virtually given up practice, but he still came to his rooms, and his tall, spare figure might be seen walking along King Street, enveloped in his long, furlined cloak, and his umbrella, which he carried like a musket over his shoulder, in military style.

At this spot, too, was the old Money Order Office, before it was removed to the Post Office in Brown Street, from which it was then separate and distinct, and close at hand Doveston, the then fashionable upholsterer, had his establishment with its large attractive showrooms.

On the opposite side of the street, and where the Reform Club now stands, there used to be the offices and buildings of the West of England Insurance Company, and in connection with which one recalls with pleasure the forms and features of its agents, Frank and Tom Jewsbury. The very sound of those names reminds anyone who knew them, of their bright, genial personalities, and of the privilege it was to come into contact with them, either socially or in the way of business.

A little lower down, on the same side, Fullalove, the auctioneer, had his place; the name is now almost forgotten, but at one time he had an excellent business and connection, and the sales at his rooms were always well attended. Next door came the china shop of John Rose and Co, which is now to be found near Cross Street; but when they were at the old spot they had the cream of this trade, whilst now there are many other firms who are competing for it.

One almost requires to be told that the present Reference Library was at one time the Manchester Town Hall, for it appears almost incredible to realise that the whole civic business of the City could possibly have been conducted in a building so small and in every way inadequate, and this so lately as thirty years ago, for it was only in the year 1868 that Alfred Waterhouse's[17] plans for the New Town Hall were approved by the Council. There used to be a temporary lock-up under the old Town Hall, facing to Cross Street, and here, too, for a yearly fee, the keys of the leading warehouses could be deposited for extra safety.

---

17 - Alfred Waterhouse (1830-1905), designed the Assize Courts (1859) and Town Hall (1868). He went on to design the Natural History Museum, London.

THE TOWN HALL, MANCHESTER 1875

THE OLD POST OFFICE, BROWN STREET 1879

Brown Street provides some interesting facts connected with its former days. At the Market Street end there stood the "Commercial" Hotel, which has only just lately been pulled down. Fifty years ago, and no doubt from a much earlier date, it was a regular coaching establishment, where conveyances started for Derby, Buxton, Macclesfield, etc, and many a time have I stood and watched the preparations for the journey. Coaches also started from the "Royal" Hotel, the "Angel," the "Talbot," and also from other places, such as the "Thatched House" and the "Boar's Head," in Withy Grove. Although railways were then in existence, they were, comparatively speaking, in their infancy, and there were many places to which they did not run at all; so, to such as I have named and others, travellers had still to depend upon the old stage coaches, the railways slowly replacing them as they extended their lines in various directions. I can remember when I made my first journey to Buxton, over forty years ago, the railway only then extended to Whaley Bridge, where the coach met us and took us on to our destinations in the old-fashioned style.

Next to the "Commercial" Hotel came the Borough and Magistrates' Court, where prisoners were taken each morning after having been temporarily locked up in the police cells for the night. When I first went to business it was my duty to go to the Post Office in the morning for the letters, and on my way to or fro I often used to see the prison van deliver its load at the door leading up to the Court. Sometimes I was there just as the policeman unlocked the door of the van, and I saw the prisoners hurried out, and up the steps of the Court to await their turn to be dealt with in one form or another. Although many of the women were brazen creatures and practically shameless, still there were others who did realise their position, and endeavoured to hide their faces from the gaze of the public. There were also callous, vicious faces amongst the men, but occasionally you would notice some who had unmistakably seen better days, or had even been gentlemen born. Such as those would slip down the steps of the van, cast a furtive glance around them, and slink hurriedly out of sight as quickly as possible. At times I would hear the yells and the shouts of the women from the cells in the van as they were driven along, and then as they stepped out into the street, they would put on a bold face and treat the whole thing as a great joke which they were enjoying. As a rule the men of this class were quieter and better behaved than the women, and, apparently at least, felt their position more keenly. The policeman who rode on the step of the van was a familiar figure in the streets of Manchester. He was a full-bodied, grey-haired man, to all appearance stolid and unimpressionable; it is probable that long acquaintanceship with the class of people with whom he had to deal had knocked out of him any little sympathy or sentiment with which he might have been originally endowed. As the van rattled up into Brown Street it was always followed by a crowd of idlers, so that the policeman could always depend upon a promiscuous surrounding large enough to prevent any prisoners escaping.

Next to the Borough Court came the General Post Office, a very much smaller and more ordinary looking building than the present structure, which covers a much larger area of ground. Still for the postal arrangements and requirements of that time it seemed fairly adequate. Then the private box department ran down a passage at the side, and not in front and across as at present. In the morning you had to wait until the officials had sorted the letters, when the row of green curtains which hid them from view was drawn aside, like the opening scene in an entertainment, or a conjuror about to show you some tricks, revealing the pigeon holes and their contents.

In glancing at a Post Office list of fifty years ago, the changes, improvements and economies seem almost romantic, for so prosaic a subject. To avail yourself of the penny postal rate for the United Kingdom, letters had to weigh under half-an-ounce, now you can send four ounces for a penny. For business purposes envelopes were then almost unknown, letters being written on large, square, double sheets of paper, and folded so as to make the outside sheet a substitute for an envelope. Wafers were then used to fasten the letters at the back, but if you wished to do things in the best business style, you sealed your letters with red wax, impressed with the firm's name. There was really a sort of dignity about the appearance of your morning bundle of letters, which is sadly lacking in the present day, when everything in this way is so intensely commonplace.

Then if you wanted to register a letter a fee of sixpence was charged; now you can do the same for twopence. But it is in the foreign postal arrangements that the most remarkable changes have taken place. At the time to which I refer for many places abroad the letters had to weigh under the quarter-ounce to be franked at the initial fee, and what these fees were, a very few instances will illustrate. To Constantinople the rate by certain routes was 2s. 3d., or at the lowest 1s. 1d.; Alexandria, 1s. 8d.; Madeira, 1s. 10d.; Buenos Ayres, 2s. 7d.; The Brazils, 2s. 9d.; Mexico, 2s. 3d.; Gibraltar, etc, 1s. 9d.; and other places in similar proportion. It is no wonder that people crossed their letters in those days, and tried to get as much on to a sheet of paper as they possibly could. I have seen letters on the thinnest of paper, not only crossed, but every blank space filled in, until it was heart and temper-breaking to decipher what was written, for which you required the patience of Job and the eyes of a lynx. In addition to all this you had to possess your soul in patience waiting for answers to your letters, seeing that it took about four months for a letter to reach India, and still longer to reach Australia. Now a letter takes about a fortnight to get to Bombay, and a couple of days longer to get to Calcutta. Now you can write every week; then there was only one mail each month. But, wonderful as all these changes are, the telegraph eclipses them all, when we realise that a message from India arrives in Manchester in some hours less than no time, electricity practically annihilating distance.

The Bank of Manchester, which used to have its premises adjoining the General Post Office, passed out of existence many years ago. In 1863 it was broken into and robbed, and after a somewhat chequered career, it was absorbed, the Consolidated Bank taking over its business. John Farrer was its manager, at one time a well-known figure in our Manchester streets. He was somewhat quaint in appearance, being short of stature, with a florid complexion and iron-grey whiskers; and you could always tell him from afar, as he walked along in a sort of spread-eagle fashion, with his feet turned out and his hands spread abroad as if he might be going to embrace you. Mr. Farrer was an old man when he retired, and possibly for this reason his ideas on banking may have become somewhat antiquated, and hardly progressive enough for the requirements of the times. But be that as it may, he was always considered a thoroughly straightforward, reliable man, and if he did not altogether meet the views of customers (and where is the banker who does?) he would always conscientiously carry out whatever he had promised or arranged. Mr. Rice was sub-manager with him in the Bank of Manchester, and when the Consolidated took over the business Mr. Rice was transferred with it, where he remained for a number of years before he also retired.

CHAPTER XXXVI

Market Street – Piccadilly – London Road Station.

ALTHOUGH Market Street, as a whole, like all other portions of the City, has witnessed many changes during the last 50 years, yet the street itself has not altogether lost its former aspect. The alterations of necessity have been circumscribed, and so the street is still today far too narrow and confined for the traffic, human and otherwise, which crowds into it. New buildings have replaced the old, and many of the once familiar names have altogether disappeared; but on the whole the general features of Market Street have not varied very materially. Even to Piccadilly the same remarks apply, except as regards the Infirmary and its surroundings. The old Infirmary pond has long ago vanished, to be replaced afterwards with a wide esplanade where fountains played during certain hours of the day. These were removed later on, to be succeeded by further alterations and improvements, resulting in present-day developments, and where many of our City statues have been provided with a home.

It is only when we arrive at London Road Station that the old inhabitant is particularly struck with the changes which have taken place, and to these I wish to draw attention. Of course even now, with all its latest additions and improvements, the station and its surroundings are anything but imposing, but no doubt with the limited space at the Company's disposal they probably did the best they could at the time, and, compared with what it once was, we have much to be thankful for. In writing of London Road Station I wish to refer to the time before the M, S. and L. Railway, now the Great Central, joined with their rivals, and, like Abraham and Lot, divided the land between them. It was then a truly dreary and melancholy looking place built of dingy red brick, with an approach to it as sad looking as the station itself. There was a long narrow roadway which you reached after mounting the incline, and which was just broad enough to turn a cab in after setting down its fare. Here you entered the booking offices, which were fully as cheerless as the outside of the station. I should imagine that when young married couples arrived here and took their tickets prior to their departure for their honeymoon, the dull, unattractive surroundings would be sufficient to give them a fit of the blues, from which it would have been impossible to extract any germ of pleasure or gaiety. However, on such occasions no doubt bridal couples are blind and oblivious to anything but their own immediate concerns, and so the dreary booking offices and unrestful looking waiting-rooms would not be able to damp their spirits.

The railway carriages also were anything but luxurious, even the first class compartments being only moderately comfortable, whereas the thirds were about as uninviting as they well could be. In these there was a general feeling of bare boards and cheerlessness as you entered them, and if you were travelling in the winter time they gave you a kind of cold shiver. Even the windows were but small square apertures, giving the most limited view possible of the outside world. The seats were cushionless, and the longer you sat upon them the harder and more unyielding they seemed to grow, and as third class passengers had no such luxuries then as foot-warmers, it may readily be supposed that on a cold day you arrived at your destination chilled to the bone, and probably not as amiable as you might be. There was no railway competition in those days, so you had to take what was given you and try to be thankful. Now there is plenty of competition and the various companies vie with one another in trying to make all their passengers as comfortable as possible. Of course I am quite prepared to grant that at the time of which I am speaking railways were in their infancy, and that it was really impossible to give the advantages which are now so common. But I am writing of things as they were, so that those who get along so quickly and easily nowadays may realise that things are not "as they used to was." Passengers were then more or less in the position of suppliants and were often treated by the officials like so much "goods and chattels." Providing that railway companies carried you to your journey's end at sometime or another, there was not much attention bestowed upon your comfort or convenience.

Then as regards the length of a journey; you certainly required to possess your soul in patience until you had actually reached your final destination. Trains stopped at every little place on the way; you were shunted here and shunted there, or you found yourself resting peacefully in some lonely siding for what appeared an age. At other times you were kept whistling and letting off steam in a very angry fashion just outside some station, where you had been congratulating yourself that you had at last reached a point in your journey where you could stretch your aching, weary limbs, and refresh the inner man. So it was more than tantalising to find yourself within measurable distance of your goal, and yet in the matter of time very far from it.

In pointing out the tediousness of railway travelling, I am reminded of an anecdote, which probably many of my readers may have heard, but some may not, so I give it. There was an old lady from the Far North, who was taking her journey by rail. She was travelling, I believe, by the North British Railway, which was formerly noted for taking the longest possible time for running the shortest of distances. Well, the old lady was in a train which was proceeding at the good old orthodox speed, namely, crawling along from point to point, and station to station, until, to use an Irishism, it had never done stopping. There was a male passenger travelling with her in the same carriage, but, according to the usual social custom of the country, no word had passed between them. At last, wearied and worn out, they arrived, at long length, at some terminus, where they were obliged to change, only again to find themselves occupants of the same compartment in another train. This at last thawed the heart of the male passenger, and so, in a highly-communicative mood, he ventured to ask where she was going. "Ganging," says she; "Well I'm ganging awa to China, but eh, mon, I'm mair na thankfu' that I've gait the wairst o' the journey a'er."

Or there is still the older joke of the American, who, travelling in a remarkably slow train, on being asked for his ticket tendered a child's half, and on the collector objecting, he replied: "Wa-all, stranger, I guess the ticket's all right; but the fact is, I've been so long travelling on this mighty slow train that I've grown up on the way."

CHAPTER XXXVII

Manchester Coach, Cab, Omnibus and Tram Traffic, past and present.

IN connection with Piccadilly it may be of interest to know that the first cabstand in Manchester was started here in the year 1839, when a man of the name of William White commenced to ply for hire on the 5th of August; W. H. Beeston, of Tib Street, being the maker of the first coach which thus started its solitary career. Personally my recollections of cabs do not carry me quite so far back as this, but the impressions left upon me are that the coaches, or growlers as they were often called, were heavy and lumbering, and you could never be mistaken as to when there was one about, as the noise they made rattling along could be heard from afar. This was no doubt partly owing to the fact that nearly all the streets were paved with large, round, cobble stones (and indeed, for the matter of that, many of the pathways also). This being so, and for the reason that the springs were not much to boast about, the clatter of the vehicles did not add to the music of the streets; and like the march called "The Turkish Patrol," the volume of sound increased as they approached and diminished as they receded.

Owing to the scarcity of conveyances it might be concluded that riding in them was somewhat of a luxury, but I imagine the present generation would hardly think so, as the amount of jolting to which passengers were then subjected was anything but a joke, and it, together with the incessant rattle, prevented any ordinary conversation. Therefore, when you required to speak to your fellow passengers you had to shout at them as if they were stone deaf, and even then it was no easy matter to get them to hear or understand. It was also difficult to get very enthusiastic about the breed and general appearance of the animals which worked this traffic. Some of the horses would have looked more at home in the shafts of a cart, whilst others bore unmistakable evidence of being on their last legs, many of them being knock-kneed, spavined and broken-winded. This was more especially so with regard to those vehicles and animals which were told off to work the railway station traffic; and the horses were certainly not such as would have been selected to lead a forlorn hope in a charge on a battle-field; whilst the conveyances made you wonder where some of them had been unearthed. They looked so seedy, damp and mildewed, with doors which oftentimes either refused to close at all, or if you managed to get them closed, refused to open.

There were then no cabmen's shelters, and as you passed along a stand on a wet day you would see the men with the rain dripping from their hats, and they themselves enveloped in a cloud of steam. It was no wonder that these unfortunate men were continually taking nips at the handiest public-house, to try and counteract the cold and the wet. They could not even indulge in waterproof clothing, for this was then only in its infancy. Yes, a cabman's life was under such conditions a dreary existence, with little or nothing to break its weary monotony, and a working day would run to something like seventeen or eighteen hours. Under such circumstances the tavern with its warmth and brightness was their only refuge. Still on a quiet fine day the men would gather in a quartette in one of their cabs on the rank and indulge in a game of "all fours," and quite enjoy the little variety.

The old-fashioned multiple cape, which some of the old "jarvies" wore as a protection against the weather, is now almost a thing of the past. They are seen at times on the coachmen and footmen of those who keep their carriages, and the present generation of ladies occasionally adopt this style of cape, but of course it is more dainty and elegant in style.

What a wonderful change we are now able to point

to in relation to the various matters on which I have been dwelling. Now as a rule the cabs and coaches are roomy and comfortable, clean and sweet. The railway station vehicles do still perhaps lag behind and in a measure reflect the old state of things, but even in these a very material improvement is to be seen. The cab horses are now mostly healthy-looking, sound and in some instances even stylish in appearance, more especially those driven in hansom cabs, which in the old days had no existence. What would the young people of the present time think of having to do without their hansom to sport about in, when they are oftentimes too lazy to walk?

In all parts of the City and suburbs there are nowadays comfortable shelters for the cabmen, where they can eat their meals in privacy, and not as formerly, when they usually had to sit on the doorsteps of their vehicles, the contents of their basins exposed to the gaze of every passer-by. Sometimes they would retire to the inside, but if they did so they ran the risk of missing a fare, and in any case the odour of dinner left in the cab was not altogether agreeable to the next occupant. In wet weather, too, these shelters protect them from the elements, and in the coldest seasons they can be warm and cozy.

In every respect the typical cabman of today is a vast improvement on his ancestor. He is educated, sober and obliging, and his better surroundings and advantages have helped to develop his own self-respect, whilst the public have ceased to regard him as only an extortionate toper. The naturally lowering and almost degrading phases of his calling exist no longer; and as the dinner hour arrives it is a pleasure to see bright, intelligent, well-clothed children going along the roads carrying their fathers' dinners and jugs of hot steaming coffee or tea; and to witness the happy little interchange of affectionate greetings on both sides. In addition to all this the hours of continual labour are shortened, or at anyrate arrangements are made by which the men can enjoy the luxury of "off time," instead of the weary, dreary drudge from early morning until all hours of the night.

But great as the improvements have been in these matters, they have been fully as numerous and important in connection with the omnibus and tram traffic of the City. Some of my readers will call to mind the old type of 'buses which used to carry the passenger traffic. They were narrow and cramped, the seats often forming a semi-circle at the top end, so that when the 'Bus was full with an extra stout party or two at the sides, those at the top end had a very uncomfortable time of it. Then whoever occupied the seat of president in the middle at the top was in close communication with the communicator and bell to the driver, which caused unpleasant vibrations in your ears, head and back every time the wire was pulled. These omnibuses, too, had a musty smell, with wisps of straw laid underneath the feet in wet weather, which gave the interior a strong flavour of the stables. Then, to still more confine the air, doors were attached which had to be opened or shut whenever an entrance or exit took place. The windows, too, shook and rattled away as the heavy wheels jolted over the metalled roads; so I imagine that if passengers of today had to return to the discomforts of the old omnibus, there would probably be a little more walking done than there is now.

The accommodation for outside passengers was also very primitive and unsatisfactory, there being a kind of knifeboard arrangement which ran along each side and covered a portion of the windows, thus not only obscuring the light, but presenting to the passengers inside an array of boots and shoes of all shapes and sizes. To mount to the top you clambered up some muddy, and often greasy steps, and if the vacant seat happened to be at the far end of the knifeboard, you had to plant your hands betwixt the necks of each man as you worked along. If you managed to escape treading on the feet of the row of "outsiders" in getting to your place you were fortunate, but if you succeeded in finding out the exact locality of someone's favourite corn it was as well to appear "as one that heareth not." If you considered yourself on friendly terms with coachee, he handed you a leathern thong or strap by means of which you hoisted yourself into position.

This was a fair sample of the ordinary omnibus of the period, so when, in the year 1852, a man of the name of MacEwen took Manchester suddenly by storm, and introduced his new omnibuses they quickly caused the old ones to make place for the new. These vehicles were much larger, longer, wider and more airy, having no doors, and were accessible outside by a neat iron ladder. The seats were raised on the top, and the feet consequently had not to dangle down in front of you, thus doing away entirely with the ugly, awkward knifeboard arrangement. The new omnibuses looked very spic and span after the dingy ones to which we had been accustomed, being painted in the gay, tartan plaid of the MacEwen clan. They were well built and finished off, and soon won themselves into popular favour. When they first commenced running, they started from the corner of Sherbourne Street, in Strangeways, just to avoid the toll-bar, which was then in existence, and ran to All Saint's, in Oxford Road, the fare being threepence. At the time of their introduction, John Greenwood, the large coach, cab, and omnibus proprietor, had almost a monopoly of the traffic, and he saw wisely that it would never do to let himself be beaten off his own ground, so he came to terms with MacEwen, and eventually the Manchester Carriage Company was formed, which developed into such a prosperous undertaking.

Before these later omnibuses were merged into the tramway cars, there had been many improvements made in them in various ways, as was also the case in the tramcars. The original tramcars were long, ugly, unwieldly looking things, with a quantity of painted metal about them, which with wear and tear soon became dingy and dirty. The drivers had to unyoke their horses on arriving at the terminus, and to walk them round to the other end of the tram, thus making the head the tail or vice versa as required. It looked stupid to see the drivers hauling about their horses with the long crossbar attached as if they were taking a team to plough. It was at this time that Mr. Eade, of the Manchester Carriage Company, introduced his new patent car, which was smaller, more compact, revolving on its own axis, and was in every respect a very great improvement on anything before it; and I think I am expressing the opinion of most people that at the time Eade's patent car was introduced it was the best and handsomest of its kind to be found anywhere.

In the days of MacEwen's omnibuses I remember he used to stable some of his horses and put up the omnibuses at Emanual Hird's Livery Stables, which were then in Booth Street, before Brown Street was opened out into Booth Street from Chancery Lane. I knew this locality well in those days, as the firm with which I was associated migrated from Lower King Street to Booth Street about 1853, and I must say the prospect which was presented to me daily out of my office windows was anything but attractive. Right in front were the stables of Emanual Hird, old and dilapidated, and flanked by a number of wornout tenements, whose occupants were not too respectable. Here, as usual, there was a plentiful supply of beerhouses, which always flourish in disreputable surroundings. Perhaps the only cheerful bit of colour to be seen in the landscape was the bright gay tartan of MacEwen's omnibuses as they stood in the stable yard, which still remains with me as a pleasant contrast to the tumbledown, decayed-looking surroundings. As I have said before, it is unfortunate that sketches were not made of some of these old spots, before they were demolished, in order that people of today might realise more clearly what is, and what has been.

CHAPTER XXXVIII

Ardwick Green and its Surroundings.

AS you saunter along from London Road Station towards Ardwick Green, the changes are widespread and unmistakable, and the amount of old decayed properties and buildings of all descriptions which have been cleared away is enormous. Whitworth Street is altogether new, and also Fairfield Street on the right; and although Granby Row is still there in name, an old habitue of the place would have some difficulty in recognising it. After crossing the Medlock, however, some traces of what London Road was at this point are still to be found. For ordinary business purposes Manchester and Ardwick Green are practically one, but in my young days I used to think it was quite a long walk from town to the Green. When you did reach your destination you felt that you were really in the country, and that you could ramble about and enjoy yourself. But this is hardly the sensation which impresses itself upon your mind as you find yourself at Ardwick Green at the present time. No doubt the place has had a large amount expended upon it, and in some respects it is greatly superior to what it was, but the old simple country look of the spot as I first knew it, has altogether vanished. My earliest recollections of the Green are associated with the May Day processions, this being a favourite locality for these gatherings and very nice it was to see the children gaily dressed and fitting about amongst the trees and foliage all in their fresh Spring attire. Here, too, on the 1st of May, the chimney-sweepers had their annual procession, and I can recall the boys with their sooty faces, whilst they themselves were dressed in all the colours of the rainbow, and very proud they were of their motley appearance as they marched about with their poles and garlands of flowers. One has now almost ceased to realise that there ever was such a day in the calendar, and the remark of the hatter in "Box and Cox": "I bought this candle on the 1st of May, chimney-sweeper's day, calculating it would last me three months," etc, has for the bulk of present-day theatre goers little point or meaning.

With the increase of the population came also an increase of the urchins and street arabs who invaded the Green, and this no doubt helped materially to despoil it of its natural charms, to such an extent that it was at length found necessary to close it, except to those families who lived around it, and who had keys to admit themselves to the space enclosed.

It would be amusing to glance into the face of someone who had lived in Ardwick Green sixty years ago, and who now again re-visited it for the first time. I can fancy the look of melancholy surprise which would depict itself upon his features as he gazed around him and saw how the whole character of the place had changed. The sweet country air and aspect gone, most of the old handsome family residences demolished or commercialised in one form or another, and the entire locality delivered over to a kind of physical melancholia, so utterly different to what it once was, that the words of the old hymn would probably most aptly express his thoughts: –

"*Change and decay in all around I see.*"

However, St. Thomas's Church is there as of old, with the three small cottages, which, considering that they were built in 1822, show the hand of time as little, or perhaps less, than anything else about. These were erected when the Reverend Cecil Wray was connected with the Church, and long before he became one of the Canons of the Cathedral. As a whole, the north side of the Green presents fewer changes than the others, and many of the old houses remain, although they have been renovated and otherwise modernised.

Alexander B. Rowley, the attorney, lived, at the time of which I am writing, on the Green; but it was perhaps more as the father of a large family of noted cricketers that he was widely known. The sons were members of the Manchester Cricket Club, and were a great strength to it as very capable exponents of the game.

Henry Charlton, the calenderer and finisher, whose descendants are still with us, also lived close by.

John Rylands[18] at one time lived at the north end of the Green, and I wonder, as he dwelt there so quietly in the old days, did he ever dream of what the business which he built up would develop to in the future? That he saw its possibilities under his fostering care I think there is little doubt, but probably even he hardly realised its immense future. But be that as it may, it was not with the idea that his wealth, if he made it, should be lavished on himself or his belongings in luxurious living or selfish gratification, for to the last he lived a simple unostentatious life. But if he did not spend his money on himself, that did not prevent him being a generous giver to the charitable and other philanthropic institutions of the City and locality. What he commenced and continued in his lifetime his widow has amplified by the magnificent gift to Manchester of the Rylands Library, where there is gathered under its roof one of the finest collections of books in the Kingdom – a veritable earthly paradise for the true student.

John Rylands was no speaker in the ordinary acceptation of the word; he spoke by deeds, not words. I remember so well on one occasion, at the Boys' Refuge, on the opening of an important addition to the work to which he had liberally contributed, he was called upon to preside. This he did in the very simplest way, commencing the proceedings by reading reverently a portion of God's Word, his own remarks being few, but practical, which

---

18. *John Rylands (1801-1888) - Known as "Manchester's First Multi-millionaire", made his vast fortune in the textile trade. Owner of 17 mills and the employer of 15,000 people he played a decisive role in the construction of the Manchester Ship Canal. His legacy funded John Rylands Library.*

he always was.

Ardwick Hall[19], where John L. Kennedy used to reside, is still in existence, though it is now railed off from the old grounds which were attached to it, but which are still lying fallow. A few of the old shrubs are still trying to struggle for life, and the borders which enclosed them are yet to be traced here and there, but the charm of the place has altogether vanished. How it would have grieved the heart of the old gentleman to see this once pleasant country residence now a dreary waste. The house itself has been better cared for, and seems to be in good habitable condition. It is strange how often mentally a man becomes associated with us, from some special, and at times trivial, circumstances, with which the name had been linked. J. L. Kennedy in business was a calico printer (succeeding J. Graham and Co.), and at the time of which I speak he did a very large and profitable business in what were called pink and purple pads. The firm had established a very enviable reputation for this class of work; and to this day in my mind the name of J. L. Kennedy is directly associated with this particular style of calico printing, with which I formerly had to do.

Henry Houldsworth, of the old-established firm of T. Houldsworth and Co. (now absorbed into the Fine Cotton Spinners' Association) lived at Ardwick Green for many years before he removed to Oak Hill, Cheetham Hill. He must have known Ardwick almost at its best, as he was resident there in 1836, and probably earlier than this. People liked to live near their places of business in those days. Thomas Houldsworth, the other partner, lived at Portland Place, Piccadilly, which was just beyond the "Queen's Hotel," then being erected.

Turning round from the Green you come to Burgess Terrace, where there lived a man who was for many years very closely associated with the municipal life of Manchester. I speak of Abel Heywood[20], a man who,

---

19 - Ardwick Hall was demolished in the early 20th century. A Great Universal Stores warehouse was built on the site.

hard working, energetic and clear headed, threw himself actively into every scheme which he considered was for the benefit of his fellow-citizens and the community in general. Having once made up his mind that a certain scheme ought to be carried out, whatever it might be, he was not easily turned aside from his purpose by any difficulty, and so he was a leading spirit in most of the great improvements and developments of the City. He was Mayor in 1862, and at one time had every prospect of being elected member for Manchester. At the last moment, however, just a few days before the polling took place, Edwin James, Q.C, came down from London and took the constituency, as it were, by storm, and was elected member. Had he not appeared upon the scene, there is little doubt Abel Heywood would have been successful, as large numbers of the Conservative Party had arranged to vote for him. He was a man who held a high place in the Council Chamber, and in his later years he was presented with the Freedom of the City.

There are very few of the good old houses left around the Green, but here and there you get just a trace of what the place must once have been. It was here that most of the well-to-do and even wealthy people of Manchester resided, as is seen by the number of coach-houses and stables attached to many of the houses. Some of these have had to suffer the indignity of having shop fronts tacked on to the ancient frameworks standing in the rear, and the gardens being transformed into stonemasons' yards, and depots for wood and coal; but a few of the old-fashioned houses are still to be discovered, with their quaint gabled windows, almost hidden away from sight by hideous erections of many kinds; and as you ponder these things and linger regretfully over the past you are disposed to give utterance to the words of the old song:–

"The light of other days is faded,
And all their glories past."

---

20 - Abel Heywood (1810- 1893) was a publisher, political radical and Mayor of Manchester (1862-63 & 1876-77).

CHAPTER XXXIX

Plymouth Grove – Lime Grove – Greenheys Lane.

AS certain diseases and epidemics appear indigenous to certain places, so, too, particular localities seem to show a special weakness for certain names. For instance, at Hampstead I have often been struck by the great number of "Crescents," which are to be found there, the name cropping up in all directions. In Glasgow, "Terraces" are more in vogue, whilst in Dublin I have noticed the people incline to Rows. (No joke intended.) Then again other localities show a leaning towards "Banks," others for "Avenues" and "Places." And so we find that in Chorlton-on-Medlock, a very strong predilection is manifested for "Groves," and in whatever direction you take your way there they are to be found. To enumerate a few of them there is Plymouth Grove, which of them all had, I think, originally the greatest claim to the title. But in addition there are Richmond, Hyde, Swinton, Lincoln, Thorncliffe, Pembroke, Stanley, Lime and Alexandra Groves, besides others which are scattered about all over the district. Of course a Grove has a very pleasant sound to the ear and senses, conjuring up thoughts of luxuriant trees, flowers and foliage, with sweet, pure, country surroundings, with life untainted by the smoke, turmoil and bustle of town and its deadening influences; and to a certain extent this is the impression of Groves left upon my young mind, when I used to ramble about amongst the Groves of Chorlton-on-Medlock. For example it was quite a charming walk out to Plymouth Grove, when it was situated in the heart of the country, and shaded by its pretty avenue of trees, and vocal with the song of birds. Now, alas, these trees are many of them black and grim, some of them dead, whilst others are trying to live out a very fitful existence. The Grove itself has lost almost all its old charm, and its inhabitants have also changed with the times, for of those who lived there in 1850 I cannot trace one that is left at the present time, they have all vanished, and the place that knew them knows them no more. The inhabitants of Plymouth Grove were then quite a select little coterie, living in handsome, well-appointed residences. Amongst those who had settled there was Thomas Kendal, of Kendal, Milne and Co.; also Richard Cope, the wine merchant whose place of business was in Exchange Street, with a vault outlet in St. Mary's Gate, the licence of which was lately acquired by Parker's, next door. Matthew Curtis, too, had his house there, and in 1860-1861 he was elected Mayor of Manchester. Ernest Reuss, Wainwright Bellhouse, and Ivie Mackie also lived there, the last-named having been thrice called to the mayoral chair. Then, too, there were S. Meyer, George Spafford, of Spafford, McConnel and Co, and A. S. Sichel.

There were others, of course, but these I have named were well-known Manchester people. Perhaps some of my older readers may remember the ponderous form of A. S. Sichel, as he came waddling along the street. He was a well-known foreign merchant, with an extensive business, but amongst the community at large he was probably more widely known, as the man with an appetite. All sorts of anecdotes were current about his capabilities when he was a prominent Manchester figure; and I almost think he prided himself on the wonderful name which he had made for himself as a noted gourmand. I believe that some of the restaurants declined to cater for him except on special terms. Hotel proprietors trembled when he entered their portals, and a dinner from the joint meant little or nothing for anybody else after his first introduction to it. A leg of mutton with him was perhaps a little too much for one but not enough for two, and it is said that his cooks at home had a busy and anxious time of it, as he was not too amiable if things went wrong in the culinary department.

Since the days to which I refer there has been a large increase in the number of houses in Plymouth Grove, but the new agreeth not with the old. It is a pity to see fine old family residences, with pleasure grounds attached, followed by rows of ordinary-looking, cheap-rented houses, where the object of the builder has been to crowd as many tenements as possible on to a given space, regardless of the deterioration of the property surrounding. Although I am not one of those who get madly enthusiastic about the "good old times," still I am very much inclined to think that many present-day builders have little or no consideration for what may be termed general effects. Their object is to get the best return for their money, whereas in the old days those who built house property endeavoured in some measure at least to consider the general surroundings, and to aim at some harmony of style. Even now there are still parts of Plymouth Grove which remind you of what it once was; but when you reach the Little Sisters' Home for the aged and infirm, at the corner of High Street, all such sentimental thoughts vanish, as you glance at this unlovely-looking building. All praise to those who are in this Home caring for the poor and needy, but surely some attempt might have been made to make the outside appearance a little more attractive. Could not some ivy be trained about it to try and hide its barrack-like appearance?

Turning to the right out of Plymouth Grove into High Street, past Richmond Grove, you are conscious that all about you is modern in style, until you reach a point somewhere about half-way between the Grove and Whitworth Park, when your attention is drawn towards a very old farmhouse and homestead, which speaks unmistakably of the "good old times," when this part of the country must have been purely pastoral. This relic of ancient days goes by the title of Blackstake Farm, and its appearance so interested me when I first saw it that I made enquiries about it. I am told that it dates back some two hundred years, and in confirmation of this I have seen by a map of this locality of 1730, a copy of which was published in the *City News*[21] on the 3rd of January, 1903, this Blackstake Farm is one of the places mentioned upon it as being then in existence. An old woman, who lived on the farm between sixty and seventy years ago, stated that at that time the fields extended from this point as far townwards as Rusholme Road. The farm is well worth a visit, as it forms a link with a past separated by centuries.

There is another Grove off Oxford Street, which, from early associations, recalls happy days spent in and about it. I refer to Lime Grove, which, although it was not perhaps either so aristocratic-looking or extensive as Plymouth Grove, still the sound of its name revives pleasant memories, and speaks to me of the country in all its purity and sweetness. It is now, alas, a very sad-looking place, and the freshness and charm which once distinguished it have altogether vanished. At one time there were not more than half-a-dozen families living in it, so there was ample space for all, and room for trees and foliage to flourish and abound. Today Lime Grove is nothing but a very ordinary street, the old houses going rapidly to decay, whilst the newer ones, including a small Welsh chapel, add in no way to its beauty; in fact, it seems a sort of mockery to call it a grove, and as you pass through it, if you have not known it before, you wonder how anyone had the courage to give it a name which suggests something after the nature of Claude Melnotte's beautiful but imaginary palace, "with orange groves and music from sweet lutes."

Some well-known Manchester people resided at one time in Lime Grove, who no doubt considered – and rightly so too – that they were then quite out of town. There were William Bellhouse, the timber merchant, William Sharp, of Sharp Brothers, the engineers, Thomas Potter, the attorney, and Lewis Langworthy, of Langworthy Brothers, all located here. Of the other members of the last-named family and firm, George Langworthy lived at Heath House, Lower Broughton Road, and Edward Riley Langworthy (who was Mayor of Salford from 1848 to 1850) lived in Victoria Park. What a splendid business these Langworthy Brothers built up by their energy, determination and integrity; and yet it seems strange to say that, although the firm exists as of old, there is no representative of the family having in our locality at the present time; of course Mrs. Langworthy, of Victoria Park, is only lately dead, but I think she was the last of the name who lived amongst us. The dear, good old lady was a great loss to the community, as she had a heart big with generosity, and her "drops in the bucket," as she used to call them, were ever dropping in the shape of handsome donations to the charities and institutions she most favoured. The Boys Refuge lost a good friend when her life came to a close, for she never wearied of sending her "drops" to help forward the good work. She was one of those who believed in giving whilst she was alive, and although she gave freely, she did so with humble simplicity as a steward of God's good gifts, to be used in His service.

James Sewell, the banker, was another dweller in Lime Grove, and continued to be so for may years. He was a quiet-looking, grey-haired man with a sparse frame, who took life soberly and methodically, and with a placid equanimity which was not easily ruffled. He had the reputation of being as good a judge of a trade bill, and its discount value, as any banker in Manchester. When anyone went to him they had not to wait long for his decision on any matter; he soon made up his mind, and he expected his customers to do the same. As his health failed him he took his nephew, a Mr. Walker, into partnership with him, and the firm became James Sewell and Nephew. Mr. Walker did not live long, and when James Sewell died, this banking business fell into the hands of Joseph Sewell, a relative who had been employed in the Bank. He was a keen, shrewd man of business, and under his direction the Bank prospered, and at the time of his death in 1887 he was a comparatively wealthy man. Eventually this private banking concern went the way of most of the others, in these days of Syndicates, Trusts and Amalgamations, and it was absorbed into the Union Bank of Manchester.

Perhaps the most melancholy and bewildering place for an old Manchester absentee to find himself in, after a lapse of half a century, would be Greenheys Lane and fields, for the whole physical aspect of the place has so completely changed that there would be every reasonable excuse for getting lost in his surroundings. Say that you approach Greenheys Lane by way of Burlington Street, and, by the way, the mention of Burlington Street reminds me of an episode in the life of a friend of mine, who, like myself, is journeying down the hill of life. He told it to me as an illustration of the style in which business was carried on in our young days. At the time the affair happened he was about sixteen years of age, and he had been sent by an uncle, in whose place he was, to collect an account, a large one, from some firm whose hours of payment were from 8 in the evening until any time. The amount he had to receive was about £3,000, and after he had collected it in cash, notes and cheques, he had to take it to his uncle's house, which was some distance down Burlington Street.

The street was in those days very indifferently lighted, only sufficiently so to make darkness visible, and as soon as he had turned down out of Oxford Street, he felt sure he heard footsteps following along after him. He hurried on, but the quicker he walked, the more quickly the steps were heard following on behind him. At last in a state of sheer fright he took to running as hard as his legs would carry him, and when he reached his uncle's door, he thundered at it as loudly as possible. When it was opened and he got inside the lobby, he could hardly speak from fright and exhaustion, and something had to be given him to bring him round. Then he told his tale about being followed,

21. *City News* newspaper 1864 to 1934, 1934-36 & 1937-1955

but he said he never could be quite sure whether this was so or not, or whether it was that having this large sum of money upon him he had magnified some ordinary sound behind him into an actual pursuit. However, his uncle was so impressed with the circumstance, that he saw the firm who paid from 8 to 11 in the evening, and remonstrated with them for paying accounts at such unearthly hours. They told him that they were not going to change their hours just to please him, and so owing to a disagreement on this matter, they ceased doing business together for some time. Just fancy any firm at the present time doing business in this sort of way; why, collectors would be on strike in no time, and rightly so, too.

But to return, after this digression; when you reached Greenheys Lane you were at once in the country, and close to Greenheys fields, with a nice brook meandering through them. Now the fields are gone, and the Lane? Well it is nothing less than sheer mockery to give it any such pleasant title. It is now simply a common street, with not one atom of attractiveness about it. The handsome gothic houses, where the Sidney Potters, the Wolffs, the Lieberts and the Schuncks resided, have altogether disappeared; and even an old tree, a worthy occupant of one of the gardens of these houses, which had been left standing, spared, I presume, by the hands of the "ruthless invaders," has been removed from the pathway where it stood in solitary grandeur up to a short time ago. At one time Sam Memdel lived at Greenheys Abbey, a fine residence in the old days, but to visit Greenheys now and glance around you and to think of it ever having been associated with an Abbey seems ridiculous. After all there is a life lesson in such a transformation scene. Father Time is digging, diving, delving and reaping about us in all directions, until at last we, like the tree of which I have been speaking, find ourselves, as old age creeps over us, standing well nigh alone, old companions and friends gone from us, and we, too waiting for our own call.

CHAPTER XL

The Manchester Art Treasures Exhibition, 1857.

SOME little time back, when glancing over some old papers which had lain undisturbed for many years, I happened to come across a season ticket belonging to the above, and as I looked at it, oh, what a crowd of pleasant memories came trooping back. Forty-eight years have since then, come and gone, and yet the recollections of many happy days spent within the walls of that wonderful Exhibition float back to me, clear and strong, and it is difficult to realise that so wide a gap of time divides the then and now. 1857 was a red-letter year for Manchester, for although there had been previous exhibitions both at home and abroad, the one held in Manchester was unique amongst them all, for there was then gathered under one roof a collection of the rarest and most valuable pictures which had probably ever been seen side by side.

It was the outcome of a National effort to bring together the best representative specimens of Art of all kinds, but more especially paintings and statuary from the earliest times up to the then present day. It was really astonishing how easily owners were induced to lend their gems, many of them of priceless value, in order that this Exhibition should be worthy of the Nation. In doing so they probably hardly realised, in the first rush of the pleasurable excitement of getting such a collection together the enormous risk they ran of losing works of Art, which if destroyed, or in any way damaged, could not by any possibility be replaced. It was after the accomplishment of the effort, and when the pictures hung in their places on the walls, the statuary filled the aisles, and the costly and unique works of Art of every kind, crowded the cases prepared for them in that beautiful building, that the risk of holding such an Exhibition impressed itself upon the minds of the people, and explains why it has been impossible to get up another exhibition of its kind. A fire in such a building, stored with so valuable a collection, would have been nothing less than a National calamity, for no insurance, however large, could have ever compensated for the destruction of such treasures. However, fortunately, no accident happened, and the Exhibition came to a happy and successful close, and the priceless collection was restored to the rightful owners safe and sound.

The happy hours and days I spent in that building at Old Trafford are even to this day a delightful retrospect. The only regret I have is that I did not make more use of my opportunities. The Exhibition was opened by the Prince Consort on the 5th of May, but the great public event in connection with it was the visit of the Queen on the 30th of June. I was fortunate in securing an excellent position to witness the imposing ceremony associated with it. I was just at the side of the large organ, looking straight down the main aisle along which the procession advanced, so I had the Royal party right in front of me as it approached the dais prepared for Her Majesty. She looked every inch a Queen as she walked quietly forward, and as she entered the far end of the aisle Clara Novella commenced singing the National Anthem.

Perhaps it may have been my feelings which swayed me, but to my mind I never heard "God Save the Queen" sung before or since as she sang it on that day. Her voice, full, clear and melodious, rang through the whole building, and as she came to the last words of the verse, she phrased them as follows: – "God save – The Queen." The last two words issued from her lips with such intensity and yet with such sweetness that they send a thrill through the thousands of people assembled to give Her Majesty welcome. I am sure the Queen was herself affected, as she could not but feel the warmth of her Lancashire greeting when the cheers burst forth on all sides. Lord Palmerston was the Minister of State who attended her, and his pleasant, genial face and bearing added to the historic charm of the ceremony. Sir Joseph Heron, as Town Clerk, was also in attendance on Her Majesty, and it was, I think, at this time that he was knighted. He was tall, handsome and aristocratic-looking, and was certainly at that time the most important man in the Manchester Corporation. His will was virtually considered law in all civic matters, and he was a courageous man who attempted to thwart or act in any way in opposition to the Town Clerk. At this time it was, I think, a very common public belief that Sir Joseph Heron was not only Town Clerk, but Mayor and Corporation all in one. However, be this as it may, there is no doubt he was a sound lawyer, a polished gentleman, and in all respects an able representative of the City interests in London, and therefore it was quite natural that much of the power and authority in connection with municipal matters should be left in his hands.

To attempt to enter into a detailed description of all the beautiful paintings which hung in profusion on the walls of the Exhibition would, of course, be a simple impossibility, nor indeed can the enthusiasm and intensity of feeling which is so great a part of one's nature at the age of twenty be so readily warmed up to the old temperature when getting on for seventy. The old glamour is gone, and what remains is a sense of remembered delight and gratification, which it would be hardly possible to transmit to a prosaic everyday reader. Another matter to take into consideration is, that to put the same Exhibition before the people of today might not of necessity raise the same amount of enthusiasm or give birth to the same pleasurable feelings. In writing thus I would leave aside one's convictions and impressions with regard to what are termed the old masters, as these live more or less for all time. But in respect to some of the Victorian era painters, what may have had a great charm for us in 1857, might not appeal in the same way to the present generation. There would not probably be much difference of opinion as to

THE MANCHESTER ART TREASURES
EXHIBITION BUILDINGS 1857

the merits of such painters as Turner, Stansfield, Landseer and the Linnells; but there are others who at the time of which I am writing created quite a sensation, who would, I think, now not stand very high in the estimation of the public.

As an example of what I mean, there was Frith[22], the artist, who made a reputation for himself by paintings such as the Railway Station and the Racecourse, and round whose pictures in the Exhibition a crowd was nearly always to be found. But after looking carefully now at one of these you are not disposed to be so enthusiastic about them, and you are inclined to consider them stagey and therefore disappointing. They have, as it were, outlasted their welcome, and it is so with other painters of the early Victorian period, both of figure and landscape, who, although admired and run after for a time, have ceased to retain any attraction for the present generation. One appears to have lost touch with their work, and as you look at some of the paintings which formerly you admired, you wonder now how and why you did.

There is George Cruikshank[23], for instance, I can remember when his sketches were in great public favour, and yet now as you glance at most of them you are struck by their coarseness and lack of style and finish. John Leach, too, for many years held sway over the public taste for his sketches and drawings in *Punch*, and rightly so, too, for they were full of life and vigour; but when you compare them with the work that is being produced at the present time you cannot but be greatly struck with the immense strides which have been made amongst artists of this class.

Then it is doubtful if art critics of today would altogether follow us in our admiration for much that appealed to us in the Exhibition of 1857, more especially when we ourselves find that our own artistic taste has become more educated and refined; but after making allowances for all this, still there was gathered there such a superabundant wealth of artistic gems of every kind that such deductions as I have named formed but a small percentage of the whole.

This Exhibition, however, was not an attraction from an artistic point of view merely, but as a social function on a scale never before attempted by Manchester; it was an undeniable success. Manchester was, for the time being at least, a centre of wealth, dress and fashion. Ladies from near and far vied with one another in the richness and elegance of their costumes, and in this way also added to the general charm of the place and its surroundings. It was, of course, a special rendezvous for young people of both sexes, and although there is a saying that marriages are made in Heaven, there can be no manner of doubt that the Art Treasures Exhibition of 1857 was a splendid training ground, and many marriages were very happily prospected there. Many social family treasures and gems were to be found within its turnstiles, and ties were formed which were not dissolved when the doors of the Exhibition were finally closed on the 17th of October, 1857.

During this year Manchester was overrun with visitors, and it was astonishing to find the number of friends and relatives who were dying to come and stay with you, not, of course, for the sake of the Exhibition, but just out of pure love and affection. Houses were in most instances crowded to their full capacity, and certainly ours was no exception to the rule. We endeavoured to make it as elastic as possible so as to find accommodation for its numerous occupants, and it was certainly a time of pleasant companionship and much social merriment.

Those were Pickwickian days when practical joking in households was a much more common thing than it is today. In fact, I am afraid young men of the present generation would consider it quite out of place to descend to any such amusement. I must confess that it was without doubt a failing in our family, which perhaps arose from the fact that we hailed originally from "The Emerald Isle," and therefore probably inherited a special tendency in the direction named.

When, therefore, our house was full of visitors, all of whom were on intimate social terms, it was not easy to avoid some of the traps which were at times laid for the unwary. For example, at that time many beds were laid with wooden lags which could be taken out of their sockets, leaving only the bedding, and anyone getting into bed when these lags had been removed would slowly but inevitably come to the floor; and it was not easy from the appearance of the bed to discover the work of those who had laid the trap. Again, if after you had got comfortably into bed and were just dosing off to sleep, you found the upper bedclothes slipping gently from the bed towards the window, you would come to the conclusion that your tormentors were at work, and had probably locked themselves in securely in another room, and with cords attached to your bedclothes were drawing them away from you through a slit in the window.

A nice fresh bit of prickly holly was a pleasant thing with which to tickle your bare feet as you landed into bed, or a well and judiciously flour-dusted pillow gave you a start in the morning when you looked in the glass and discovered that your hair and face had assumed a somewhat pale and piebald appearance from contact with the pillow during the night.

Talking about prickly holly, I remember staying away one Christmas with friends at Wolverhampton, and as there were a number of visitors in the house three of us, all intimate friends and companions, had to sleep three in a bed, which was fortunately a large one. I was the last to retire, and I found my bedfellows had kindly left me the centre place, for which I was grateful, as the night was bitterly cold. Well, I got into bed, and as was

---

22 - *William Powell Frith (1819-1909), a painter specialising in portraitd and Victorian Era narratives. Elected to the Royal Academy 1862.*
23. *George Cruikshank (1792-1878), a caricaturist praised as 'the modern Hogarth'.*

my custom on a winter's night, I at once tucked my limbs as close up to my chin as I could in order to concentrate the heat as much as possible. Somehow this arrangement of mine did not appear to find favour with my friends, who urged me to put down my feet, but as there were about 20 degrees of frost outside I declined their repeated solicitations. Although they derided me, they failed to make any impression upon me, and they at length jumped out of bed, when it came to light that a very substantial bunch of holly had been placed in our bed, and as each of my companions pricked themselves with it as they got into bed, they bore the discomfort silently, and planting the holly just where my feet would meet it, they chuckled over my anticipated trouble. Innocently I had escaped the trap set for me, and next morning at breakfast I had all the laugh against them.

On another occasion, when our house was extra full, two male cousins were staying with us and had to occupy the same room. In the morning the one who had first risen saw, as he thought, a pot (unused) of Jewsbury and Brown's toothpaste on the dressing table. On lifting the lid he hardly thought the contents of the pot looked like toothpaste, but being distinctly labelled so, he broke into it and put some on his toothbrush. It appeared to him to have an uncommonly greasy taste, and he appealed to the one who had not risen on the matter. He replied in a half sleepy way that it was all right, at the same time smothering his laughter under the bedclothes, as he saw the mistake he was making. Later on the early riser was surprised to see his cousin, who had then risen and was dressing, using the contents of the same pot as a pomade for the hair. However, he said nothing, but, chuckling to himself, went down to breakfast, telling us with great glee that his relative had been using toothpaste for pomade. When the latter appeared the early riser found that it was not he who had got the worm in this instance, for he had been using a special home-made pomade which was filled into Jewsbury and Brown's old toothpaste pots. Satisfied that he was this time the victim, he retired to try and get his mouth into a more comfortable condition.

I began with the Art Treasures Exhibition, and I find myself concluding the chapter with toothpaste and pomade; it seems a funny mixture, but memory is fickle and flighty, and old men are proverbially garrulous.

CHAPTER XLI

The Great Flood of 1866.

ON the 17th of November, 1866, a great and disastrous flood occurred which caused widespread and terrible damage to property both in Manchester and Salford. From the present racecourse at the Cliff (but which at that time had been transferred to Old Trafford), right away to The Crescent, Salford, there extended one huge lake of turbid water, rushing irresistibly along, and carrying with it in its course everything which it was capable of rooting up or dislodging from its place. It was a truly magnificent sight to those who could from some point of safety stand and take in the panorama of seething waters which lay stretched out before them. But to those who had life and property at stake it was a day of disaster and never-ceasing anxiety and dread. In Broughton Lane, and in many other places, the inhabitants might be seen sailing about from house to house in boats and on rafts, and, in fact, upon any thing that would float and carry them to some place of security. In many dwellings the water was not only in the cellars and in the living rooms, but might be seen rising up into the bedrooms. Hundreds of families were crowded together in the attics and upper rooms of their houses and cottages, looking with alarm at the water as it mounted higher and higher, lapping against the stairs and cutting off any retreat from their watery prison.

It was a serious and anxious sight on the afternoon of that day, to watch the rapid swirl of muddy brown water as it came shooting along past you, and carrying away on its angry-looking bosom all manner of incongruous things. Imagine seeing a dead pig, a family group of cocks and hens perched disconsolately on an old hencoop, in company with a host of miscellaneous articles of all

THE OLD BLACK BRIDGE
Swept away by the great flood in 1866

shapes and sizes, household and otherwise; dog-kennels, trees, bandboxes, furniture of all descriptions, hats, wooden boxes and floating crockery, all rushing wildly along and at times jostling and falling foul one of another, as if they were hurrying on and away from some relentless foe who was driving them to destruction, and from whom they were powerless to escape.

    In Strangeways the water lay deep in the roadway, and passengers in the omnibuses at places had to put their feet on the opposite seats, to try and keep clear of the water which came lapping in as we drove along. I saw one courageous cabman driving a hansom with his fare inside, attempt to breast the full force of the flood as he entered Broughton Lane, but he had not proceeded far before the depth of the water forced him to turn round and beat a hasty retreat, as had he not quickly done so the consequences might have been serious. Fortunately the flood reached its height somewhere about three o'clock in the afternoon, for what the misery and loss of life would have been had it continued to rise after darkness had set in it would have been hard to say. But as the day closed the waters began to subside, and many an anxious mind was relieved. The sight presented next morning was truly pitiable; the furniture and household belongings in hundreds of dwellings were hopelessly damaged or destroyed; the trees which lay in the course of the flood looked as if they had been fishing on their own account and had had a good haul in the shape of straw, rags, paper, old baskets, etc, in fact anything appeared to be fish which came to their net by finding a lodgment in their branches.

What the feelings of the women must have been when they descended to the lower rooms on that morning may perhaps be imagined, for with everything caked in slimy mud, "putting things to rights" must have been a sorry experience. But, bad as things were at the time, the after effects were even worse. The damp got into the walls and foundations of the houses, and for years hardly a dry or healthy habitation could be found where the waters had had full play. Sickness and a high death-rate were of course, only a natural sequence, and newcomers avoided Lower Broughton almost like a plague spot. As may readily be supposed, property owners had a very bad time of it; tenants had to be tempted with exceptionally low rents, which I fear would be counterbalanced by bad health and increased doctors' bills. For years the flood line could be seen in many places, and possibly may even yet be traced; whilst in Peel Park a notice may be seen there indicating the high water mark at the Crescent terminus of the flood.

On the afternoon of the day when the waters were at about their highest point, I remember walking down Great Clowes Street from the higher ground, and a little below Upper Camp Street I was unable to advance, for at this spot the waters commenced, lapping lazily at my feet, and right away from there to Peel Park there was an unbroken deluge of turbid brown water, houses and all kinds of property surrounded by it. It was at this time that the Black Bridge, as it was called, which crossed the Irwell from the Broughton side, just at the foot of Fitzgerald's Castle[24] (lately demolished), was swept away. It had never been an ornamental structure, but it served the purpose of conveying people across to the races when they were held there, as they are again at this time. The old racecourse and stands were very primitive in their character, as compared with the buildings and stables which have been erected on the old site. In some measure this is to be accounted for by the large sum which the Ship Canal Company were obliged to pay the Racecourse Company for the ground at Old Trafford[25].

---

24. *"Fitzgerald's Castle" was not a castle but is described as a "large castellated brick house built in 1826 by John Purcell Fitzgerald, then owner of Pendleton Colliery". It was demolished in 1902 when racing returned to the Castle Irwell site.*

25. *The 'Old Trafford' site referred to was the race course at New Barns, Weaste, a section of which was demolished to make way for the No. 9 Dock on the Ship Canal - a site now occupied by the Lowry Centre.*

CHAPTER XLII

Our Manchester Moors.

A GLANCE at the above heading might perhaps give the reader the impression that he is going to hear something about grouse shooting, or of a pleasant ramble amongst purple heather, over hill and dale, in the pure, fresh, country air, tuneful with the songs of birds. This, however, is not my intention, although before "developing my panorama" I would like to say a few words on behalf of the only stretch of moorland, which has still been left us in close proximity to the City. I allude, of course, to Kersal Moor, which, though it lies less than a couple of miles from the City boundary, can even to this day boast of its purple heather and its blackberries, as may be seen if you will only trouble to stroll about over its less frequented slopes. True, the heather may not seem equal to what you come across on Axe Edge, or some Scottish Moor far away North, and doubtless the blueberries may be few and far between. Still I have often seen these slopes on a mellow, sunny August day, thickly carpeted with heather bloom, and the blueberry plants, with their dainty scarlet-tinted leaves, helping to give a bright tone to the surroundings. I would even go so far as to say that I have seen a ripe blueberry, but I may as well at once confess that I do not think it would pay anyone to send to market the crop which might be gathered on Kersal Moor.

And yet I know of those who, living within a stone's throw of these moorland slopes, are ignorant even of their existence. They are "too dull, too thankless, and too slow to catch the sunlight ere it flits away," and so they fail to enjoy nature's gifts which are lying close around them. Let me tell such that there are less pleasant ways of whiling away a lazy half-hour than by taking a stroll on the heather slopes to be found on Kersal Moor on a bright sunny morning when the larks are singing gaily high in the air.

I regret to say, however, as year after year passes, the space covered by the heather becomes "small by degrees and beautifully less." It cannot be otherwise when many of those who frequent the Moor seem only happy when destroying something just for the love of doing so; and so crowds of young people of both sexes may be seen tearing up bunches of this pretty heather by the roots and either carrying away, or wantonly throwing aside what they have just gathered. It certainly does seem a pity that some means cannot be devised by which, if it be found impossible to increase the area of its growth, what is still left may be in some way protected and preserved. But I have been wandering away from my original intention, which was to dwell for a little, not on Kersal moor, but on the Ancient Moors. When I say ancient it is a comparative term, as I am going to refer to the Moors who settled in Manchester, or rather commenced to do so some forty years ago. But "Ancient Moors" has a good ring about it, and so I may as well adopt it. Early in the sixties as you passed along the business streets of the City, you would suddenly come in sight of some white turbaned individual, whose gay Eastern dress appeared in such strong contrast to the sombre hues of the attire of all those about him. At first the sight of one of these men in Moorish garb was a very uncommon occurrence, and people would stand and smile as one of them passed along. But now they have ceased to be a wonder, and so they go to and fro and do their business in their usual quiet way, and make their purchases at the shops without more than perhaps a casual glance from the passers by.

When these Moorish pioneers first appeared as the precursors of those who afterwards settled amongst us, their numbers might have been counted almost on the fingers of one hand; but after the first plunge had been taken, they steadily increased in numbers, until at their full strength they formed quite a compact little business community.

My connection with them commenced with the first arrivals, as they were purchasers of my class of goods, and for this reason I became very friendly with them all. When a new arrival came upon the scene he was always easily distinguishable from the rest, as he would be seen shod with Oriental slippers, to which he had been accustomed in his own country. But it was quickly realised that such footwear was not serviceable in a climate like ours, where a wet day would play sad havoc with those gay-looking slippers without any heels; so one of the first lessons to be learned by a new arrival was to get his feet encased in boots with more understanding in their nature.

Most of these Moors seemed to learn English almost as quickly as they changed their footgear; or at any rate they were soon quite capable of making a bargain, and able to buy their goods at the cheapest possible prices, in fact bargaining seemed their English grammar, and excellent use they made of it. If for a short time you did succeed in getting a trifle more margin on your sales to a newcomer, he very soon posted himself up in matters, and you found out that, however limited his knowledge of English might be, he always knew enough to be able to beat you down in price.

I think the first English house to introduce these Morocco Moors in any number to the Manchester market was Thomas Forshaw, who then had his place of business in Norfolk Street. Here, if you had any business to transact with any of these clients of his, you would usually find them congregated in his entrance lobby, where there were benches lining the sides, on which they would be seated, as it were, in general council. It was quite an Oriental picture to see them grouped around in their quaint, picturesque attire, surmounted by the white turban or the red fez. I believe they were not entitled to wear the full white turban unless they had made at least one pilgrimage to Mecca. If you had any communication to make to any of their number you were often obliged to make it in the presence and hearing of the entire conclave; and as a rule there was no disposition to keep their transactions secret from each other, and at times they would consult amongst themselves before the one in treaty with you would make up his mind as to placing an order. At times this was somewhat embarrassing to the seller, but their manner of doing business was pleasant and easy enough when you had once been admitted to their general friendship. They first of all required to have confidence in your mode of doing business, but having once had the "open sesame" pronounced in your favour you could go in and out among them and get along with them very comfortably.

As the years went by, and their friends in Morocco found out that their country men were doing so well at this side, the numbers increased; but Thomas Forshaw gradually lost his hold upon them, for the Moors discovered by degrees that they could go into the market and buy in their own names, thus saving the commission with which he charged them. I am afraid credit was granted them too freely, and they were thus encouraged to trade beyond their means. However, the consequences of this appeared later on, and in the meantime the number of white turbans to be seen in the streets of Manchester steadily and perceptibly increased.

One of the first of these Moors to establish himself in business on his own account was a man of the name of Bengelun. He was a handsome man, although somewhat short of stature, but for his height he was one of the fattest men I had then come across. He seemed to carry a very mountain of adipose matter in front of him as he came paddling along the street, and swaying about from side and to side; and you could not but sympathise with him as you saw him panting for breath as he slowly mounted the stairs to his office. After the first established council broke up little by little at Thomas Forshaw's, it seemed to naturally transfer itself to the offices of Mr. Bengelun; so that if you could not find your man at his own place of business you would nearly always be safe in looking for and finding him at Mr. Bengelun's, where the bulk of them would be congregated together, filling the rooms to overflowing, some sitting, some reclining, whilst others would be squatted about Eastern fashion, with their legs doubled up underneath them, and here they would hold their midday palaver. These Moors came from various quarters; Tangiers, Mogadore, Larache, Casablanca, Fez, etc, and when they all got talking, more or less together, with their various intonations, accents and gesticulations, it was really quite entertaining to be in their midst. Associated with these Morocco Moors were some of their co-religionists from Cairo and Alexandria. Amongst the latter was a Mr. Benani, a very clever, intelligent, capable man of business. He also took quite a lead amongst them, and after the death of Mr. Bengelun, the daily meetings used to be held at his offices.

Taken as a whole, these Moors were a thoughtful, peaceable, kindly and sociable set of men. Mohammedans by faith, one could not but admire and respect them for their strict observance of all that their religion enjoined. Of course, there are black sheep in every fold, but as a body of men they set an example to many Christians of sobriety and religious zeal, with which those who came closely in contact with them could not but be struck.

During their long fast of Ramadan, the most of them neither ate, drank or smoked during the day. In their own country this was not such a serious matter as it is with us, as in Morocco the days and nights are more nearly equal in the summer months, when this fast takes place, than is the case in England. Here they required to fast from about three in the morning until about eight in the evening, which constituted a great strain upon the system for many weeks. This fast commenced with the new moon, and so strict were they that they should not err as to the time for starting the fast, that rather than make any mistake about the exact time of the new moon in their own country, they would begin fasting the day before. Many of the Moors who flourished here in the past have altogether disappeared, many are dead, others have left the country. Their names, too, would sound strange to English ears, such as Luarzazi, Elofer, Benquiran, Lehluh, Benabsolam, Dris and Benassi Benani. Benani and Tassi were two of the most usual names amongst them, and, I presume, answered to Smith, Jones, and Robinson in this country. Then there were such names as Guessus, Lushi, Meecoe, Bomar Larashe, Benabdislam, and Benmassoud. The Bens were prolific as the sons of many ancestors. Where there were several of the same surname they were recognised by some personal peculiarity. For instance, one man was called Big Tassi, on account of his almost gigantic proportions; and yet although he was large physically, he was particularly mild and gentle-looking in appearance, but he was not so soft-hearted that he could not drive a very keen bargain. There was also Black Tassi, so called from his swarthy complexion. He was as keen as a knife and as sharp as a needle, but I am afraid his heart partook of the nature of his complexion, for there came a day when he suddenly vanished to the tune of "The debts I left behind me."

Meecoe, bright and cheery in nature and disposition, came with a long purse, and with the impression that his purchasing power was unlimited. For a short period he was quite the darling of the Manchester Market. He bought, and bought, and bought; and we sold, and sold, and sold, just as dear old Manchester loves to do. And we should all have continued happy if, after the long purse became empty, we had not wanted payment for his more than liberal purchases. Waiting for those proverbial "remittances from the other side" is at the best a dreary and unsatisfactory business. Yet our friend seemed quite cheerful and happy, and if reiterated promises and offers of fresh orders for goods could have only satisfied creditors all might have been well. When these at length failed to give comfort and contentment, our dear friend betook himself to Morocco, so that he might try and hurry them up on the other side, but unfortunately his people abroad declined to be hurried up, and so his departure was followed by further delay, disappointment and eventually loss. His long purse had not proved long enough for its purpose, and Mr. Meecoe's light-hearted pleasantries could not convert themselves into bank notes, or even dollars which with wool was the usual mode of remittance, and so the creditors had to whistle for their money (in vulgar parlance), and that was the end of it.

There was another man amongst these Moors so diminutive in height that he might almost have passed for a dwarf. He had a sallow complexioned face and shifting eyes, and was not altogether attractive in appearance. He could be very oily and sweet when he wished to get his own way in some matter of business, but a very firebrand when anything went wrong. The greater his passion the yellower he became, probably he was of a bilious nature, which may have accounted for his extreme irritability. I remember on one occasion when I had to insist upon him doing what was right in some transaction between us, the oily smile with which he first tried to have his own way gradually disappeared as he found he could make no impression upon me; a gloomy scowl was succeeded by such a fit of rage that he actually foamed at the mouth. When he had arrived at this stage, the only thing of which he seemed capable, was to point his finger at his tongue and cry out: "Look at my tongue, look at my tongue." Why I should do so I cannot say; the whole scene was very comical and would have made a splendid photograph. Slowly he cooled down and eventually retired, but there was no look of love in those shifting eyes as he passed out of my office.

Such an incident was of quite an exceptional nature, and for many of these Moors I had a very sincere respect, doing their business as they did, in a quiet, almost placid kind of manner. Some of this white-turbaned fraternity are still to be found here, but their numbers have considerably diminished. Bad government, coupled with the demonetisation of silver have well-nigh killed this once prospering and promising trade. They were, and are, a class of men who, if circumstances had favoured them, were capable of developing a satisfactory business; but the government of the Sultan of Morocco was so wretchedly bad that it was impossible for them to make any headway. At times official intimation would be received by one of their number that he must return to act in the capacity of a tax gatherer in his own country, a position very abhorrent to most of them, as to make an existence in such a calling, after paying the Government the sum for which the taxes had been farmed to such an one, extortion, cruelty and robbery were a necessity. When these calls were made upon them they tried to get appointed as nominal agents for English firms, so that they might claim the support and protection of the English Consul abroad.

In connection with the way in which these taxes are collected in Morocco and elsewhere, I remember coming across an old friend some years ago in St. Ann's Square, of whom I had lost sight for a long time. I knew he had been knocking about the world pretty much in the character of a rolling stone, so I asked him what he was doing. "Doing, my dear fellow," said he, "I have been farming taxes for the Sultan of Morocco." "I am afraid that's a poor business," I replied. "Not at all," my friend remarked. "Why, how do you manage to collect them from the poor people," I said. "Collect them, oh, very easily," he answered, "I go to a village and make my demand, and if they make any objection, I just plant a piece of cannon at the head of the main village street and fire away, which, of course, soon brings them to their senses." This was an epitome of our conversation, although not perhaps the actual words. Of course, my friend may have been drawing the long bow in what he was saying, as I had known him do before, but as to the fact that in Morocco and Turkey the taxes are gathered and wrung out of the impoverished people in some such way, there is really no exaggeration in his statement of the case.

CHAPTER XLIII

The Late Queen's First Visit to Manchester.

ON the 9th of October, 1851, the Queen paid her first visit to Manchester, accompanied by Prince Albert, the Prince of Wales (now the King), the late Duke of Wellington, and others. It was a great event in the life of our city, and every effort was made to do honour to the occasion.

The Royal party stayed with the Earl of Ellesmere, at Worsley Hall, and on the following day drove about and saw what was most worth visiting in Manchester and Salford. I was one of the 80,000 school children who gave her a warm welcome as she drove in an open carriage through Peel Park – a welcome to which she afterwards referred in one of the books she wrote as having made a deep impression upon her at the time. Certainly it was the most wonderful sight of the kind I have ever seen, and it never can or will fade away from my memory.

Fancy listening to the voices of 80,000 children singing together "God Save the Queen!" It was something at once heart-stirring and thrilling, the sort of thing to make a lump come into one's throat. As the Queen approached and that huge choir of treble voices burst out into the first verse of the National Anthem the effect was almost electrical, and as she drove slowly along and glanced up at the crowds of children lining the terraces above, they could no longer contain themselves, and the singing suddenly changed into one grand chorus of cheers, the unrestrained outburst and expression of pure child love for their Queen.

Of those 80,000 little ones who filled Peel Park on that eventful day, many have altogether passed out of existence; others there are who have developed into the men and women of today, and some again are rapidly going down the hill of life. But today, when Manchester's memorial to our beloved Queen, in the shape of a handsome statue[26], is being unveiled by Lord Roberts, it is very pleasant to recall that unique gathering on the banks of the Irwell. I do not think it is possible for any human being to have lived more completely in the hearts of her people than did her late Majesty. During her long reign, as she herself has said, it was the personal realisation of this feeling which sustained and enabled her to bear with fortitude and resignation all her griefs and anxieties. In the same year that the Queen visited Manchester the first great Exhibition was held at the Crystal Palace in Hyde Park, and although I was only a boy of fifteen I was fortunate enough to get a sight of it. And, as may be supposed, I was in a state of considerable excitement when I was told that I was going to be taken to see it. I had never been in London, and this of itself was a great event, and kept me in a state of fever-heat until the time for going arrived.

We went by a trip train starting about 6 o'clock in the morning, and timed to reach our destination at about 10 o'clock at night. There was an immense crowd on the station when we left London Road, and I was in mortal dread that after all I was going to be left behind, being jostled and knocked about in all directions. Eventually our party fought their way into a carriage, and although it was already full to overflowing I was dragged in through the window, and the occupants tried to make the best of things under the circumstances.

An ordinary train to London took then, I think, about seven hours, but a trip train was truly a dismal experience. You started when they were ready to let it go, and you arrived – when you got there. In this instance we were considerably over eighteen hours on the way. We were shunted and sided, and sided and shunted, and kept ages waiting here, there, and everywhere, until the whole charm of the journey had been completely knocked out of

---

26. *Edward Onslow's Victoria monument in Piccadilly Gardens - unveiled 1901*

it. It would have been bad enough even in a moderately-filled train, but with carriages nearly bursting with their living contents the long drawn out "pleasures" of this particular journey to London may to some extent be imagined.

Still there was always the goal to look forward to, and the great fact that at some time I should arrive at that wonderful place – London. The thought consoled me for much suffering and discomfort. When we reached Euston, it was dark and dreary, and I was unable to satisfy my longing soul with a sight of anything. All was bustle and confusion as the crowds dispersed to their various destinations.

Tired, dirty, arid hungry we arrived at our lodgings, where friends who had preceded us to London had thoughtfully ordered us some hot supper. After waiting some time for the meat to appear, the bell was rung and the domestic entered the room. Our friend remarked, "I asked you to heat the steak, why don't you bring it." The reply was, "Oh, yes, mem, you asked me to heat it; and I've heat it long ago thank you, mem." This was cruel; however, we just had to make the best of matters; take what we could get, and then seek the rest of the weary.

My recollections of the Exhibition itself are very confused; there was so much to see, and such a short time in which to accomplish it, that I really saw nothing properly. The general effect when standing at the commencement of the main aisle and looking down its full length was very striking. The long lines of the most beautiful statuary which bordered both sides, gracefully back draped with bright, crimson cloth, together with the wealth and abundance of the many objects of interest which caught the eye on all sides, made a delightful picture. The fountains, the trees, the plants, the flowers, and the bright gay attire of the spectators, coupled with the full, rich swelling tones of the great organ, gave to the whole an appearance of fairyland.

Being the last days of the Exhibition the crowds

were enormous, and it was almost impossible to move about or see anything in detail. If you wanted to get to a particular point, you had almost to fight your way to it, and, when you did so, you had to content yourself with a glimpse of this and a glance at that. I managed to get a sight of the great Koh-i-Nor diamond, which at that time was making such a sensation. It was placed in the centre of a large brass or gilded circular cage, and cushioned on crimson silk velvet. Candidly, to me it had very much the appearance of an ordinary crystal, and secretly to myself I was obliged to own I was disappointed. But to have returned home and confessed not to have seen the Koh-i-Nor would have been almost tantamount to not seeing the Exhibition. I remember one of the tricks of the pantomime that year was an imitation of the cage and the diamond, and the clown and pantaloon trying to grab it; as soon as their hands got inside the cage the Diamond suddenly disappeared, their hands were caught by steel springs, whilst a policeman suddenly appeared from below and captured the culprits in the very act.

What a fascination even the name of London has for a young English mind. There is a mysterious charm attaching to it, which is only dispelled to a certain extent when the first visit has been paid to the Metropolis. My dream of the great city was that it was grand, beautiful, palatial, something infinitely superior to what I was leaving behind. Whereas my first impressions were distinctly disappointing; the streets in many instances being dirty, gloomy, dingy, and the houses and shops to match. Of course, half a century has made a wonderful transformation, and one might almost now say that London is a new city. The improvements during that period have been simply gigantic, and the feelings experienced by anyone now visiting London for the first time must be very different to mine in the year 1851.

But, after all is said, there is no city in the world like London. Paris may be handsomer and gayer; Vienna more elegant, with its marvellously clear atmosphere and its magnificent white buildings lining the boulevards which might have been built but yesterday; New York is more regular and roomy-looking, with its broad, straight streets and avenues; Constantinople more delightful with its lovely situation and climate, its mosques, minarets, and marble palaces. But, somehow, there is a charm about London which none of these possess. There is such a sense of reality about it, a length, and depth, and breadth; the visible configuration and consummation of national progress and industry. For example, where is there anywhere in the world such a place as Westminster Abbey? The history of our country written in stone, and written, too, very powerfully and attractively. As we wander through its aisles, and look at the graves and monuments of the great men who have made our history for us, a thrill of pride runs through our veins for we are gazing on the memorials of those ancestors who have made our country what it is.

CHAPTER XLIV

The 5th of November – St. Valentine's Day.

AT one time the 5th of November was a great day in the calendar of the year, and is immortalised in the words of the old song:

"Oh, please to remember the 5th of November, The gunpowder treason and plot,"

a rhyme that was very familiar to my ears in my young days. Now there are not very many who can call to mind this great anniversary in its palmy days, when it used to be celebrated with so much "pomp and circumstance," and for which such elaborate preparations were made. Still, there are even yet a few people who try to imagine that they are commemorating the day by the display of some feeble-looking fireworks for the amusement of the little children. But in the old days for months before the festival, a small army of young people might be found manufacturing "guys," gathering wood, and concocting all manner of noisy and sometimes even dangerous explosives, and in many other ways preparing for the worthy celebration of Gunpowder Plot. We used to form ourselves into a kind of Joint Stock 5th of November Army Corps, for the purchase of all requisite materials. I really forget how many loads of coal, and the number of tar barrels there were, which went to make up the necessary supplies for our bonfires; but some idea of the fires may be formed when I say that they often used to keep burning for days after the eventful night had passed. The stacking of the bonfires was a matter of deep concern and thoughtful consideration to the generals in command; and when we had finished our labours we should no doubt have made excellent candidates for troops of Nigger Minstrels.

When all preparations had been completed, when we

had made our fireworks, which we succeeded in doing without loss of limb or life, having only at times to mourn over a scorched face or the loss of an eyebrow, and a fair percentage of damaged hands or fingers. When all was ready, we waited with feverish impatience for the night of the great day.

I am afraid it was not always a day of pleasure to all, invalids and nervous people must have dreaded its arrival, for the sky was aflame and the air big with the sound of cannon firing, and the unlimited discharge of everything that would make a noise, either big or little. I remember on one occasion when a choice party in our back sitting-room, responding to a call to arms which had been proclaimed, considered that, like Nelson, everybody must do his duty. So we banged away out of the window for all we were worth. Each one of the party doing his duty nobly, loading, ramming, priming and firing. The row we made was deafening, and when at full swing a message came from a neighbouring house saying that a lady was ill and would we desist. We did so, but it was with great regret that we ceased our bombardment, as we felt what a splendid exhibition we had been giving of our capabilities as an amateur artillery company.

The most successful Guy Fawkes we ever manufactured was at the time of the Russian War in the year 1854. It was a representation of the Emperor Nicholas, and was quite a supreme effort on our part, and when we contemplated our handiwork completed, we felt that we had in the matter of Guys altogether immortalised ourselves; just like some author or painter when fame has come to him with some special and particular manifestation of his genius.

Our Guy was no ugly effigy, but a really lifelike and attractive likeness of the Emperor, so that when we paraded it round the neighbourhood it called forth a chorus of general admiration. I may as well confess that a large amount of our success was due to a lady's handiwork, one of my sisters rendering us material assistance in bringing this work of art to such a satisfactory completion.

There was nothing mean or shabby about our Guy, he was an Emperor every inch of him from top to toe. He was habited in full regimentals, with helmet, a real sword and other accoutrements, all of the most elaborate construction. He stood about eight feet high, and in his high military boots he had quite an imposing, aristocratic appearance. So remarkably true to life was our Guy, that an incident in connection with his introduction to the Broughton community may be related. Acting as his body guard, our party arrived at one of the houses in Homer Terrace, then occupied by William Turner, a son of James Aspinall Turner, one of the old members of Parliament for Manchester. It was shortly after William's marriage with Annie Payne, of the Theatre Royal. When we reached the door of the house, we placed his Imperial Majesty carefully on the front step and rang the bell, which was answered by the domestic. Of course it was night, and when she opened the door and saw this tall, lifelike form close before her, she gave vent to a wild shriek and rushed into the house. Mrs. Turner hearing her screams quickly appeared upon the scene, when she, too, saw it, she rushed back into the house screaming. Last of all came the husband and when he realised the situation, he got into a terrible passion and, running into the house, declared he would shoot us. So whilst Mr. Turner went in search of his weapon, we thought discretion was the better part of valour, and therefore beat a very hasty retreat with our friend Mr. Nicholas, in order that we might not run the risk of having our brains blown out.

 I think we all experienced a kind of pang when, on that particular 5th of November, we had to commit our handsome Guy to the devouring flames, and it did seem a pity that the careful, patient work of months, should be consumed in a few minutes. But the law "of the Medes and Persians altereth not," and so, too, we in like manner had to carry out Gunpowder Plot Law. Thus our lovely Guy had to be fastened to a stake and devoured of flames; and so the Emperor Nicholas, placed in the centre of a huge bonfire, met his fate like a man, silently and without uttering a single protest against the fate for which he had been prepared.

There was another anniversary which at one time had a wonderful charm and fascination for nearly all young people of both sexes, but which now, although it still occupies its old place upon the calendar for the year, passes by almost altogether unnoticed, unhonoured and unsung: I refer to St. Valentine's Day. It was a custom in the old days that for weeks before the arrival of the 14th day of February, those who were blessed with a poetical turn of mind, should devote their capabilities in that direction to the production of some tender and touching doggerel wherewith to delight the heart of some fair maid, whom for the time being they had enthroned as their idol. Others there were who exercised their faculties in a humorous direction; whilst others again, who had no personal qualifications as poets, had to content themselves with what the shops could supply them, to express the feelings of love and adoration by which they were moved. But in some form or another from one corner of the land to the other, people of all classes, young and sometimes even the old, rich and poor, as St. Valentine's Day drew near, seemed to be brought under the spell of the God of love, and appeared compelled to give expression to their pent-up feelings. The shops were filled with all manner of costly and elaborate designs, and shopkeepers had a busy time of it satisfying the demands that were made upon them.

When you entered an establishment where valentines were sold, the very air was laden with the scent of these varied works of art. The deep fringe of laced paper which surrounded the verses of love which were found nestling in the centre of the productions, were often extremely pretty, but as fragile as they were beautiful, and to protect them they had to be packed in specially manufactured boxes. These verses of love, if not always of the highest order, were usually fervid enough, and could not but appeal to the heart of a fair young maiden; more especially when printed on white satin in letters of gold, silver, or violet, as the case might be. It is an easy matter in these prosaic days of ours to make little of these effusions, and poke our fun at what we term the foibles of our ancestors, but St. Valentine's Day had a delightful charm of reality about it as I first remember it, and even to this day I should not be surprised if in the ransacking of old desks, work-boxes and secretaires, some of these tender, fragile missives were yet to be found, capable of calling a blush or a pleasant smile to some wrinkled face. As time went on senders became more practical in their effusions, gloves, handkerchiefs, books, flowers, or some dainty little article of jewellery, represented the love or admiration of the sender, until at last even these came to an end. Now there are few shopkeepers brave enough to lay in a stock of valentines, as the demand for them has practically ceased. Occasionally you may see in some side street a few large, common, vulgar specimens in a shop window, probably an old resurrected stock, of which the owners are trying in vain to get quit. We shall probably soon forget that there ever was such a day, for the old poetry associated therewith has died out of it, and "St. Valentine's day in the morning" has practically no meaning for the present generation.

CHAPTER XLV

**Mental Epidemics – Table Turning – Spirit Rapping
– Clairvoyance – Dark Sceances –
The 15 Puzzle – The Comic Song Craze –
Other National Periodical Weaknesses.**

DURING the year 1853 an epidemic broke out in this country in the form of table turning, and very severe it was whilst it lasted; most people went mildly cracked on the subject. It was written, talked, quarrelled, and, I fear, even in some cases fought about, until it was really hardly safe to go into some houses unless you were mentally, right or wrong as the case might be, on the vexed and disputed question of table turning. It was very amusing to enter a room and see a large table surrounded by a number of ladies and gentlemen, with their fingers stretched out and touching each the other, all looking painfully serious and with a very determined expression of countenance, as if they were in some trouble. It was the creed of the disciples and believers in this new mystery that you must all, individually and collectively, "will" that the table should turn, or not an inch would it budge. Again, should there happen to be an unbeliever in your midst his want of faith would knock success on the head. If you happened to be slightly incredulous and you ventured to "smile a little smile," you were at once roundly rated by a general chorus of the true believers, and promptly besought to get up and go away; in fact, you were in a sense excommunicated.

Well, after a deep, solemn effort of "will," you would see the table beginning to tilt up on one side, or making a circular movement. At this awful moment the people would slowly rise from their seats looking as serious as judges, and you would see them following the vagaries of the table and the call of the spirit wherever it chanced to lead them. A visitor from some other sphere looking down on one of these assemblies might have been excused if he came to the conclusion that he was witnessing some playful demonstration by a band of harmless lunatics.

From the foregoing remarks it may be naturally supposed that I was an unbeliever in these mystic rites. At first I did try to school myself into the belief that there was something strange and supernatural in this table turning, but I ended in becoming a scoffer. I presume my "willing" powers must have been defective, and so to make up for this when the table did not respond as I thought it ought to have done, I am afraid I gave the spirit a helping hand just by way of encouragement.

After all we are strange mortals, and it appears that at times a sort of craze of one kind or another seems to take possession of us. Once it has obtained a lodgment in our brain it spreads rapidly just like an epidemic of measles or scarletina, or any other infectious disease. For instance, I remember there was quite a rage in the direction of mesmerism. Everybody about you was either getting mesmerised or else mesmerising other people. An elder brother of mine was a very successful operator on other people, and I was much impressed when a friend of ours whom he had mesmerised, was supposed to be able to tell us what was happening in other parts of the house, whilst he himself lay apparently fast asleep on a sofa.

Then at another time spirit rapping was all the rage, with dark seances, the Davenport Brothers making quite a sensation by their apparently supernatural demonstrations. Their meetings were crowded, and people fully believed that these brothers were actual spirit mediums. But when the whole business was exposed, men and women quickly recovered their senses.

Then thought reading seized upon the popular imagination, and it was believed that certain individuals had the power of reading your thoughts, and many ladies might be seen at "At Homes" doing all sorts of wonderful things. One man of the name of Cumberland drew large audiences to see him rushing about with another man's hand on his forehead, chasing about coupled together, in order to discover the hiding place of a wretched little pin, which was of no earthly use to anybody when he had found it. Of course he was always successful in his search, and crowds flocked to see him, and the papers wrote long accounts of his wonderful gifts, and then he disappeared and made way for some other fad to take possession of the public mind.

The 15 puzzle was another craze, in regard to which nearly the whole of the people in America and in England went practically off their heads for a time. Wherever you went, at home or abroad, men, women, boy a and girls all had their little boxes with 15 blocks of wood in them, trying to work them out aright. Even as you went along the streets you would see the office boys and little nippers going on their errands or sitting about, working studiously away at one of these puzzles. I have myself sat up late at night, like numbers of other demented creatures, trying to get those wretched little blocks in their proper places. Whilst this attack lasted it was very pronounced, and one is almost ashamed to acknowledge the large amount of time bestowed by the peoples of America and England on the childish manipulation of a senseless trifle like the 15 puzzle.

This same kind of craze develops itself in many directions. Sometimes, and indeed very often, it is a song, often a stupid, witless effusion which, as it were, tickles the national brain, and for the time being runs riot there. Everywhere you go you are haunted by that song; it has taken possession of you and apparently of everybody else with whom you come into contact. At home, in the concert hall, on the barrel organs, by thousands of the boys in the street who can, or who as often cannot, whistle, that dreadful song pursues you. It may be "Uncle Ned," "Old Dog Tray," "The Ratcatcher's Daughter," "Jeannette and Jeanot," "Villikins and his Dinah," or, to come to more recent times, "High-tiddledy-high-ti," "Maggie Murphy's

Home," "Ta-ra-ra-boom-de-ay," "Tommy Atkins," or one of the latest pantomime songs. It matters little what the song may be, or what its merits, providing only that it happens to hit the popular fancy for the time being.

Many of these songs, which often make the fortunes of those who compose them, and those who sing them, are the veriest rubbish, and meaningless to a degree; but they catch on in some unaccountable way, and strike some responsive chord in our nature, the citadel of our reason surrenders, and, as if by some power of magic, the whole nation bows down and worships the latest musical idol it has set up. Of course elderly people "pooh, pooh" the thing, and say, "How absurd it is to be carried away by such wretched trash." But the probability is that if you were able to follow the mental workings of the individual who thus expresses himself you would discover that when the national fever is at its height this staid head of a family finds himself when he awakes in the morning (unconsciously) steadily tum-tumming at the words and tune of the very ditty which he says he holds in such contempt. As likely as not he shaves himself and brushes his hair to its refrain or chorus. It accompanies him probably on his way to business, and when he gets to the office he finds himself adding up figures, drawing cheques, or going through some particular calculation to the tune of "Maggie Murphy's Home" or "The Tin Gee-gee."

I presume this sort of thing is an infirmity of the flesh, but, nevertheless, it is a fact that the same infatuation takes possession of people with regard to new games or tricks. I remember a circus clown who was exceedingly clever at balancing all sorts of things on his head, his nose or his chin – from enormously heavy weights to a solitary straw. This at once took on with the public, and wherever you went you found people balancing anything that happened to come in their way – chairs, sticks, long clay pipes, straws, etc. A boy would be seen coming along the street dodging his head about in all directions as he tried to balance a long straw on the end of his nose, and in all probability he would finish by running into some old lady or gentleman, as he wandered on with his eyes intently fixed on that precious old straw.

Another thing that hit the popular fancy many years ago was a light fancy ball, fastened to a long elastic thread. You threw the ball sharply from you and if you knew how to direct the throw the ball would return to your hand with the rebound of the elastic. There was really nothing in it, but these balls for a time met you everywhere, and makers and vendors reaped a harvest. At almost every street corner men were to be found selling them to the passers by, giving at the same time an illustration of how to do the trick; and so as you passed along these gay-looking balls were to be seen shooting about you in all directions in a rather aggravating sort of way.

Of course many of these catchpennies are of mushroom growth, here today and gone tomorrow, but some of them die hard.

Then as regards new games, I remember when croquet first came in people went almost wild about it, and wherever you went the cannoning of the croquet balls was to be heard, and a game of croquet was for a time the *piécè de résistance* at every summer entertainment. Household duties were neglected and despised, whilst the entire family would be seen deeply immersed in some hand-to-hand encounter with mallets and balls on the garden lawn. People became so infatuated with croquet that they would play when the dew was lying heavy upon the grass, and when it had become so dark that candles were placed over the hoops to show where they were. The gong would sound for meals, but food had no attraction until one side or the other had beaten its opponents. But gradually an element of laziness and satiety crept in; some girls played because it was the rage, and not because they were fascinated by the game; they never knew where their ball was nor on whom they had to play, and they usually had to be called up to where they were required from some corner of the green, where they would be deeply engaged with some young man in discussing the weather, or perhaps something more interesting. And so by degrees the croquet fever declined until it almost died out altogether. Of late years croquet has come to the front again, and it claims a number of devotees, but it is not played with that feverish earnestness which characterised its introduction.

Lawn tennis followed croquet, as the next national pastime, and from its earliest days up to the present time it has steadily gained in public favour. It did not launch itself upon us in what may be termed epidemic form; but from the first it appealed to both sexes as a game where they might meet in pleasant competition on fairly equal terms. Lawn tennis has many elements of attractiveness about it; it is an especially healthy and thoroughly enjoyable pastime, and I consider there is little doubt that, in conjunction with cycling, it has helped materially towards the physical development of the gentler sex during the last twenty-five years. Even the most casual observer cannot, I think, but notice with pleasure that women and girls of today are stronger, more vigorous, and in every way more able for the battle of life than were those of the preceding generation.

Then there is golf, an old game revived, at any rate in England, although I can recollect quite well when, more than fifty years ago, golf was played over the whole of Kersal Moor, and prior to the building of St. Paul's Church; but those who took part in it did so in a very quiet, undemonstrative kind of way. There was none of the wild excitement which we see so often exhibited by its present devoted followers, who make golf a very material and important part of their existence. Talk about a man having "a bee in his bonnet," as an illustration of this commend me to a whole-hearted enthusiast holding forth to the world on his wonderful deeds of arms accomplished at golf. I was down at Matlock Bath some time ago, with a friend who was then suffering badly from a severe attack of golf fever. Poor fellow, he was bad. There were then no golf links in the district, so he engaged a field all to himself, in order that he might practise there alone, as there was nobody else to play with. Here day after day he would go and knock the balls about, seemingly quite happy. I accompanied him once, but I confess I found it rather slow work; but he never tired and would go at it quite contentedly for hours, and it was a difficult matter to get him home even to meals. On the occasion when he persuaded me to join him, as we wended our way homewards he obliged me with what I have no doubt was a clever and convincing dissertation on the game, and concluded by telling me that in golf there were no less than thirty-nine different variety of strokes. I thought it was a pity that another one could not be discovered, if only to make them up into the even forty. But I suppose this only shows how almost painfully particular golf players are to be strictly accurate in any thing relating to this wonderful game. I was almost afraid that my friend was going to describe to me the whole of the thirty-nine strokes, but he spared me that, and to this day I am still, shall I say in happy ignorance, as to what constitutes their various delicate gradations and minute differences. Fortunately a little later on this friend of whom I have been writing developed another fever in a botanical direction, which happily operated like a counter irritant, and so for a time at least the golf idol was deposed, and he was enabled to go about his regular occupations like any ordinary mortal. But at the time when the golf fever was at its height, he was comparatively lost to his family. He would go out early in the morning and spend the day on the links, and at dinner in the evening he was prepared, if there was anyone to listen to him, to recount the events of the day with its successes and its failures. Then after dinner he would retire to furbish up his clubs, etc, so as to be ready for the next day's fray, and I believe such a programme as this is a fair representation of the golf enthusiast's daily routine.

    I began this chapter with some remarks on table

turning and find I am ending by rambling away to the golf links, and on the surface the connection between the two does not appear to be very close. But in making these observations the dominant thought in my mind is: that on the whole human nature is subject to what may be termed fits of periodical mental vagaries, a species of fireworks on the brain. Dormant at times, but ready when fired by some spark of general excitement or unreasoning enthusiasm to burst into flame, and, like some prairie fire, carry everything before it, and "Their's not to reason why." That is to say, given certain conditions, we are all more or less prepared to be a little bit foolish, not considering too carefully the folly which we allow to possess us, whether it be table turning, the 15 puzzle, a comic song, or golf.

CHAPTER XLVI

Stage Recollections – A Few Introductory Remarks.

BEFORE proceeding directly to speak of my theatrical recollections I should like to preface my remarks by a few words on the stage in general, and my own views thereon in particular. This question of the stage and its bearing on society as a whole has, as everybody knows, been a vexed theme of discussion from time immemorial, and it is more than likely that I may have nothing original to say upon a subject which has engaged the attention of so many able writers on both sides. Still it is possible that what I feel and think may find an echo in other minds, and may not therefore be altogether worthless as a basis of some new development.

I think there are very few people who will deny, even those who are most bitterly opposed to the stage, that there lurks somewhere within the human breast a natural drawing to, and fascination for, the stage in some form or another; and this is more especially the case when we are young and impressionable, and when everything in and around us has a charm altogether its own. Then everything is warm, bright and fresh; the emotions are more quickly stirred, and any appeal to them meets with a ready response; and after all there is no denying the fact that a pure, healthy play, ably written and worthily interpreted, is not only absorbingly interesting, but it conveys with it in the acting a direct visual and objective lesson which is thrown on to the screen of the mind with a power which is oftentimes never effaced.

I am aware that even to this day there are some good people who are shocked, almost horrified, at the bare thought of entering the doors of a theatre, who believe, and quite sincerely too, that it is nothing less than a very hotbed of iniquity, and that those who attend theatres are not only doing themselves a great moral wrong, but that they are also setting an example to others, to be blamed and deplored. Of course it cannot be denied that there is much connected with the stage, which would be "more honoured in the breach than in the observance," and it is also unfortunately true that there are many unworthy plays which find a place upon its boards; but we have to do with the broad fact that the stage does exist, and not only so, but that it has the power of attracting within its influence a very large proportion of the human race for good or for evil as the case may happen to be; and its votaries are drawn from all sorts and conditions of men and women, from the young and the old, the rich and the poor, the good and the bad.

It seems to me, then, that it would be well if those who have set their faces against countenancing the stage under any circumstances or conditions, would thoughtfully reconsider the position of determined hostility which they have taken up in regard to it. And recognising the fact that from the earliest days of the civilised world, the stage has formed a very important part of its daily life, and that as far as we can see it is likely to continue to do so as long as it lasts, would it not be wise to join hands with those who, though not antagonists, are most anxious to see it purified from all that is hurtful and pernicious? Making it an instrument for raising the moral tone of the people, in place of debasing it, as is, and has been, unfortunately, too often the case.

We know that in the olden times even the Church recognised its power, and in such plays as "Everyman" the stage exercised a widespread moral influence over the people. For myself, I am quite satisfied that the better part of our human nature can be stirred and elevated in the witnessing of some pure and noble play, powerfully and intelligently performed; or, on the other hand, that physical dullness can be chased away by the clever and amusing representation of some innocent weakness or foible belonging to our social existence. And after all, too, it is well that we should not get away from this fact, that although but few of us are to be found actually upon the stage, still we are all more or less actors in the drama of real life, and that as Shakespeare says:– "We have our exits and our entrances, and one man in his time plays many parts." I think many of us hardly realise how very true this is of us, as regards the whole course of our daily life. We have each been apportioned our special gift or talent, whatever it may be, and its cultivation and development partakes of in a measure the acting of a part. The world, as we present ourselves to it, has put us down for a certain role in our particular pathway in life, and everyone is, or at least should be, trying to make it a success.

For example, one man has been dubbed a hearty good fellow, and day by day you will see him acting the part in which, so to speak, the world has clothed him. In all he says and does he tries to act the character he represents as closely as may be, until it becomes instinctively interwoven with the whole texture of his existence; until even he himself may be unaware how naturally he avoids all that would mar the present harmony of the part he has assumed as his life role.

Then there is the individual who prides himself upon calling a spade a spade. He is blunt and brusque, and when, as he says, he puts down his foot, there is no mistake about it. In his character of the candid friend, he shows very small consideration for the opinions, feelings or failings of others; but after all he is simply acting his part, and so he assumes the garb that harmonises most closely with the embodiment of the plain, blunt man.

Another man is noted for his merry, jovial disposition, a disposition which no doubt was in the first instance a plant of natural growth, but by degrees he realises that this is the role which the world has assigned to him, and so he does his best to be a successful actor of the character which he has to support. He slaps people on their backs, and is "hail fellow well met" with all with whom he comes into contact. His laugh is almost infectious, and wherever he goes or whatever he does, you invariably find him acting the character of the jolly good fellow.

There, too, goes the man who has the reputation of being one of the best-dressed men in town. He feels that, having posed as such, he is bound to live up to it. Having once placed himself on the pedestal of fashion, he must of necessity act and dress accordingly. He realises that the world, having tacitly acknowledged his right to the character to which he has laid claim, he is bound to perform his part to the best of his ability. His tailor therefore has a busy time of it, whilst at the same time he keeps the world interested and sometimes surprised at the novelties he is capable of presenting to its notice. Even in the higher walks of life the same spirit of living up to a certain standard is discernible. For instance, say that a Minister has won for himself the reputation of being a powerful or eloquent preacher. He accepts the position which his talents have in the first instance made for him; but in doing so he understands that from that time forward, to retain the pre-eminence to which he has aspired, he must not fail to act up to the standard of excellence expected from him, and this, too, no matter at what cost it may be to him of time, mind, body or natural inclination.

In political life the same conditions prevail. Some man makes a name for himself in some particular line, whatever it may be; but the character, once assumed and acknowledged by the public, he has at all times to perform the part to which he has laid claim. Should he pose as an enthusiast, an enthusiast he must perforce continue to the end. There is every reason to believe that the deep and abiding hold which Mr. Gladstone exercised over the English people was greatly strengthened and developed by the intense fervour and enthusiasm which he was capable of throwing into all he said and did. Had he allowed these to fall below high water mark his popularity might not have been so widespread and lasting, but he knew his gifts and his possibilities, and he acted up to them with wonderful success.

In the same way Sir Wilfrid Lawson has, by his speeches, allowed himself to be dubbed a political humourist, and so wherever he goes and whenever he speaks, people look to him to take up the role of the political jester.

There are some of the Irish members of Parliament who have made their reputations as political firebrands, and so in all that they say or do we are really almost disappointed if they fall away from the full measure of their acting capabilities in their special line. Even Mr. Chamberlain without his orchid and eyeglass would hardly be the same individual, so closely have they been associated with the whole course of his political existence.

In the very world of crime, too this acting of a part up to some preconceived standard is to be found all the world over. One ruffian lays claim to the jaunty, unabashed, defiant criminal style, and we see him act the part even to the mock heroics at his trial; and we may listen to the jocular farewell to his companions in Court, as his sentence, perhaps even of death, is being passed upon him. Amongst women more especially this desire for a theatrical finish in a Court of Justice is very noticeable. They dearly love something dramatic or humorous which will appeal to their listening friends in the gallery. Some emotional outburst, or some sarcastic witticism, a few honeyed words, or a mocking laugh, with perhaps a curtsy of thanks to the judge, and they feel that they are ringing down the curtain with true dramatic success.

Yes, I think we cannot gainsay the fact that we are all more or less, as the case may be, imbued with the actor's instincts. We may be a success or we may be a failure, as is the case on the mimic stage; but do as we will, we cannot altogether eradicate that which is inherent in our nature. "What is bred in the bone, will never come out of the flesh." And so the result is, that the stage has for most of us an instinctive charm and fascination which it is almost impossible altogether to resist.

I would, therefore, urge upon those who still regard the stage and all connected with it with hostility and aversion, to adopt towards it a wiser and more generous policy. Let them not entirely hold aloof, but try by every means in their power to purge it from its dross, and give their countenance and encouragement to those who, recognising its immense power for good or evil, are earnestly striving to raise its tone in every possible way.

Let those of our literary men who have hitherto declined to have anything to do with the stage, possess the courage to come forward and give of their best. Let them write as they have never done before, with a sense of responsibility, and resolve that as far as in them lies, they will make a supreme effort to raise the taste of theatre-going people to a higher and more refined level, by producing plays which shall not only do honour to those who write them, but shall also do good to all those who may witness them. Christian men and women must realise the fact that they are face to face with a great problem, and it is this: that the stage is with us and is certainly going to remain, that its tendency is often, even at the present day neither elevating nor modest. That its serious side is occupied in many instances with plays which, although usually ably written, are often concerned with the portrayal of unhealthy and unnatural phases of social life; whilst the humorous side is given up to the production of plays musical and otherwise, liberally supplied with vulgarities and indelicacies, which can only disgust, the pure minded and lower the moral tone of those who witness them. Let those who write for the stage refuse to pander to the vitiated tastes of those who would bring it down to the level of their own corrupt thoughts and desires. At the same time it is necessary in order that plays should be successful and popular, that they should be clever, vigorous, witty, and interesting. But they require also to be pure and healthy in their nature, so that in their performance they may not put our wives and daughters to the blush.

Then, again, some of our good people are very much disposed to look upon actors and actresses as a species of moral lepers, from whom it is necessary to keep as far apart as possible. It is but fair, however, that they should bear in mind that although there are, of course, black sheep in every fold, there are numbers of people connected with the stage who lead pure, honourable, virtuous lives, and such men and women would gladly welcome anything done in the direction of the purification of the stage. Let them, then, feel their hands strengthened by giving them healthy material to work with, material that is not morally tainted at the fountain head. Let them further disabuse their minds of the impression that by a certain portion of the world they are, so to speak, "passed by on the other side," but allow their lives to speak for themselves. For even at the present time there are some people who would be almost horrified at being brought into direct personal contact with either an actor or actress.

I would now sum up these remarks with a final appeal to all who are opposed to the stage to recognise the fact that their present attitude is only adding to the difficulties of those who are longing and striving after its purification. That as humanity clings to the stage as a part of its existence, from which it refuses to part company, the next best thing to do is to try and make it in the future all that its reformers wish it to be. And so I would urge upon those who now decline to have anything to do with the stage to come forward and assist those who, whilst acknowledging a predilection in its favour, are also desirous that all that is pernicious and hurtful in connection with it should be done away with, in order that it may eventually become a real power for good in the world.

"Whose end, both at the first and now, Was and is to hold as 'twere, The mirror up to nature, To show virtue her own features, Scorn her own image, And the very age and body of the time, His form and pressure."

CHAPTER XLVII

Stage Recollections, continued.

My earliest recollection of the stage is being taken to witness a ballet called "The Mountain Sylph," suggested by an old opera of the same name. At that time ballets were more or less plays in dumb show, with a plentiful supply of music and dancing; and these are coming into fashion again at the present time. The one to which I refer was very romantic in its development, and was just the sort of thing calculated to make an impression on a young mind. The plot, as I remember it, had something to do with a Fairy Queen, beautiful beyond description (in my eyes at least), who fell madly in love with some mortal, as handsome he, as she was beautiful. They appeared to be delightfully happy together, as they danced and pirouetted gracefully about the stage. But, unfortunately, their happiness was but of short duration, as the subjects of the Fairy Queen found out all about her love affair, and were determined to put an end to it. They therefore danced themselves into her presence, disturbing an interesting tete-a-tete in a most unkind manner, and then proceeded to tell her, in the cruellest manner possible (but, of course, all in dumb show) that as she had stooped from her high estate and had dared to love a mortal, she could no longer continue to be their Queen, and must therefore be deprived of her wings. Then these hard-hearted fairies proceeded with their dreadful work, and my heart was filled with sympathy for her, under the distressing circumstances. And it seems to me at this long distance of time that I can still hear the crushing together of those gossamer wings, as they were torn away from her; and then as she sinks feebly to the ground (for her life ebbs away from her with the loss of her wings), her lover rushes in only in time for her to die to his arms, and I was no doubt very unhappy as the curtain slowly descended. I think I was about eight years of age when this happened, and if so, this performance must have taken place at the old Theatre Royal in Fountain Street, which was burned down on the 7th of May, 1844. The theatre stood on the ground now occupied by Daniel Lee and Co. and John Munn and Co. I can remember visiting the ruins of the Theatre Royal after the fire, but there was little left to denote what it had once been. There is, however, always a fascination to the young mind in any thing connected with the stage and its surroundings, and I sought for hidden treasures amid the charred remains, but with little success, as the fire had done its work very effectually.

Recollections of subsequent visits to the theatre about this period of my existence are both misty and scrappy; a confused medley of pantomimes rises up before me, and, strange to say, most of these are still doing duty at the present day, although some of them, "Jack the Giant Killer," "Gulliver and his Travels" "Sinbad the Sailor," and "Jack and the Beanstalk" do not do duty perhaps quite as often as they used to do in the days of old. I remember seeing Sims Reeves in, I think, "Fidelio," in London, when I went to see the great Exhibition of 1851, but any really distinct recollections of the stage commence about the year 1853, and are then principally associated with the Stock Company of the Theatre Royal, in Peter Street, where it was rebuilt after the one in Fountain Street was destroyed.

I had always a strong predilection for the stage, so when the way was clear and the state of my exchequer permitted it, I wended my way to the doors of the Royal, having first fortified myself with a sumptuous repast in the form of a bun and a glass of milk, usually partaken of at Howarth's shop in Cross Street. After the ordinary struggle amongst the first comers to get into the theatre, I used to try and secure my usual seat in the middle of the front row of the pit, price one shilling, with the additional payment of one penny for a bill, and promptly settled down with great satisfaction to enjoy myself; and it must not be forgotten that a pit was a pit in those days, the seats running right up to the orchestra, there were no intervening stalls to deprive a poor fellow of what he had fought for so nobly outside, namely, the best place for seeing and hearing in the theatre.

A few remarks about the personnel of the Theatre Royal Company may not be without interest, and more especially to old theatre-goers. First and foremost then, there was the invaluable Mrs. Horsman, who was as versatile as any manager could possibly desire. She could take parts without number, and do credit to them all. From the Queen in "Hamlet" to Mrs. Sowerby Creamery in "The Serious Family," or "Dame Quickly" in "The Merry Wives of Windsor," and in each role she was equally at home. She was truly a splendid old actress, and it was pleasant to see the mother and her son Charles (for he too was one of the Company) acting constantly together. Although Charles had not the varied gifts of his mother, he was a fairly good actor in the numerous characters which fell to his lot.

It is interesting to know that Augustus Harris was, in 1853, a member of the Theatre Royal Company prior to his migration to London, and, amongst other parts, I saw him in Doctor Caius in "The Merry Wives of Windsor," and he and Mr. J. Wood were a merry, noisy couple, the latter taking the character of Sir Hugh Evans.

John Wood and his charming little wife were a very important couple for some years at the Theatre Royal, and they contributed to most of its successes. They appeared equal to any demands that were made upon them, and these demands were legion. Tragedy, comedy, burlesque, farce and pantomime all came alike to them, and they never failed to rise to the occasion. As a comic actor J. Wood excelled, and was both quaint and funny; nature had provided him with features which were unmistakably plain, but he made the most of them;

in fact, they constituted a very important factor of his stock-in-trade. His wife was as pretty as he was plain. She was a delightful little actress, and there was a charming naivete about all she did which helped to make her a great favourite with the public. Her impersonation of Little Red Riding Hood in the pantomime of the same name was quite bewitching in its way. Her husband always took the villain in pantomime, and seemed quite to revel in crime.

W. H. Stephens, another member of the Company, was also a man of many parts; what Mrs. Horsman was in female, he was in male parts; but indeed I am afraid that most, if not all, of the members of this Company had to be ready at very short notice to do all and sundry. I think perhaps the best impersonation given by Stephens was that of Polonius in "Hamlet," in fact he made it so true to life that he positively aggravated you by his tedious senile verbosity. His Justice Shallow in "The Merry Wives" was an excellent performance, whilst at another time he would appear as the First Witch in "Macbeth" and be quite at home in it. One night he would shine out as a very creditable Sir Peter Teasle, the next he would hide his light under a bushel by enacting some indifferent character, a sort of dummy to some star. There is no doubt that Mr. Knowles saw that he got full value from his actors and actresses for the salaries they received, and which, I am afraid, did not err on the side of generosity.

There was a Mr. Harker, a very painstaking member of the Company, perhaps not so diverse in his impersonations, but as the Ghost in "Hamlet" he was remarkably good and scpulchral. He also made an excellent Sir John Falstaff, and a good Duncan in "Macbeth."

Mrs. Bickerstaff was a veritable maid of all work, bright, cheery and ubiquitous; a piece never flagged while she was on the stage, and although she was never brilliant, she could always be relied upon to make a piece go with a swing.

Swinbourn occupied the position of first tragedian at this time, and was a conscientious actor, though somewhat heavy in his style, and wanting in the more delicate touches of light and shade. His countenance was gloomy, and he was certainly any thing but prepossessing in appearance. To see him in Melnotte in "The Lady of Lyons" made one wonder how Pauline could make up her mind to fall in love with such an unattractive gardener.

There was another very interesting group in this company who were all great favourites with the Manchester public. I allude to the Payne family. There was H. Payne, the father, a capital clown of the good old type; his son, W. H. Payne, was a graceful dancer, and usually took the part of Harlequin; another son, F. Payne, also occasionally performed. There were two daughters, Annie and Harriett; the former of these two was the celebrated danseuse who took the part of Columbine in the pantomime for some years. She was a most graceful dancer and very attractive in appearance. The family were much respected, and Annie Payne eventually married William Turner, the son of James Aspinall Turner, formerly one of the members for Manchester.

I come now to speak of Amy Sedgwick, who first made a name for herself at the Theatre Royal, some time before Buckstone secured her for his Company at the Haymarket. One of the first occasions on which I saw her was in October, 1855, when I saw her take the character of Julie Lesurque in the "The Courier of Lyons."

To those who were privileged to watch the development of Amy Sedgwick from her modest beginnings into a great actress, there is a peculiar charm even in the very sound of her name, recalling, as it does, many pleasant recollections. She appeared amongst us without any flourish of trumpets, but she came, and saw, and conquered. She was a woman who put her whole soul into all she said and did, and so the characters she impersonated seemed to live before you. She had the power of communicating to her listeners all that she herself felt. Her laughter and her tears were alike infectious, and all the passions that fill the human breast seemed to flow from her as from a natural spring in a voice full, rich, and deep. Every movement of her body was easy, lithe, and graceful, and there was an absolute freedom from anything of a studied or mechanical nature. Perhaps the actress who at the present day reminds one most of Amy Sedgwick is Mrs. Kendal, and who as Madge Robertson in the Haymarket Company probably took her as her model in her youthful days.

Amy Sedgwick's impersonation of Pauline in "The Lady of Lyons" was one of the finest pieces of emotional acting I have ever witnessed. Of those who were privileged to see her in this play, who can forget the scorn which seemed to move her as she paced the stage uttering the words:

"*This, then, is thy palace,*"

or the heartbroken sob of wounded pride mingled with love, as she gazes down at Melnotte from the head of the staircase leading to his mother's room.

There is no doubt that Amy Sedgwick had a splendid education at the Royal, for she had to assume a very wide range of characters in tragedy, comedy, and even farce, and Tom Taylor, when he wrote such plays as "Still Waters Run Deep," "The Unequal Match," and others, was very fortunate in having such an actress as she was to interpret his heroines.

In 1856 Walter Montgomery also joined the Company, and so for a period of about twelve months Manchester was happily provided with two stars of such brilliancy that she was quite content with her theatrical lot. It was said that although Amy Sedgwick and Walter Montgomery had often to be such ardent lovers before the footlights, there was not much love lost between them when off the stage. Be that as it may, and possibly the report may have been nothing but idle gossip, they certainly left nothing to be desired in their acting together.

Walter Montgomery was not only a highly-gifted actor, but he was also a Shakespearian reader of exceptional dramatic power. Such plays as "Hamlet," "Othello," "Macbeth," "The Merchant of Venice," and "As You Like

It," he seemed to know off by heart. And in some respects it was a greater treat to hear him in one of his recitals than to see the play enacted, for with him every character in the piece seemed to live before you, impersonated in its best and truest form. Whilst he remained in Manchester he was a great favourite both socially and as an actor, and there was a general feeling of regret when in 1857 he and Amy Sedgwick took their farewell benefits and severed their connection with the Royal. He took for his benefit "Virginius" and "The Honeymoon," and she chose for her farewell, "As You Like It" and the "Wicked Wife."

Amy Sedgwick, afterwards as a member of the Haymarket Company, still continued to visit, from time to time, the haunt of her earlier triumphs, but as far as I can remember, Walter Montgomery never again appeared on the Theatre Royal boards. Somehow he did not fulfil the promise of his early days; I fear he was spoiled by the flattery and adulation of his friends in Manchester (where the lady portion of the community made him a sort of idol). In any case he did not make the name for himself of which his natural gifts gave promise. Eventually he married, but he had no sooner done so than he put an end to his existence, and so the name of Walter Montgomery become a thing of the past, a blurred and painful memory.

W. Worboys, a very amusing little comic actor, who joined the Company about the same time as Amy Sedgwick, was said to be her brother, but with what truth I cannot say. There is generally much that is romantic in the lives of those who adopt the stage for their profession, and what is lacking gossip is ready to supply.

At this period of its existence the Stock Company of the Theatre Royal reached what may be considered its high-water mark; for with the departure of Amy Sedgwick and Walter Montgomery, although it still numbered amongst its members such names as George and Henry Vandenoff, T. Mead, J. G. Shore, G. F. Sinclair, Isabel Adams, Sarah Lewis, as well as those to whom I have already referred, there were no particularly shining lights to redeem it from what might be termed ordinary mediocrity.

Then, too, theatrical advertising was a very modest affair, as compared with the elaborate posters, pictorial and otherwise which now crowd the walls and the hoardings of our towns and cities. Then a few bills about 18 by 8 inches, coarsely printed and pasted on some iron frames scattered throughout the leading avenues to the city, were practically the only public announcements made, or inducements held out to visit the theatres or discover their attractions. Now, on the walls and hoardings, and in the shop windows, you can have your histrionic appetite whetted and very appreciably developed by coloured representations of a most exciting nature, occasionally pleasantly attractive, but often gruesome or intensely vulgar, and which are to be found staring at you in a most defiant and obtrusive fashion wherever your eye happens to rest. The old, quiet way of advertising a performance or a play, would be really quite refreshing compared with the coarse, offensive, pictorial exhibitions which are now so common. It is no wonder that the enjoyable shilling pit has had to be abolished, in the face of the enormous expenditure which is now considered necessary to draw audiences to the various entertainments. However, although the present mode of advertising may have its drawbacks, there is certainly no fault to find with the mounting of plays now as compared with the old days of the Theatre Royal, both as regards scenery, dresses and properties. Then the same old background would have to do duty for years. It had to serve for tragedies, comedies, operas and farces, until at last little of the original paint remained, and it was left to your imagination to supply its deficiencies. Stage carpets were then a luxury, and after any unusual commotion on the boards, the stage flunkey had to appear, long brush in hand, to sweep away the dust at the close of the scene. I do not know how it was, but the moment that unfortunate man would appear, clothed in his purple velvet, silver-braided coat, scarlet knee breeches, and white stockings, the gallery always received "Jeames" with wild hootings, accompanied by whistling, and jocular enquiries after his mother. He used to suffer from a species of stage fright whilst he remained, and was glad to get done and away.

Then with regard to stage accessories, it often happened that a plain wooden table the worse for wear, and a couple of chairs, had to do duty as the entire furniture of a room or some interior. The eatables and drinkables, too, were of the most unmistakably wooden or pasteboard description. Even to the uninitiated, stage feasts were palpable mockeries, and you sympathised with the actors as they tried to chink make-believe goblets, or sat down to partake with a jovial air, of some wooden-looking repast. Actors and actresses had then to rely on their exertions and talents for success, and by no means on stage accessories, whereas at the present day it often happens that the resources of some of our best artistic house furnishers are taxed to the uttermost to provide the elaborate mise en scene of a single play.

The wardrobe of an ordinary actor forty years ago was anything but extensive, and the same costume had to do duty again and again, in characters many and diverse, until at last you came to recognise it as an old friend. Now an actor in the same piece will probably appear in four or five different changes of dress, all of which are expected to be faultless in cut, excellent in quality and in every particular of the latest fashion. A leading actress who now sends to Paris for most of her dresses, had in the old days to content herself with the stage seamstress and her mother at home, who had often to turn, alter or remodel some costume which had probably long before lost all its pristine freshness and style.

Audiences under these circumstances were disposed to be very lenient; they came to see the acting, and if that were good they went home quite satisfied. There was, however, one thing they did appreciate, and that was a good long bill of fare, and I have seen Charles Mathews act in as many as three and four pieces on one night; people liked plenty for their money, and they got it. Fancy a leading actor taking Hamlet or Othello or Richard the Third, as the case might be, and finishing up with Katherine and Petruchio for a single night's work. Not only so, but there would be a change of programme nearly every night, so that there would be, as may be supposed, precious little playtime for actor or actress in those days. It is a very different matter now, when the same play will occupy the boards of a theatre for six, twelve or eighteen months at a time, and in this way allow the performers more time at their disposal.

CHAPTER XLVIII

Stage Recollections, continued.

AT first, the Theatre Royal Stock Company depended largely on their own native talent in catering for the theatrical public, now and again reinforced by the visit of some favourite star; and of those who came in that capacity there was none who could count upon a more hearty welcome than the fascinating and versatile Charles Mathews. When I first saw him about 1853 he was, I should imagine, at the height of his popularity, and whenever he made his appearance in Manchester he could always rely on crowded houses and a reception not only warm but even affectionate. He seemed to be thoroughly happy and at home with his audiences who gathered in such numbers to welcome him at the Theatre Royal. It was said that Mr. Knowles, the lessee, had a call upon his services for monetary favours received, but be that as it may, he always seemed very happy when he came amongst us.

There was no one who could approach him in his day in his particular style of acting. He was easy, graceful, and amusing, and his humour never descended either to coarseness or vulgarity, he was a perfect gentleman in all he said and did; and he dressed, too, as he acted, to perfection. He was happily gifted by nature with a marvellously young-looking face, which remained with him as a very valuable stage asset long after he had passed into the "sere and yellow leaf." He was possessed of a very mercurial temperament and the characters he portrayed partook of the same nature; in some of them, such as "Patter *versus* Clatter," "A Practical Man," "A Curious Case," and others, he carried you along with a sort of breathless rush. But, however rapid he might be he always kept his audience in touch with him; he was clear, crisp and finished, and coupled with a remarkable elasticity of mind and body, he had a charm of manner peculiarly his own. The only actor of the present day on whom his mantle appears in a measure to have fallen is Charles Wyndham, who in his easy, gay, nonchalant style of acting reminds one pleasantly of his prototype.

Unfortunately, Charles Mathews, being an extravagant man, was often in financial difficulties. I saw him on one occasion in a piece called "Before Breakfast," in which he took the character of a discharged servant, appearing with a stick and a small bunch of clothes hanging therefrom. His opening words were: "Well here I am, discharged from my last place, ready to start the world afresh." This remark was received with great applause, and I discovered afterwards that he had just been released from Lancaster Gaol, where he had been confined for debt, and he was making merry with his audience on that account.

Another time he was acting a piece which was an amusing take-off of Professor Anderson, the conjuror, who was called the Wizard of the North. As the curtain rose Charles Mathews came forward holding in his hand a very dainty green silk umbrella, which he most carefully hung up by a cord which descended from above, near to the footlights. He begged his audience in a most mysterious manner to keep their eyes steadily fixed upon this umbrella, and then proceeded with the play, which was clever and amusing. Of course we naturally kept a close watch upon the umbrella, expecting he was going to perform some special trick with it; but at the tag of the piece he merely came forward and thanked the audience for their kind reception of "the great gun trick," and was then about to retire from the stage. The people, however, who did not want to be done out of the umbrella trick which they concluded he had overlooked, called out "Umbrella, umbrella" Then he turned back with a smile as if he had quite forgotten all about it, and said in his blandest of manners: "Oh, thank you so much, ladies and gentlemen, for reminding me of my umbrella, and especially for having kept such a close watch upon it;" then, with a confidential stage whisper, he went on: "The fact is, as you see, I am rather particular about my umbrellas, and really I have lost such a number lately that I thought the safest plan was to put it in your care instead of leaving it in the green-room. Thank you so much for keeping your eyes upon it; it's very good of you." And he retired with one of his charming smiles. Then as the position dawned upon us we smiled too, feeling at the same time how delightfully we had been taken in.

For many years he was able to fill the Theatre Royal to overflowing, and he seemed to defy old age. But there came a time at last when that wonderful elasticity of step deserted him, and when the paint, no matter how deftly applied, failed to hide the ravages of old age. He became at length a mere wreck of his former self, and, although he continued to cling to the stage as if he could not part from it, it was a melancholy sight to see him as a weak, feeble, tottering old man, trying still to assume the gay, jaunty style, which at one time had been so irresistible. After Charles Mathews there was no one to whom I was more attracted in my early theatre-going days than to Miss P. Horton (afterwards Mrs. German Reed), who was a charming actress with the additional gift of a sweet, melodious voice. She had also a pair of merry, twinkling eyes and a happy debonnaire style about her which was very taking. Her most popular impersonation was, I think, that of Ariel in "The Tempest," in which her acting and singing left nothing to be desired. Perhaps she may have been a shade too robust for such an aerial representation, but you lost sight of this when you saw her in the part, and heard her singing, especially that delightful song "Where the bee sucks."

As a burlesque actress she was very clever, although not of the present-day style in this class of entertainment. Then burlesques could be amusing without being coarse or vulgar. She was content to dress modestly but attractively; she could be bright and merry without being fast, and anyone who has seen her in "Ivanhoe," "The Little Demon," "The Man at the Wheel," or "The Fair One with the Golden Locks," will, I think, allow that they leave behind them very pleasant memories. I am not quite clear if Miss P. Horton took part in the burlesque of "Lalla Rookh" or not, but one of the songs in it clings to my memory, and may serve as a sample of what "took on" in those days. It was sung by Khorsanbad, a man without morals:—

"I have not a sixpence and I have not a friend,
I have not one good quality myself to recommend.
Oh, I'm a rascal and a thief,
And of ruffians I'm the chief,
And the badness of my character surpasses all belief.
Sometimes I live by hook,
And sometimes I live by crook;
And I think I'm just the husband for the lovely Lalla Rookh."

"I've every bad habit in a husband you could wish,
I smoke like a limekiln, I drink like a fish;
Oh, I gamble and I bet,
I'm over head and ears in debt,
I play billiards, loo unlimited, blind hookey and roulette,
So I'm sure you'll all agree, with such qualities to book
That I'm just the sort of husband for the lovely Lalla Rookh."

Miss P. Horton took farewell of the stage whilst her powers were still undimmed; but as Mrs. German Reed she and her husband started a drawing-room entertainment in which they were very successful. Still, although this was so, nothing she did in this way had the charm which was associated with her stage life, where her bright sunny manner and her rich mellow voice were not easy to replace. Henry Irving made his first appearance at the Theatre Royal in a play called "The Spy," in which I saw him act on the 8th of October, 1860, and I must say that nothing I saw then or afterwards whilst he remained in Manchester would have led me to think that he would have attained to the high position which he now occupies in the theatrical world. His mannerisms and peculiarities both of voice and gait, which were more than noticeable as a novice, still cling to him even at the present day, and were, I always considered, material drawbacks to his success. Of course I am aware that most people are prepared to go into ecstasies about him, but I must humbly confess that I am not one of the number. When he formed one of the stock company at the Royal, I saw him many a time and oft, and my opinion is that the success of Henry Irving is to be attributed in a great measure to a fixed determination on his part to become a master in his profession rather than to the inborn gifts and natural genius of the man. But there is no doubt that what he lacked naturally he replaced by an intense and enthusiastic love for his work, which, coupled with a keen appreciation of the art of stagecraft, enabled him to present his productions to the public in such a costly style and with such wonderful perfection of detail, that any apparent shortcomings in the actor have been lost sight of in the brilliancy and realistic setting of the representation.

There was one particular incident in the life of Henry Irving which brought him very favourably before the notice of the Manchester public, and it happened in this way. Some individuals styling themselves the Davenport Brothers had been going about the country for some time giving very wonderful dark seances, declaring that they had direct communication with the spirit world, and that these manifestations were produced through the medium of spirits. They were creating quite a sensation, and many weak-minded people believed in them. It was at this time that three actors, Henry Irving, Fred Maccabe and Philip Day (the two latter from the Prince's Theatre), formed the determination to expose these men. First in the Athenaeum and afterwards in the Free Trade Hall, this accomplished trio gave a series of sham seances, and so cleverly was the whole business exposed that the Messrs. Davenport Brothers suddenly disappeared and their dark seances along with them. This incident was, I think, the turning point in the careers of both Irving and Maccabe; as the people of Manchester felt that they had done a service to the community by their able exposure of the tricks of these charlatans.

I think the last play in which I saw Henry Irving act at the Theatre Royal was "The Ticket of Leave Man," in which he took the character of Jim Dalton. This was in October, 1864, soon after which, I conclude, he must have gone to London. Although I may not have been able to trace in him the great marks of genius which others do, still I must say that he was one of the most conscientious actors the Theatre Royal possessed when he served his apprenticeship there.

Fred Maccabe, who was at this time at the Prince's Theatre, eventually brought out an entertainment entitled "Begone Dull Care," which proved a great success, and for many years he was a very prosperous man. Then, alas, the "dull care" which he helped to drive away from others settled on himself, and poverty came along with old age. I saw him at Blackpool some years ago in his once inimitable character sketch of "The Wandering Minstrel with a top note," and it was sad to see him feebly trying to galvanise into life, the ghost of a former triumph.

Prior to 1860 there was really only one other theatre in addition to the Royal which could be dignified with the name, and that was the Queen's, which at that time stood at the corner of Spring Gardens and York Street. It is true there was another place called the City Theatre which stood near the Royal, but it had only a short existence, and need not be taken into account. The Queen's was under the management of Mr. and Mrs. Egan, and was essentially the theatre of the "gods," and for whom they especially catered. Those who frequented the Queen's liked something of a highly melodramatic flavour, and they usually got what they liked. F. B. Egan was a tall, powerful-looking man about six feet four in height, whilst his wife, a pretty-looking, buxom little body, was as short as he was tall, and the couple formed a striking contrast when seen on the stage together. They stood high in the estimation of the "gods," and were quite alive to their own individual and collective importance. If their friends in the gallery were sometimes disposed to be rather too boisterous and unruly, Mr. and Mrs. Egan were not afraid of speaking their minds; but on the whole the gallery were very loyal to their favourites.

I remember on one occasion during a performance, and in the course of some very tragic business on the stage, an individual in the gallery had the audacity to throw down a piece of orange peel, which happened to fall at Mrs. Egan's feet. Interrupting the action of the play, she called her husband's attention to the stray piece of peel. Egan at once took the hint, and, stepping forward to the footlights, called out in his stentorian voice, "Who threw that orange peel?" Of course it was not likely that the culprit would discover himself, but the gallery at once showed their appreciation of Egan's actions by shouting out, "Chuck him down." Fortunately for the miscreant he could not be identified, and was thus able to avoid the tender mercies of the gods. After a withering glance upwards in the supposed direction of the offender, the orange peel was kicked aside, and the tragedy proceeded from the point of interruption, just as if nothing had happened.

The last time I saw G. V. Brooks was in July, 1854, at the Queen's, where he came to fulfil a farewell engagement prior to sailing for Australia. It was indeed a farewell, for he never saw England again, being drowned in the "London" on the passage, together with all on board. He often paid long visits to Manchester and had the reputation of a great actor, but I cannot say that he greatly impressed me. Possibly when I saw him he was past his best, so that my judgment may hardly be a fair one. There was to me, too, much sound and fury in his acting, and he tore, as it were, his passions to tatters. In such plays as "Othello," "Macbeth," and "A New Way to Pay Old Debts," this was more especially the case, and in the last-named tragedy he made demands upon his voice and lungs which must have taken them all their time to satisfy. In the dying scene, which was painfully protracted, you were apt to wonder where, as a dying man, he was able to keep on hand such a large supply of physical force and energy. His throes were so prolonged that you felt inclined to echo the Lancashire remark, "Here, oi say, owd chop, ween had enoo' o' this, get forrard wi' thee deein', mon." I saw him in the character of Richilieu during this visit, and I considered it a much more satisfactory performance; in this play he was, in fact, quite at his best.

Those who knew Barry Sullivan in his best days will, I think, agree with me in saying that he was, of his time, the finest tragic actor who walked the boards, and also the ablest and most intelligent interpreter of Shakespeare. His Hamlet was exceptionally fine, and although far from being what might be considered a handsome man, he had been endowed by nature with a noble presence, well-formed limbs, an easy carriage and (if I may use the term) a poetry of motion which, coupled with a melodious, tuneful voice, won your attention and sympathy as soon as he had appeared upon the stage. Who that has seen him as he came down the boards on his first entry in "Hamlet" can forget the charm even of his opening sentence?

"*A little more than kin and less than kind,*"
or again,
"*Tis not alone my inky cloak, good mother.*"

"Hamlet" may, I think, be considered Shakespeare's masterpiece, both as a dramatic conception and an inexhaustible mine of poetic wealth; and to see it worthily interpreted by such a man as Barry Sullivan in the past, or by Beerbohm Tree and Forbes Robertson in the present day, are pleasures to be remembered. Barry Sullivan, although seen to the best advantage in such plays as "Hamlet," "Othello," "Richard the Third," and "Macbeth," was a good all-round actor. In "Katherine and Petruchio," "Don Caesar de Bazan," "Damon and Pythias," "The Hunchback," "The Stranger," "Money," and "The Gamester," he was especially fine. He used also to act in a play called "Woman's Heart" with Miss Vandenhoff, written by the latter.

CHAPTER XLIX

Stage Recollections, continued.

MR. AND MRS. CHARLES DILLON often visited Manchester, and were great favourites. The pieces in which they excelled were the pathetically emotional. Their greatest success in this class of play was "Belphegor, the Mountebank," in which they appealed so forcibly to the susceptibilities of their audiences that handkerchiefs were much in evidence amongst the ladies, whilst even the sterner sex could not altogether disguise their feelings. "Don Caesar de Razan," "Masks and Faces," "The Three Musketeers," and "William Tell" were plays in which they shone; whilst in "Othello" and "King Lear" Charles Dillon was well worth seeing.

I must not omit to mention Mrs. Stirling, who occasionally came amongst us. She was a most finished actress, and although when she acted in "King Rene's Daughter" her figure was hardly as slim as could be desired for the blind girl, still the charm of her performance blotted out all incongruities of a physical nature.

I now come to speak of Mr. and Mrs. Benjamin Webster, or, as the latter was generally known, Miss Woolgar. They were both talented, but Miss Woolgar was especially gifted. Her acting was most realistic, intense, and powerful. In the year 1860 I saw them in a play called "The Dead Heart," one, I think, of the most heartrending pieces I ever witnessed. The acting was most powerful, and as the cast included Charles Calvert as the Abbe Latour, it was a performance to be remembered; and the encounter between Benjamin Webster and Charles Calvert, in one particular scene, was very thrilling.

Shortly, the plot (which is reproduced in "The Only Way ") is as follows: Robert Landry, after languishing in prison for twenty years, is released at the storming of the Bastille. On regaining his liberty he finds that the man who succeeded in getting him sent to prison is dead, but that a son of his enemy is alive, and on whom he has vowed to be revenged. He accomplishes his purpose, and gets the man condemned to death. The night before his execution, the mother (Miss Woolgar) visits Robert Landry and makes such a powerful and touching appeal to her husband's enemy, that he at length consents to save him.

There is only one way in which this can be done, which is by putting himself in his place and dying for him. This he does, and the curtain slowly descends as you see Robert Landry walking calmly along the plank to place his head beneath the knife of the guillotine, which stands before you in all its hideous reality. To anyone who is never so happy in a theatre as when he is miserable, let me recommend "The Dead Heart"; should this not satisfy him he must indeed be hard to please.

Robson was an actor quite unique in his way; he was serio-comic in style, but the two gifts were so happily blended that they formed in him one harmonious whole. In one breath he could move you to tears, in the next to laughter. At one moment he startled and astonished you by some grand tragic outburst, in the next the tragedy became a screaming farce. Then he was at his best Madame Ristori had won fame for herself as a tragic actress of rare ability. One of her finest efforts was the impersonation of Medea in the tragedy of the same name, and in which I was privileged to see her. Robson took it into his head to get up a travesty of this play, and did so with such success that people flocked to see him in it wherever he went. At times his imitations of the great tragedienne were so clever and close that you could have almost thought it was Ristori who was speaking. But hardly had this idea taken possession of you than the tragic burst of declamation was as rapidly changed to something utterly farcical and ridiculous. So successful were these impersonations of

Robson, that Madame Ristori went herself to see him, and was as delighted and amused as others at his wonderful and grotesque copy of herself.

Another of his burlesques after Ristori was "Norma" and it was very rich to see him come on to the stage as the priestess, with a wreath stuck jauntily on the side of his head, and dragging two little brats of children by the hand, in the street ballad style. His acting of the Porter's Knot was exquisitely touching, and his impersonation of Desmarets in "Plot and Passion" the very acme of all that was cringing, mean, crafty and subtle.

Mr. and Mrs. Barney Williams, who introduced to the English stage a number of amusing American sketches, were very taking in their particular line. Mrs. Barney had the American nasal twang to perfection, whilst the husband had a rich Irish brogue as a contrast. Mr. and Mrs. Florence, who followed them a little later on in the same style, were fully as good. Some of their songs (highly poetic?) still cling to my memory, and have done good service as cradle songs thirty years ago. That my readers may judge of their quality I give a few examples: –

"*a lobster in a lobster pot,*
A blue fish wrigglin' on a hook,
May suffer some, but oh no, not,
What I due feel for my Mary Anne.
"*Oh, don't you see yon tur-tile dove,*
A-sittin' on yonder pine,
Lamentin' the loss of his own true love,
As I am duin' of mine, Mary Anne?"
Here is a verse of another: –
"*Down in Skytown lived a maid,*
Sing song Polly, wont you try me oh,
Churning butter was her trade,
Sing song Polly, won't you try me oh?"
CHORUS.
Keemo, Kimo, dar oh whar,
Me hi, me ho, me in come Sally,
Singing sometime periwinkle,

Ling-tum, Nip-kat,
Sing song, Polly wont you try me oh?
And last but not least: –
"*On one fine day in August last,*
A bobbin' reaund, areaund, reaund, reaund,
As Josh and I went to make hay,
Then we went a bobbin' reaund.
Sez Josh to me, let's married be,
A bobbin' reaund, areaund, reaund, reaund,
And I kissed Josh, and Josh kissed me,
As we went a bobbin' reaund."

These effusions speak for themselves, and in competition with them the present Poet Laureate is not in it.

Some thirty years ago the Haymarket Company was the most popular combination of actors and actresses in the country. Wherever they went they were an unbounded success. The great charm of their acting was, that every part in a play from the smallest to the greatest, was filled with the best talent available; and anyone getting a position in this Company his or her theatrical career was henceforth considered secure. They revived a number of the best old English Comedies such as "The School for Scandal, "The Rivals," "She Stoops to Conquer," "The Love Chase," and others, which were staged and acted as they had never been before. These, with such additions as "The Hunchback," "Still Waters Run Deep," "As You Like It," "The Unequal Match," and others, made a feast of good things, of which the public was quite ready to partake. Buckstone, as managing director, was a host in himself, and was at the same time the best comic man of the company. A strange thing is, that for many years of his life he was so deaf, that he could not hear even his cues on the stage, and had to depend almost entirely on the dumb show on the stage to find out when his part came on.

It was whilst the Haymarket Company were on one of their tours in Manchester that Kendal and Madge Robertson were married. They were very quietly made one, in the morning at the Cathedral, and in the evening they played together in "As You Like It." I happened to be at the theatre that evening although I was not then aware of the event. But ever after this it seemed as if Mr. and Mrs. Kendal were Manchester's special theatrical children, and we all took quite a fatherly interest in them. They used to act together in most of the plays written by Robertson, Mrs. Kendal's brother, "Caste," "Society," "Ours," "School," etc. These plays had quite a successful run for many years, and as performed by the Haymarket Company they were seen at their best.

I went to see some of these plays acted again a short time ago, and I must confess I was greatly disappointed with what at one time I so much charmed. I considered them very thin and crude, and they certainly do not bear comparison with the same class of plays written at the present time. In saying this I do not refer to the plots of many of the plays now produced, the moral tone of which has, I think, degenerated. But it is as regards finish, style, terseness, humour, delineation of character, and the development of stage groupings and effects that authors of today are so much in advance of those of a generation past. Take up any plays at random which were written then, and I think you cannot but be struck with the fact that with few exceptions, they show a want of concentrated and constructive thought, a general carelessness of style, and a feebleness and want of literary acumen in the delineation of character.

For example, compare "School," or "Society," or "Ours" with, say, "A Pair of Spectacles" or "The Last of the Dandies," and you cannot but be convinced of the marked literary difference between them and all in favour of the latter. What passed muster then would not be tolerated at the present time. What can be more really unnatural, wordy, and stilted than the greater portion of the play called "Money." Listening to it now after a lapse of many years, as I did some time ago, I was inclined to feel very angry with that gentlemanly prig, Evelyn, as he gives utterance to sentences sometimes nearly half a page in length of what might be termed moralising clap-trap. And yet I can remember when "Money" was considered a first-class comedy, and was selected by such actors as Barry Sullivan and Walter Montgomery for their benefit performances.

When first Mr. and Mrs. Kendal visited Manchester as travelling stars, they were very happy in their selection of plays, and were always sure of a hearty welcome and overflowing houses. However, afterwards, unfortunately, they produced pieces of a different type, lacking in their plot the clear, wholesome charm which distinguished their earlier productions. Where, for example, could there be found a more enjoyable comedy than "A Scrap of Paper?" The acting of Mr. and Mrs. Kendal in this delightful piece is, I consider, as near perfection as it is possible to be. I think it is a pity that the plays which they placed later before their audiences for a time dealt more with social problems, which, however good the acting may be, have no attraction for those who consider that it would be well if the stage avoided the production of plays dealing with these unhappy, and, let us hope, exceptional phases of human existence. However, recently they have reverted to their old style of pieces and brought out "The Elder Miss Blossom." It was a real pleasure to see Mr. and Mrs. Kendal at their best in this deeply interesting, and at the same time amusing, comedy. In places where the incidents border on the pathetic Mrs. Kendal played upon the feelings of her audience with that same old charm, so characteristic of her more youthful days, coupled with all that delicate finesse and skill which has come to her with maturer years. May "The Elder Miss Blossom" long hold a place in Mr. and Mrs. Kendal's repertoire.

CHAPTER L

Stage Recollections, continued.

I COME now to speak of an actor who from the year 1860 and onwards for some years did more to advance the best interests of the stage than any other actor previously connected with Manchester. I speak of Charles Calvert, who in the joint capacity of actor and stage manager, first at the Theatre Royal and then at the Prince's Theatre, threw himself with such whole-hearted energy, zeal, and devotion into the work of stage development and reform. The first play in which I saw him perform, I think, was a comedy called "Lost and Won," which was given for the benefit of Chambers, manager of the Royal. This was on the 28th of March, 1860, and on this occasion his name appeared as stage manager. His wife also made her first appearance on this evening.

There is not the least doubt that he and his wife served an apprenticeship of downright hard work whilst they remained at the Royal. The almost nightly change of programme was a very severe strain on all actors and actresses at that time; but Charles Calvert was a man who worked with a will, and with the determination that whatever he put his hand to, should be done to the best of his ability. An enthusiastic lover of Shakespeare, he longed for the time when his plays should have justice done to them, not only as regards their acting, but also artistically. He had come to realise the incongruity of staging these masterpieces with tawdry, worn-out dresses and indifferent scenery, and where many of the minor characters were filled by veritable dummies, who neither looked nor acted the parts they professed to represent. As stage manager at the Royal he did all he could to institute reform, but I am afraid Mr. Knowles was at this time disposed to run his theatre on the cheese-paring principle, and could not be persuaded that to get, he must give. In this respect Charles Calvert found his hands were tied, but he struggled on as best he could, and although the results of his labours were not what he could have wished, he sowed seed which bore fruit in after years. I remember visiting him in his little dressing-room at the Royal, where he chatted away in his brisk, energetic style, donning the while his anything but brilliant attire for the character of Rob Roy.

He remained at the Royal until 1862, and there he took his benefit on the 2nd of April. The plays he selected were two of Tom Taylor's, "The Fool's Revenge" and "Nine Points of Law." His impersonation of the fool, Bertuccio, in the former, was perhaps one of the cleverest things he ever did. I can see him now as like a sprite he darts about the stage, dressed in black and orange tights with cap and bells to match, and with the clever mocking jest upon his lips watching his opportunity to be revenged on the man who has torn his daughter from him, and on whom the whole passionate love of his nature is concentrated with almost painful intensity. Shortly after he left the Royal (where he felt he had no scope for the development of those stage reforms on which his heart was set) he became manager at the Prince's Theatre, and there, with a freer hand, he was enabled to carry out the numerous Shakespearian Revivals with which Charles Calvert's name in theatrical Manchester has been more especially associated. Still, although he was apparently a strong man, I am afraid he was not altogether what he looked. And, after all, these revivals involved a great amount of physical and mental wear and tear, as well as anxiety as to their ultimate success financially. I have the impression that there were many points of similarity between Charles Calvert and Augustus Harris. They were both men with determined wills and actuated by a desire to get all and every thing connected with the stage into a healthier and more satisfactory condition. They had a firm conviction that starving a piece in any way was false economy, but that if it were adequately represented the extra cost of production would repay itself in the long run. These two men, therefore, had the courage of their opinions, and were not afraid to spend money to make their productions as attractive as possible. Still, I have little doubt that their many anxieties from time to time told upon them and probably tended in a measure to shorten their lives.

On glancing through my old play bills, I see that it was in July, 1854, when I saw Helen Faucit (who only passed away in November, 1898), perform in "The Hunchback," and although this is over fifty years ago, the impression her wonderful acting made upon me is still present with me. I think it will be acknowledged by all those who were privileged to see her act that there was no other actress who seemed so completely to absorb into her nature the characters she impersonated as did Helen Faucit. Her whole soul appeared to breathe forth from her in all she did, and she was endowed with all the gifts and graces which help to make up the perfect actress. Her elocutionary powers were not only of the highest order, but they were matched by a voice which thrilled you with its emotional and sympathetic qualities. Her features, although not beautiful, were a vivid and faithful index of the passions which stirred her; in addition to which, every movement of her body was characterised in her lighter moods by charming naturalness and buoyancy, yet easy refinement; whilst in her sterner efforts she was the embodiment of all that was dignified and impassioned. In fact, there was such a fascination in Helen Faucit's acting that when you saw her in any of her characters the stage appeared almost in a sense empty, when she was not present on it. By her life and example she did much to raise the tone and the morale of the stage, and when she quitted it she carried with her the respect and admiration of the English nation. To the present generation she was better known as the wife of the late Sir Theodore Martin, but to those who can look back to the fifties the name of Helen

Faucit has a very special charm and attraction unique in its character.

It is now some thirty years ago since Sothern made his great and phenomenal hit in the character of Lord Dundreary in "Our American Cousin." When it was first produced the play was only moderately successful. Sothern, however, so developed the part of Lord Dundreary that all other characters in the piece became of no account. Wherever he went the crowds rushed madly after him, until at last the country developed a very severe attack of Dundreary on the brain. His impersonation of a gentlemanly idiot was quite unique in its way. The limp, the lisp, the drawl, the stutter, were irresistibly comic, whilst his dress and make-up were veritable works of art. He was not only present with you at the theatre, but you carried him home and, mentally, even to bed, with you. You became so inoculated that you found yourself gradually gliding into the Dundreary limp as you walked along; you stuttered and drawled and lisped, until at last you ran the danger of lapsing into a state of helpless Dundreary idiocy. Perhaps the most amusingly clever thing in the whole performance was the reading of "Bwother Tham's" letter. It was worth going to see him again and again if only for this one episode, which was quite an acting gem in its way. Another favourite impersonation of Sothern's was David Garrick, in which he was very good; but his name and fame will always be associated with Lord Dundreary when everything else in connection with him is forgotten.

As an actor J. L. Toole stood high in the public estimation as the very impersonation of animal spirits and grotesque humour; and in all he did he had the faculty of appearing to enjoy the fun he made upon the stage quite as much as did his audience.

When I first saw him he came down to Manchester with Charles Dillon's Company from the Lyceum. This was in October, 1857, when Mr. and Mrs. Dillon starred in such plays as "Louis the Eleventh," "Belphegor," and

"Othello," whilst Toole wound up the evening with "My Friend from Leatherhead," "Domestic Economy," "The Spitalfield's Weaver" and similar productions. Although the pieces in which he usually performed were often of the flimsiest description and crammed full of the most glaring improbabilities, he simply made them go by his drolleries and his inexhaustible supply of animal spirits. In the plays in which he performed he was seldom off the stage, and during the whole of the time his energy never flagged; he seemed to be here, there and everywhere at the same time, bubbling over with all sorts of original comicalities. And yet Toole could be pathetic as well as humorous, and in a number of pieces his acting was tinged with almost a tragic vein. In "Dot," for instance (an adaptation from "The Cricket on the Hearth"), his interpretation of Caleb Plummer was full of quiet, gentle, genuine pathos, and at times there were not many dry eyes amongst his audience. Like Dickens in his writings, Toole on the stage had the great gift of combining successfully the humorous with the pathetic, without destroying or spoiling either the one or the other.

He is still with us, but his acting days are now over; the last time I saw him was in "Walker, London," and it was sad to see the man who could once rollick about the stage like an india-rubber ball, only able to move to and fro with care and caution, obliged to husband his strength as much as possible, in order to avoid a breakdown. When he began to star on his own account Toole always included his old friend Paul Redford in his company; and it was touching to witness the old actor's affection for his pupil, whom, in his deep-toned voice, he usually designated as, "My dear boy."

As a rule, in speaking of any particular play, it is as often as not associated with the name of some actor or actress; but there is one piece which, I think, won its way into public favour entirely on its own special merits, on account of the sentiment embodied. This was "Uncle Tom's Cabin." Of course, it was preceded by, and had its origination in, the book of the same name by Mrs. Reecher Stowe, which, when it was written, took the people by storm both at home and abroad. When it was dramatised and placed upon the stage it was a triumphant success wherever it was produced. Everybody went to see it, even those who hardly ever entered a theatre where to be found at "Uncle Tom's Cabin." The trials of Uncle Tom, the sweet lovableness of little Eva, the laughable eccentricities of Topsy, and the cruelty of Legree appealed to the feelings of the people with an intensity seldom witnessed on the stage, and which even the book itself was hardly more capable of inspiring. As a play of an emotional and sensational nature it had a very long life, and even to this day it has a sort of flickering existence in the country and on the provincial stage. Mrs. Beecher Stowe wrote other works of fiction, but "Uncle Tom's Cabin" was the book of her life, for to its influence may be directly attributed the abolition of slavery in America

There are many other actors of whom I might speak, who were well known to the theatre-goers of a generation past. There was Miss Bateman, who made a name for herself in the character of Leah, a Jewess, who in the course of the play delivers herself of a curse so terrible and intense in its nature that it was apt to give one a fit of the blues to listen to it; and it was the fashion for people to go and see her repeatedly in this play in order that they might enjoy the luxury of hearing her in this withering and blood-curdling denunciation.

There was Fechter, the foreign Hamlet and Shakespearean actor, a man who had evidently devoted his life to the study of the great dramatist, but whose foreign accent clung so tenaciously to him that the effect produced was somewhat similar to hearing the part of Hamlet given a rich Irish brogue, if such a contretemps can be imagined.

Then there was Dion Boucicault, the author and actor, who achieved such an immense success with his "Colleen Bawn" and other Irish plays; Phelps, of Sadler's

Wells, the East London tragic pioneer, who only visited Manchester very occasionally; Miss Glyn, great in the character of Queen Charlotte in "King John." (By the way, how is it that in these days of Shakespearean revivals this play is overlooked, full as it is of powerful and touching writing and dramatic incident?) I must not forget Miss Cushman, who made her name as Meg Merrilees in the play of "Guy Mannering." There was the African negro actor, Ira Aldridge, whose pieces partook mostly of the blood-and-thunder style. There was the low comedian, Wright, who, in my mind, is more especially associated with the character of Paul Pry, in which he was clever, but at the same time vulgar. There was, too, the versatile and inimitable Compton, who seems to rise up before me in his wonderful impersonation of Rob Acres in "The Rivals." I see him (mentally) with his pistol hanging limply in his hand in the duel scene, and am inclined to think there never was anything more exquisitely amusing than his acting in this piece. And associated with Compton in the Haymarket Company there was Farren, and Howe, and Chippendale, Mrs. Fitzwilliams, Mrs. Keeley, and a host of others whom I must pass over, but who helped me to enjoy many a pleasant evening in their company in the days of my youth.

CHAPTER LI

Stage Recollections, continued.

AND now before bringing these stage reminiscences to a close, a few remarks about Italian and English opera as they were presented to the public here some thirty to forty years ago may not be uninteresting to the present generation. Speaking of music generally, its culture and development during that period has been almost phenomenal; and there is perhaps no place in England where this is more noticeable than in our own City, where the people are, as a whole, ardent musicians, and where what would have been considered satisfactory and even creditable forty years ago, would now without doubt be thought poor and elementary.

In addition to this educational advance, we must not ignore the fact that the scene painter, the upholsterer, the decorator and the costumier now add considerably to the complete success of any operatic production. In the days of Mario, Grisi, Patti (in her younger days), Cruvelli, Gassier, Herr Formes, Giuglini, Foli, Tamberlick, and others of the same period, we had to look away from the stage and its accessories, which were often inartistic and crude, and more especially so in the provinces, to the singers themselves; and so, in spite of these drawbacks, those old days bring back very many pleasurable memories, and I hear, as it were, again the echo of the familiar melodies and the sound of many beautiful voices, now silent in the grave. Perhaps it may be that youth in some way lends a charm of superlative excellence to all enjoyments, with which it is connected, and so I may be prejudiced in holding to the belief that as regards quality and timbre of voice many of the leading singers in the past were superior to most of those of the present generation.

I have before me one of my old playbills of November 25th, 1854, and as I glance down the list of the names of those who composed Madame Caradori's Opera Troupe, and of those who performed that evening in "Robert le Diable," the curtain of my memory is drawn aside, and I see and hear Carl Formes as Bertram, Mad'lle Agnes Rury as Isabella, and Madame Rudersdorff as Agnes; and I call to mind how my heart was stirred as I listened to the last-named singer in that grand old song, "Robert toi que j'aime," to my mind one of the most moving dramatic melodies that was ever composed. To this day there is no song which exercises such an influence over me, and even now when it is heard in a concert room I consider it has hardly its equal. But to hear it as I did on the stage, interpreted with all the passionate earnestness and intensity with which Madame Rudersdorff imbued it, was a musical gratification not to be forgotten.

Madame Caradori had at this time a very strong company of operatic singers under her control, and so highly appreciated was it that her seasons in Manchester would sometimes lengthen out to five or six weeks at a time. She was herself a woman of fine massive physique, full of vigour, with high Dramatic capabilities. She shone in such operas as "Norma" "Lucrezia Borgia" "Semiramide," etc, which allowed her full opportunity for the display of her powers both as an actress and as a singer.

Herr Formes was at this time at his best, and his impersonation of Bertram, in "Robert le Diable," was exceptionally fine, for he was not only a splendid "Basso profundo," but he was also a most realistic actor, one who was capable of completely losing his own individuality in the character he was portraying. And yet at the same time his own personality was present in all he did, as he was a man of marked physique, being short of stature, thick-set, with very marked features, and long, black, flowing hair. These characteristics helped to give artistic colour to all he did, but especially were they noticeable in his impersonation of Raoul in "The Hugenots," in which his acting was superb. I can see him now before me as he bursts forth into that grand old soldier's song, "Piff Paff," and which delivered with a wealth of dramatic force and fire, invariably won him an encore, and then, when the end comes, you are startled by the report of arms, and shot through the heart, you see him reel to and fro, stagger, and fall lifeless to the ground. The whole scene is so impressive, and the acting of Formes is so intensely realistic, that you might well be excused for fearing that some terrible mistake has been made, and that you are the de facto witness of an actual death struggle.

At this time Charles Hallé and E. J. Loder were the joint conductors of the orchestra, with Seymour and Shiekle as leaders, but eventually the last named became the fixed musical conductor at the Theatre Royal, and remained so for some time.

In addition to this travelling troupe under Madame Caradori, we were also favoured with occasional visits from the Royal Italian Opera from Covent Garden, which were considered musical events of some importance. In 1855 I heard, amongst others, Grisi, Mario, Didée, and Gassier; and although Grisi was then past her prime, she and Mario were still able to charm their listeners with the marvellous quality of their voices. I saw Mario in "The Hugenots," and the former in "Semiramide," and I heard, too, the great Cruvelli in this same opera. In "La Traviata" I saw the dainty little Piccolomini, who made for herself quite a reputation in this melancholy opera, but which was one for which I never cared.

It was in August, 1862, that I first heard the renowned Adelina Patti, and "La Sonnambula" was the opera in which I saw her perform. She was then, I think, under twenty years of age, but even at this period of her life, she had made a name for herself for her wonderful singing, a name which after an interval of some forty years she still continues to hold. It is really wonderful to think that at her age she is still able to sing almost as of old, and to retain a youthfulness which is akin to magical. As old time singers, she and Santley, to whom I refer later, are the two great wonders of the age.

It is strange to notice how the taste of the public generally for Italian opera has steadily declined during the last thirty years, and how Wagner, who was then practically unknown here, has now become the enthroned king in the operatic world. At the time when Titiens and Giuglini were enchanting their audiences with their magnificent singing, the operas of Wagner had not succeeded in finding here a place upon the stage; and although this was so, even when "Il Travatore" held sway in the operatic world, it was time very enjoyably spent to go and hear Titiens and Giuglini in what was then considered Verdi's masterpiece. Titiens was a great actress as well as a magnificent singer, so her success was unbounded. The opera in which I think I listened to her with perhaps the greatest pleasure was Gounod's "Faust," and although her somewhat massive proportions hardly gave one the impression of an ideal Marguerite, still in every other way she so completely identified herself with the part, that you overlooked any physical incongruities. She absolutely made the character live before you, whilst at the same time she delighted you with the wealth and richness of her vocal capabilities. To her nothing seemed an effort, and her voice welled forth as from an inexhaustible spring. Her acting and singing, more especially in the prison scene in this opera, I always considered one of her finest efforts. She appeared to completely abandon herself to the demands which the part made upon her, with her whole soul and body, and in that grand concerted climax I seem still to hear the notes of her pure, melodious voice ringing rich and clear above all the rest.

There are many names, at one time "familiar in our ears as household words" connected with the Italian opera, stage, as singers of note, such as Sinico, Carlotti Patti, Sedlatzek, Ciampi, Benedetti, Gardoni, Campobello, Tagliafico, Foli, Santley and others; but of all these probably the only one which has any true significance for the present generation is that of Santley. I can remember him when he first appeared with Titiens in "Faust," in the character of Valentine, in which he was a great success. From the very first he was a favourite with the public, and this he has continued to be for about half a century. His is a wonderful record, and it is almost marvellous to think that at his age his voice has retained so much of its old power and sweetness, and that today there is no one who is able in oratorio to supplant him. I heard him lately in "Elijah," and he sang the music allotted to him with almost all his old fire and dramatic effect, like the true artist of his profession that he undoubtedly is. Long may he continue to renew his youth, like the eagle.

When English opera first sought a home in Manchester, I fear it had a great struggle for existence, as in the estimation of musical people generally it occupied a very second-rate position as compared with Italian opera, which was then all the fashion. Still, when Louisa Pyne and her company paid us a visit they were always sure of a hearty welcome by a certain section of theatre-going people, who preferred to understand what was taking place on the stage instead of often having to guess at the plot of an Italian opera; and where sometimes in an emergency some of the stars would be singing in either French or German, whilst the rest of the company were holding forth in Italian. After the marriage of Louisa Pyne with Harrison, who was the principal tenor in her company, it developed into the Pyne-Harrison Opera Company, but I fear its success was not very great nor its existence prolonged. New combinations were formed, including such names as Fanny Huddart, Miss Dyer, Lucy Escott, Henry Haigh, Augustus Braham, Aynsley Cook, Manvers, and others. Their repertoire of operas was a fairly good one, including, of course, "The Bohemian Girl" (which has done duty as the *"piéce de résistance"* for a couple of generations), "Maritana" "Masaniello," "Fra Diavolo," "The Daughter of the Regiment," "The

Beggar's Opera" "Dinorah," and "The Lily of Killarney." Still, although one went to hear these operas with a great amount of enjoyment, the foreign article was too much in vogue to enable the various companies to lead anything but a precarious existence. The lack of support from the wealthy classes, and consequently an impoverished exchequer, prevented them from securing the best talent, or of presenting their productions in their most attractive form. It required the joint inspiration of Gilbert and Sullivan to give a new birth to English opera. Their delightfully amusing and clever productions very quickly revolutionised matters, and enabled them to place English opera in a position of security which it had never previously occupied. The whole English nation owes a debt of gratitude to these two talented men for their unceasing efforts to make light opera both pure and at the same time delightfully attractive, and, as Gilbert says in one of his lyrics, *"A source of innocent merriment."*

If authors of plays would only do for the drama what these two men have done for light English opera, the offence of the stage as it too often exists at present, would in a great measure cease.

CHAPTER LII

The Growth of Music in Manchester during the last fifty years – Charles Hallé – The Monday Evening Concerts – Catherine Hayes – Sims Reeves – Henry Russell – Mons. Julien.

THE foregoing remarks on operatic music would hardly be complete unless some reference were made to the position of Manchester from a musical standpoint, say, from about the time when Charles Hallé was conductor of the Theatre Royal orchestra. The strides which have been made by our City in the development of music during that period have been remarkable, and without doubt this progress is very largely due to the energy, devotion and ability of this man, Charles Hallé, who starting from most modest beginnings, was not content until he had awakened a desire amongst us for a more classical and refined musical standard. When he first came to Manchester he found its musical aspirations at a very low ebb, as compared with their position at the present day. But he found congenial soil upon which to work, for Lancashire as a whole was a true lover of music, and was ready to be educated to higher and better things. He it was who in the face of financial difficulties of a most trying and prolonged nature, held firmly to the resolution with which he started, namely, to cultivate a taste for the works of the best composers, by presenting them in a more complete and artistic form than had before been attempted; and to do so he endeavoured to secure the best available talent vocal and instrumental, regardless of expense. Consequently his liberal expenditure did not enable him to grow rich, and it is said that at the end of his first season, when the accounts were made up, he found himself with half-a-crown to the good. But to Charles Hallé, with his high musical ideals, financial results were a comparatively small matter, as what he aimed at was the musical education of the community. In this he was eminently successful, and there is probably no place in the United Kingdom where high-class music is listened to with greater delight than in Manchester, and I think this fact compensated him for much worry and anxiety. How Sir Charles Hallé endeared himself to all who knew him, and what a blank his death made in the musical world, is too well known to be repeated here.

The late H. B. Peacock, who was connected with the *Examiner and Times* in its palmy days, was perhaps the first man in Manchester to popularise music with the masses. He started what were familiarly called "The Monday Evening Concerts," which for some time were very successful, for at them would gather about him the floating talent of the day. The concerts were held in the old Free Trade Hall, and large and enthusiastic audiences attended them. Amongst those who were prominent singers at these concerts were Catherine Hayes, Sims Reeves, Madame Rudersdorff, Herr Formes, Madame Caradori, Fanny Huddart, Signor Delavanti, Henry Russell and many others.

Catherine Hayes was at that time certainly the most attractive and touching of ballad singers. She sang with exquisite pathos, and had the power of moving her listeners almost to tears. Her favourite songs were Irish, and amongst them her greatest successes were "Kathleen Mavourneen," "Savourneen Deelish," "The Minstrel Boy," etc. But the ballad which impressed me more than any other was "The Harp that once through Tara's Halls," which she sang with almost religious intensity. The people always flocked to hear her wherever she went, and she was a great favourite in Manchester.

Sims Reeves also at the period of which I am writing was without doubt the finest tenor in the country, and very popular with all classes. I have been given to understand that at one time he and Catherine Hayes were engaged. In oratorio Sims Reeves had not a rival, and on any great occasion Charles Hallé never felt success secure without the services of the great tenor. So much had the people set their hearts upon him that in many cases as soon as he had arrived a poster would be issued and hurriedly distributed over the whole town with the announcement: "Sims Reeves has arrived." The reason for this was that he often disappointed his audiences by not putting in an appearance, as he would never sing except when his voice was in perfect condition. There are many people of the present generation who considered that Lloyd was his equal, but for my part I have no shadow of doubt that Sims Reeves was the finest tenor of his day. As a trained musician Lloyd may have been his equal, but Sims Reeves had the gift of touching the chords of the heart as no other vocalist I ever heard was able to do. As a ballad singer no one could approach him, and I feel sure that those who heard him in his prime in such ballads as "The Death of Nelson," "Tom Bowling," "Maud," "My Pretty Jane," "The Anchor's Weighed," and "The Bay of Biscay," will agree with me that in such songs as these he was unequalled. He was twice married, the last time towards the close of his life, when he was in needy circumstances. There is no halo around his closing years, and he died practically in poverty, a sad ending to a once brilliant career, when he could do as he liked, and could almost command his own terms when he chose to sing.

Henry Russell, who is lately dead, was another public favourite. He originated an entertainment at which he dramatised songs mostly of his own composition, and to which he accompanied himself on the piano. He was what might be termed a capital pianoforte racer, at one moment thumping about in a thunder and lightning style, and then suddenly softening down to the most delicate pianissimo, just as the exigencies of the piece or song he was playing, in his estimation, seemed to require. He sat with the piano sideways to the audience, and his face turned towards them, and as he was gifted with great facial expression, doing so enabled him to give full effect to his vocal efforts.

His songs were nearly all of the melodramatic order, by turns harrowing, plaintive, patriotic or blood-curdling as the case might be, and as he had possession of a full, rich, powerful voice, he was enabled to play upon the feelings of his audience with great effect.

Although his entertainment was not what might be termed high class, it was healthy, robust and interesting, whilst it was at no time vulgar. In such songs as "The Gambler's Wife," "The Maniac," "The Ship on Fire," "Man the Lifeboat," what with facial expression, his powerful voice, and a pianoforte accompaniment in which almost every note in it had to do duty, he was usually able to rouse his listeners to the proper high level of enthusiasm, usually bringing the song to a grand climax with a dramatic top note, and a wild stampede up and down the entire keyboard of the piano, followed by some melodramatic chords, and finally closing with the usual three musical thumps, which always seem so necessary as the climax note of triumph to the society entertainer's sketches. Henry Russell always gave his audiences a most diversified programme, and some of his national songs became quite the rage. Of these perhaps the most popular was one called "Cheer, Boys, Cheer," although "To the West, to the West," the chorus of which runs as follows: –

"To the West, to the West,
To the land of the free,
Where the mighty Missouri
Rolls down to the sea;
Where a man is a man,
If he's willing to toil,
And where each one may gather
The fruits of the soil."

ran it very close. There were others, such as "The Red, White and Blue," and "A Life on the Ocean Wave," all of which were to be heard in all directions, and were particularly popular with the boys in the street, who were never tired of whistling these songs at all times and places.

Then there was the great, immaculate "Mons. Julien" and his band. He posed before the public as a composer and musical enthusiast, but I am more disposed to put him down as a musical humbug than as a man possessed of real musical talent. But he was a clever organiser, and succeeded in gathering round him (for that period) an excellent band. He knew, too, how to cater for the public taste, and how to appeal to our national foibles or weaknesses.

He centred at London, but he also toured the provinces, and when he came to Manchester, which he often did, he was always sure of large audiences. He was constantly bringing out something original and attractive and at times even startling. One of his greatest successes was his "British Army Quadrilles," which he crowded with little surprises to catch the public taste. The last time I heard these quadrilles they were performed at the Blackpool Winter Gardens, and were conducted by De Jong. He had soldiers planted in various positions throughout the Hall, who at particular stated times previously arranged to fit in with the music, fired off guns, so as to give them the true "Mons. Julien" effect of a real engagement.

It was Mons. Julien's custom to always travel about with what might be termed a certain amount of "mise en scene," the various articles being very carefully arranged with an eye to general effect. For example, he possessed magnificent fauteuil, most gorgeously upholstered in crimson velvet, with elaborate white and gold mountings. His couductor's stand, lyre-shaped and also painted in gold and white was very striking, and the wand with which he led his band was of pure white and very distinctive.

He himself was always dressed very lavishly, from the smallest and shiniest of patent leather boots which could by any persuasion be tempted on to his feet, up to the well-oiled raven black hair which fell gracefully down his back. He was short of stature, but what he lacked in height was more than compensated for in breadth. When he had ceased conducting some piece, he would gracefully sink back in a complacent, semi-exhausted state into his lovely armchair, of course being careful first to place his exquisite white baton on his lyre-shaped music stand. Thus seated, he considered himself open for full-dress inspection. The general impression left was one of white shirt front, voluminous white waistcoat, and white kid gloves. This vision of white was relieved by a massive gold chain, like a miniature cable, a large diamond shirt stud, and a handsome gold watch, which he was careful to consult from time to time, as the concert progressed.

There were some clever soloists in his orchestra, and at times when someone of them had more than realised his expectations, he would step down from his pedestal, approach the instrumentalist, stretch forth his arms, and effusively embrace him in the sight of the audience. Then he would sink slowly into his chair, and do a little white handkerchief business, just to give a finish to the whole scene.

This was the type of man and music which passed muster at the time of which I speak, so that it may be supposed there was plenty of room for improvement. It was at this period that Charles Hallé came to the front, and the people of Manchester, recognising his sterling qualities as a true musician, were, under his guidance, willing to be educated up to his standard; and so before he passed away he had the satisfaction of seeing the good seed which he had sown bearing abundant fruit. I am, of course, ready to admit that even when Charles Hallé came amongst us there were opportunities for the few at least of listening to first-class music at Chamber Concerts and at the Gentleman's Concert Hall, but these occasions were not as many as they might have been, and they did not exist for the general body of the people. Whereas now the case is quite different; high-class music is provided for all who wish to enjoy it, be they rich or be they poor; and so at the present time when any new and difficult work of some composer is brought before the public, it is not only interpreted by the best talent, but you will see crowds of the middle and even the working classes closely and intelligently following the musical score, and enjoying with true zest the treat provided for them. Dr. Hans Richter is a worthy follower of Sir Charles Hallé, and under his able baton Manchester, from a musical point of view, is supremely happy.

CHAPTER LIII

Old Manchester Faces.

I.

THERE hangs in my office an engraving taken from the original painting at present on the walls of the Manchester Royal Exchange, representing many of its old subscribers, and as I study this picture from time to time I cannot repress feelings of regret and sadness as the years creep stealthily along, at the increasing number of those who, once at the centre and very heart of Manchester's commercial life, have either passed over to the great majority or have in some other way lost touch with all that was in the old days so familiar to them.

There are of course many old forms and faces which, although not to be found in this group, were woven in and formed a part of the texture of our daily business life. And it seems to me that it might not be uninteresting to try by means of memory and reminiscence to reanimate a few of those Manchester men, who lived and breathed among us, and who contributed materially to the tone and colour of their surroundings.

And I would preface my remarks by saying that it is probably a distinct advantage that we all of us possess some peculiar distinguishing characteristics, humorous or otherwise, as the case may be. And in what I may be led to say I hope I may not offend the susceptibilities of anyone, or hurt the feelings of any relatives or friends of those who have passed away. I do not wish to write a single jarring word, or make an ill-natured reference to, any individual who may rise up before me; although at times it may happen that in order to draw a character correctly

I may have to touch upon some special point of weakness or strength, which may carry with it its quaint or amusing features. In any case I would like it to be understood that I will not "set down aught in malice; yet I persuade myself to speak the truth shall nothing wrong."

Perhaps what helps to make our ordinary life in Cottonopolis more varied and interesting than is frequently the case, is the fact that our large foreign trade brings us into contact with almost all nationalities, and makes us probably more cosmopolitan in our views. We welcome to our shores (and this is no longer mere metaphor) men from all parts of the world – Parthians, Medes, and the "dwellers in Mesopotamia, Jews, Cretes, and Arabians." Manchester makes no distinction as to creed or race. She opens her portals and offers an equal chance to all those who wish to settle here to trade and get gain. We cannot, of course, deny that at times we have cherished the wolf in sheep's clothing and have allowed our foreign friends to rob us of our "goods and chattels." There may be an amiable weakness amongst us to think "men honest that but seem to be so," a too willing disposition to give unlimited credit to some individuals of limited credentials but imposing names. Still, although the community has suffered from this excess of confidence, we have at the same time attracted to our city very many foreigners who have settled amongst us and been a strength to us in every sense of the word – men who, having made Manchester their adopted home, have been ready and willing to give liberally of their time, their money, and their energies to the promotion and furtherance of all good works, and have supported with no niggardly hand the various charitable institutions for which we are honourably distinguished.

In looking back into the past one of the first men I would like to speak of is Murray Gladstone; and in doing so a very pleasant form and figure rises up before me. At one time Manchester would have hardly seemed complete without the presence of his kindly, benevolent face, universally respected, his influence for good certainly though quietly made itself felt amongst us. His character happily combined that of a true Christian gentleman and an active and honourable man of business. His manner was quiet, genial and unassuming. Whatever your business with him might be, you could always be sure that you would be listened to with respect and patience. In his business life he acted upon the principle that "Jack was as good as his master." When he made a statement it carried conviction with it, as people were satisfied beforehand of the honesty of his mind and purpose and his complete freedom from exaggeration. Any scheme which commended itself to him obtained his support; and such support was a material guarantee of its success with the general public. Where he led they were ready to follow, and a meeting held for any purpose with Murray Gladstone in the chair had assurance of a good start from his very presence and countenance, in the double sense.

When I first came into contact with him the Indian trade, with which he was largely connected, was in what might have been termed "a fat and flourishing condition"; profits were good and exchange steady. Like the man who said he didn't know he had a liver, so in those days people hardly realised that there was such a thing as exchange; its action was so healthy and regular that they did not trouble themselves about it. But, unfortunately, this state of things was not to last. With the breakdown in the exchange came widespread competition and losses, and the worry and anxieties of business told seriously upon a sensitive and delicately constituted physical frame, and Murray Gladstone's familiar face disappeared from the group of Manchester friends. The house at Kersal in which he lived passed into the occupation of the late Bishop Fraser, and as I think of them both I cannot but note the coincidence that this house should be the home of two so similar in their natures; both good men and true, moved by the same spirit of earnest simplicity and transparent sincerity, elements so refreshing in these matter-of-fact days. His portrait which hangs on the wall of the Royal

Exchange is a very faithful likeness of him in his later years; and as you look at it, you are reminded of one who was loved and respected by all who knew him, and the mention of whose name brings back pleasant memories to a wide circle.

A good many years have come and gone since Bernard Liebert (or, as he was more familiarly called behind his back, "Old Barney ") was in the flesh amongst us, and in the midst of the busy hum of commercial life. But I can remember the time when he played a very important part in Manchester's commercial commonwealth. He was a clever, shrewd, capable man of business, and you would have required to get up remarkably early if you wanted to get the best of a bargain with him. And yet to look at him his appearance gave no indication of his capabilities. He had a slow, methodical gait, never seemed to be in a hurry, and as he strolled leisurely along he was about the last man you would have associated with anything so alarmingly active as a game of football. His manner was blunt, and at times you might almost say gruff, yet withal he was kindhearted and generous, but a man who scorned to wrap up his good deeds in gilt-edged paper. You had to take him as you found him, and his moods were not at all times the same. Of some men it is said that their bark is worse than their bite, and I think "Old Barney" came under this category. He had, in the days of which I speak, his place of business in a very unpretentious-looking building in Princess Street, the frontage having once been the entrance to an old private house. Here at various hours of the day he might be seen leaning idly against one of the pillars of the doorway, with his hand to his mouth in a peculiar attitude, as if he had nothing else to do. But I have quite the impression that he thought out many a business plan on the doorstep of that house in Princess Street, and as he gazed listlessly up and down the street, with his thumb apparently glued to his mouth, he was evolving some further development of his business. He was at one time in partnership with Sam Mendel, but it was said, that Bernard Liebert dissolved it because the latter was too go-ahead for him. Mr. Liebert had an old-fashioned way of liking to see where he was walking – he had no taste for ballooning and not knowing where he might come down. It was when the velveteen trade was in its infancy and in comparatively few hands that he saw the possibilities of its rapid development, and he struck out boldly in this department of his trade, and so was enabled to realise large profits before others were able to overtake him.

II

AMONGST the foreign shipping merchants there were few names which had a more familiar ring about them than that of S. D. Bles, who determined from his first settlement here to make this his home, and soon became closely identified with the business life of the city. It is now many years since he passed away, but I still have him mentally before me as distinctly as if he were yet with us. He laid the foundation of the present concern by persevering and systematic hard work, and although he was no doubt both clever and capable, I think he relied for success more on the results to be obtained by thus persistently "pegging away," keeping his shoulder steadily to the wheel, and gaining the confidence of those with whom he traded. To look on the outward man he seemed to take life very quietly and without unnecessary fuss. If you met him in the street he would be seen walking along with sober mien and with his handkerchief held loosely in one hand, which was a habit of his.

But if he moved slowly, he moved surely, and the love of work which characterised him he instilled into his sons as they grew up into the business. His warehouse was certainly no training ground for those who were disposed to eat the bread of idleness. When most of the places were closed and in darkness, you would, if in the locality, see their offices lit up, and if they were not actually burning the "midnight oil," with gas as a substitute, the results were the same. Although S. D. Bles was a strict business disciplinarian, and one who believed in every day for its own work, however long it might prove to be, he was kindly and thoughtful as a father and a devoted husband. In the old days the practice was for business people, in many instances, to return to their homes for the midday meal, and it was pleasant to join with the father and sons on the homeward journey, and witness the affection with which he was regarded by the whole family. My knowledge of S. D. Bles dates back some fifty years, to the time when he lived in Marlborough Terrace, Broughton Lane, and when the youngest son was a sturdy little fellow in short frocks and pinafores, with white cotton socks and ankle-strap shoes, attire which is now supplanted by knickerbocker suits, which, although perhaps healthier, are certainly not as becoming for young children.

Talking of the father's influence in the training of sons for business life, there is another instance of this which brings me to speak of a man who for many years took an active part in the affairs of the city, and perhaps has taken more share in the rebuilding of Manchester and Salford than any other individual connected with us. I speak of the lately deceased and deeply regretted Robert Neill, who, commencing life as a joiner, has shown us what it is possible for a practical, energetic, and capable workman to accomplish in building up his own fortune. The monuments of his work surround us in every direction, and a description of the many buildings he has erected would be an interesting retrospect of the history of our city. An octogenarian, he remained to the last hale and hearty, with all his faculties unimpaired and able to give his matured and practical advice on any matters of business. But he was not only a hard worker in his own sphere of labour, he also threw himself with whole-hearted energy into municipal affairs, and in 1866 to 1868 he was twice called to the civic chair. Active and energetic himself, he was determined that his sons should follow in his wake, and I do not think there could have been found two young men better trained to carry out what the father had commenced. The workmen's bell found the sons also at their posts, and after breakfast the father, with a son on each side of him, was to be seen on the road returning to the works as regular as the morning came round. Robert Neill was a man of strong, resolute will, and his very walk and the way in which he planted down his stick, which was always his companion in the streets, gave a clear indication of the type of man he was in all he said and did. His motto in life was: "If you do a thing at all do it well."

Amongst the Greeks, who were a fairly numerous body some thirty or forty years ago in Manchester, there was one who occupied a very prominent position, and who at one time did a very extensive business with the Levant. His name was Sofiano, and he was not only large in a commercial sense, but also physically; indeed he was absolutely and *de facto* one of the great ones of the city and this was fully realised as you saw him looming towards you, in form not unlike a captive balloon but in weight – well, here you felt the comparison ceased.

The Greek trade was at that time a very large and apparently prosperous one. Mr. Sofiano, amongst others, was one of its most important representatives, and his figure was a very well-known one on the boards of the Manchester Exchange. He was naturally a man of a very excitable nature, and, in spite of his bulk, quick and energetic in all his movements. He had a mind stored with a wealth of Oriental anecdote and metaphor, of which he made free use even in his business. I am not at all sure but that his wonderful capabilities in this direction had at times the power of inducing some salesmen to give him some little advantage in the price of his goods. It is astonishing what an effect a story well told and judiciously applied had in those days, even on the price of T cloths and shirtings. But then spinners and manufacturers had something like a margin on their productions. Now, when there is nothing left but the "bare bones," there is no longer a possibility of success even for the most persuasive of tongues. As easily might you hope to draw water from the flinty rock. "So waste not your sweetness on the desert air"; the days of the charmer are gone.

Mr. Sofiano was not only entertaining as a conversationalist, but he was also remarkable for his powers of facial expression and gesticulation, which always seemed to fit in most aptly and amusingly with whatever he might be saying. When illustrating his remarks he had a way of extending his arms from his sides, and gathering the ends of his fingers closely together like a bunch of sausages. Then suddenly opening them out, with the palms upwards, he would purse up his lips like the spout of a kettle; whilst his eyebrows, which were heavy, black, and bushy, seemed, in the excitement of what he was saying, to be trying to work up into his hair a tale told by Mr. Sofiano was quite a little dramatic entertainment, and I can call to mind no one of whom he so much reminded me at such a time as Father Gavazzi, who was gifted with the same wealth of physical illustration, and in comparison with which the cold-blooded style of an Englishman is tame in the extreme.

In the year 1860 the great crisis in the Levant trade occurred, and a large number of Greek failures took place. Amongst the firms who succumbed Sofiano Bros. also came to grief. Mr. Sofiano, who was naturally a proud man, felt the blow very keenly, and his carriage and horses, which had been so well known on the road, had to be given up, and he had to get into a smaller compass. After a time, however, his natural buoyancy of disposition reasserted itself, and he could still charm the ears of friends, business and otherwise, as they gathered in his office listening to his amusing gossip and happy Oriental illustrations of fact and fancy. A habit of his as he became interested in anything he was saying was to gather his legs under him, tailor fashion, which, as it may be supposed, did not in any way detract from the comicality of his remarks.

Then old age and bad health, as well as bad business, overtook him, and the Greek Sir John Falstaff gradually wasted away to a gaunt and haggard wreck and shadow of his once burly form. For some time before he died the nature of his illness prevented him using a conveyance of any kind, and during this period of his life he might be seen creeping down the road to town with a folding campstool, which the poor old gentleman would occasionally open out and sit upon, until the wearied body was sufficiently rested to resume the tedious journey. Even to the last the old fire would now and again flash forth; but it was like a fitful blaze amidst dying embers, seen only for a moment.

III.

ANOTHER well-known face on the Exchange was that of George Higgins, the spinner of coarse "extra hard twist." He had an excellent name for this class of yarn and was able to command a market for it. He spun "extra hard" when there was money to be made at it, and when the difficulty was not so much with regard to the selling as to the buying. Then it was the ordinary thing for spinners to have their production fully engaged for weeks and months to come, and often the buyer had to run after the seller; now, I am afraid, it is very much the other way. George Higgins was a good-looking, dark-haired gentleman, who looked through gold spectacles in a firm, determined sort of way, as much as to say, "Now, please understand I've quite made up my mind". If he quoted a price for his yarn you could at once realise that he meant to stick to it, unless you were prepared with argument which he considered sufficiently strong to alter his mind. He was not accustomed to beat about the bush; he knew his own mind, and he expected you to know yours. He did the bulk of his selling through his agents, Richard and Edward Broadhurst, who were for many years in partnership together. These two, and Henry, the third brother, have all passed away, but it is pleasant to recall the time when they went in and out amongst us, noted as they all were for their quiet gentlemanly bearing and their straightforward dealing in all matters of business; men of fair fame, who were an honour and credit to our commercial community.

Then there was George Oliver, who was, I think, at one time entitled to the sobriquet of "the handsomest man in town." Tall and erect, with sharp, well-cut features and a clear, pure complexion, which seemed to defy the contamination of the atmosphere of smoky old Manchester; you almost wondered, from his whole appearance, how such a man came to be mixed up with business life at all. With a gun on his arm tramping over a Scottish moor, or as an officer in the army he would have looked quite at home; but as an active Manchester merchant he might have appeared to some like the square block in the round hole. However, this was far from being the case, for he was without doubt a good, sound, clear-headed man of business. Honourable and high-principled in all his dealings, he was quite entitled to rank as one of our typical merchant gentlemen.

In the painting of the Exchange subscribers, to which I have already referred, there is a portrait nearly full length of "Tom Birch," the ever-familiar term of address by which he was known to his friends. I must say the portraiture in this instance is not by any means a happy one. It is only by a great effort that you can recognise any resemblance to the original, and this more by his well-known habit of putting his thumbs into his waistcoat armholes than anything else. Tom Birch was particularly short of stature, whereas in the painting he gives you the impression of being somewhat of a giant. Stout he certainly was, but he was likewise diminutive, and what he wanted in height he made up in breadth. He was perhaps one of the merriest and best tempered men who went on to the boards. He delighted in retailing the latest bon-mot, or any amusing little story which happened to be in the air. You would generally find him surrounded by a group of listeners who, after enjoying some of his jokes, would disperse around in search of business prey; only to be presently attracted back into his circle by some still more entertaining anecdote, which was always ready to follow in the wake of its predecessor. Tom Birch was a young school boy mentally, and the Manchester Royal Exchange was his playground. There was a merry twinkle in his eye and a light-hearted gaiety in his whole bearing which carried infection with them, even in those who professed to be somewhat shocked at his levity.

His name brings to mind some of the associates of his younger days. For instance, there was John Turner (son of James Aspinall Turner) certainly a man of weight, for I imagine he was on the heavy side of twenty stone. Then George Stellfox, a remarkably handsome man with a wonderfully quick eye for a pretty face, was another of his friends; also Will Pollard and diminutive Tom Pilling. Of the last named Tom Birch used to remark that he wore such enormously high collars that he could not look up to see the time by St. Ann's Church clock, except at a regulated distance, for fear of self-decapitation.

How fashions repeat themselves. This was over forty years ago, and now again at the present time the young men who love to be in the height of fashion are to be seen going about with their heads perched on the top of a huge white erection which goes by the name of a collar. At the time of which I am writing one citizen of Manchester, who in his "salad" days had a love for these exaggerated luxuries, and before bounteous Nature had blessed his soft downy cheek with whiskers, was vulgarly styled "chops and collars," for as he came along the road, these were the objects which loomed most prominently upon your vision. The subject of collars reminds me of boots. Why, I do not know, unless that the then craze in collars was also developed in the direction of boots – tight boots. If you wished to do the correct thing there was nothing for it but to encase your feet in the tiniest possible boots. The process involved a certain amount of wheedling, cramming, and jamming; but what of that if you succeeded in making your feet look smaller than your neighbour's. I can remember one day as I journeyed to town, seeing one of the exquisites of the day (and I could give his name) standing, supporting himself against a lamp-post in an agony of pain, as he tried to get relief by knocking the toes of his boots against the bottom of the post. Oh, the agonies that men and women will endure if they can only follow Dame Fashion wherever she may lead them! I am satisfied that at the time to which I am referring, whole acres of corns were sown broadcast, for the future punishment of those who were determined to go in for small feet regardless of physical cost.

I have mentioned in my remarks one Greek merchant, but as he was only one of a number with whom I came into contact in my early years, and who were well known in business and private circles, I will now mention a few of them consecutively as they come back to my recollection. For example, there was Theodore Souvazoglu who laid the foundation of and also built up a most successful business here. Of course, the times on which he fell were undoubtedly favourable to him, but still his restless energy, hard work, and integrity formed the main secret of his success. He was quite a character in his way. He had a quick, short, apparently irritable manner that made you feel somewhat uncomfortable when coming into contact with him for the first time. He spoke very rapidly – so much so that, with his imperfect English, it was almost impossible at times to make out his meaning. He had almost a snappish way of addressing anyone, but he meant nothing by it, and it was really only his peculiar mode of expressing himself; in fact, he rather prided himself on his brusqueness of manner; but at the bottom he was a warm-hearted, genuine man, which, the better you knew him, the more fully you realised. If he was a keen buyer (and he certainly had this reputation), he was also an excellent payer, and if prompt cash had any influence with a seller, he knew where he could get satisfaction in this respect. He was a tall, large, heavy-looking man, with black hair and sharp, restless-looking eyes, and an expression in them that seemed to say, "Oh, it's all right, young man; no doubt you think yourself very clever, but I'm up to you, my boy."

After remaining in Manchester for a number of years, he returned to Constantinople to manage the business at that end. In the year 1872, when important matters obliged me to visit Constantinople, I once more came into contact with my old friend. Except that with his absence from Manchester his capabilities for expressing himself in English had materially declined, I found him pretty much the same man as he had been in the past in temperament, manner, and bearing. Renewed contact with Orientals had perhaps helped to develop prominently his natural peculiarities. I remember being in his office one Saturday morning when he was paying the small brokers for their week's work, and truly the whole scene was as good as a pantomime. On the table was a large wooden bowl, something like a porridge basin, which was filled with money of every description. Over this Theodore Souvazoglu presided, as these poor, ill-clothed, miserable-looking creatures presented and prostrated themselves before him with their various accounts. I suspected that a number of these were pensioners rather than brokers, whom he helped to eke out a precarious sort of living.

As each one sidled in, salaamed, and explained in a meek deprecatory way the particulars of his little bill, Theodore would get excited and storm away at him as if he were the greatest villain in existence, and had come there to rob him. To this they each replied by bowing and scraping before him as if he were some superior being whom they were trying to propitiate. After this little play had gone on for some time, and Theodore Souvazoglu had apportioned out the amount of wrath suitable to each individual, he would dip his hand into the bowl of money before him and select a small museum of coins of all shapes, sizes, and values, and pay them their accounts, sending away the poor creatures happy and contented, as if he had not uttered an unkind word. On the following Saturday they would come up again and go through the same sort of entertainment, to be followed, of course, by similar results. I am almost inclined to think that these Orientals really rather enjoyed the whole thing, and would have been afraid that all was not right if they had got their accounts without a murmur.

One day, when walking with my friend from Galata to Pera, where he had built himself a large handsome marble house, of which he was naturally very proud, he had occasion to purchase a hairbrush, which he declined to have wrapped up in the ordinary way, so he walked along with me through the streets, flourishing the brush aloft as he gesticulated wildly with his hands, telling me some trivial incident which certainly did not by any means require the amount of emphasis and declamation with which it was accompanied. I was glad when our destination was reached, as we had become the gazing stock of the passers by, who could not help being attracted by my friend who came striding quickly along wholly unconscious of the amusement he was causing, laying down the law in an excited manner and brandishing his hairbrush in the air like a musician's bâton.

He would now and again pay a hurried visit to Manchester, but with all his visits he never appeared to get on any easier terms with his English, which remained to the last a funny helter-skelter sort of jumble, which few people could properly understand. On one of these occasions he asked me to go round with him to some houses, where he wished to make various purchases of linen and napery for private use. It was rather a comical experience, and my friends to whom I took him did not know what to make of him, for he was altogether so excitable and odd. If a price was asked for some article he wanted to offer about 20 per cent. less, as if he were in the bazaar at Constantinople, although it was quite as a favour he was getting what he required at wholesale prices. And all he said came tumbling out in such a funny, incoherent manner, that I must confess I was not altogether sorry when he had satisfied his wants and our ramble through the linen houses had come to an end.

IV.

THERE will, I am sure, be some of my readers who will be able to call to remembrance the tall, stately form of "Shakespeare" Frangopulo, as he was called when he lived in Manchester. As he began to descend the hill of life his likeness to the great dramatist became more and more marked; the shapely, elevated forehead, the pointed beard, and the whole contour of the face gave a remarkable consistency to the title he bore. He had what really might have been termed a noble-looking presence, and in addition to this the graciousness and dignity of the perfect gentleman. There was a quiet repose about all he said and did which, amid the fuss and bustle of the ordinary conditions of Manchester life, could not but strike one most favourably.

He was one of the wealthy Greek merchants who, like Theodore Souvazoglu, started and developed his business when the home and foreign trade was, so to speak, jumping to prosperity. Although both these men were successful, I think it would be a matter of difficulty to imagine two men who, arriving at the same goal, were more dissimilar in their whole style and bearing. The one brusque, almost rough, in manner; the other calm, stately, and polished, a man who, as he descended from his carriage at his house on Bury New Road, might readily have passed for some prince of noble blood. In the early years of his career he had brought from abroad a young Greek who formed a part of his household establishment. This man showed himself to be possessed of such exceptional capabilities that he took him into his warehouse, where he got on rapidly. He allowed him to commence in a small way on his own account in the fent trade, and in a short time he did so well for himself that he had the call of the purchase of the fents at most of the leading shipping houses in the city. At this time large profits were made in the shipment of fents to foreign markets, and in this way Paul Tambaci – the man to whom I am referring – laid the foundation of a large and important trade to the leading markets of the East. A career which might have ended prosperously terminated most disastrously, although he did not live to see the end. He was, without doubt, a clever, shrewd, hardworking man, but his misfortune was that he had made up his mind that at all risks he would be one of the big men of his generation. He died fighting for the possession of his ideal paradise. He never entered it, however, but left behind for those who followed an inheritance of misery, distress, and disappointment.

A. D. Blagomeno was another Greek merchant who between the years 1854 and 1860 shot forward into great prominence, until brought down by the Greek crisis which occurred in the latter year. At the time of the war between Russia and Turkey large fortunes were made by the shipment of almost everything under the sun to the seat of war. Constantinople for the time being became a greater centre of commerce than she had been before, and so, like other traders to the Levant, Blagomeno was able to do an extended and lucrative business. When the war was at an end he launched out in other directions, principally in trade with Egypt and India, although he still continued his connections with Constantinople, Smyrna and the Principalities. But he had too many irons in the fire for safety, and when the crisis came he, like many other valiants in the army of Greek merchants, was unable to weather the storm. During the years I was in contact with him I had the opportunity of making mental portraits of some of those who from time to time helped to make up his staff, and perhaps an outline of a few of them might not be altogether without interest, more especially to those who can remember the individuals to whom my remarks may apply.

The first one of the group who comes to my mind is a Mr. Platti, a man small of stature but almost fierce in the possession of very bushy black whiskers, which stood out determinedly from the sides of his face like so much ebonised wire; his eyebrows, which grew in two thick clusters, surmounted a pair of black piercing eyes, and had he only been attired in native Greek costume he would have worn quite a brigandish air. However, although he looked fierce, he was as a matter of fact a very mild young man, and I do not think he was disposed to do any harm to anybody. In his youthful days when I first knew him he was quite a dandy, and would appear in the streets dressed in the very height of the fashions. With faultless coat and vest, light pantaloons strapped tightly beneath his smart patent leather boots, a silk hat that almost sparkled with the freshness of its gloss, spotless gloves, a thin, pretty fancy cane, and a fragrant cigar; such was Mr. Platti when he blossomed out into full flower. When he joined Mr. Blagomeno's staff his palmy days had passed, and there was remarkably little of the gilt left on his gingerbread. He took a much more modest and practical view of things, and more especially with regard to the adornment of the outer man. The fashions had changed and he with them, as it has been and is with many another butterfly of fashion, and will be to the end of the chapter.

Later on there was a Mr. Malodi, who occupied a place on the staff, his department being the foreign correspondence, which in his time was very voluminous. He was an elderly man, stout, and with a soft, light moustache, which curled inwards until it found its way into his mouth, and seemed quite at home there. He was what might be termed a very proper man, perhaps a little pedantic in his style, but well read and a man of education. A man who was disposed to estimate his abilities at their full value, but withal kindly and good hearted.

He had a nook at one end of the office where he occupied himself with his correspondence. He wrote his letters principally in Greek, but in a large round hand, so it did not take him long to cover a sheet of paper. He had some of the tricks of an actor in his mode of doing things, and many a time and oft have I watched him from the corner of my eye rehearsing what he was going to say to a correspondent. He would mentally bring him before the bar of his judgment and address him in a most dramatic style. His body swayed from side to side in harmony with the majestic wave of the dexter hand. His lips moved and his moustache crept slyly into his mouth as his face expressed in turn anger, remonstrance, and persuasion, until at length a reposeful look of satisfaction stole over his features as he composed himself to write what had been so carefully and characteristically rehearsed. Even as he wrote one would notice sudden gleams of triumph lighten up his face as he felt how completely he was knocking the wind out of the sails of his correspondent. And then as he reached the climax of his argument he would wave his hand with the pen in it with a sort of "end of the act" flourish, as much as to say: "There, my dear sir, perhaps you will kindly let me know what you can possibly say in reply to that."

This Mr. Malodi eventually took charge of the Constantinople establishment, and another Greek occupied his position at this side. I have forgotten his name, but he, like his predecessor, was not without his peculiarities. He was a grey grizzly-bearded old gentleman, with weak-looking, faded sort of eyes, from which he gazed, when addressing you, in an absent-minded sort of way. He smoked the very strongest cigars from early morning till late at night; in fact, I should not have been surprised to learn that he slept with one in his mouth. It was not only that he was an inordinate consumer of the weed, but he appeared to completely saturate himself with smoke, both inside and out; he gave the impression that he absorbed his cigars instead of smoking them in the ordinary way. When he got into any difficulties as to what he should say to a correspondent, he would run his hand through his hair (which always stood bolt upright) in a nervous, worried sort of way, and then take a long and strong pull at his cigar. The effect of this inhalation was that for the time being he was enveloped in a dense column of smoke, and I do not think I have ever seen anyone with one draw create such a garment of smoke. It issued from his mouth and his nostrils, and curled up through his hair in such a thick cloud that for the time being he was lost to sight. As this would gradually clear away you would see him resuming his correspondence, until some further mental difficulty seemed to oblige him to go through a similar incantation of smoke worship for relief and guidance.

V.

THERE is another Greek friend who has only lately passed away from amongst us, and of whom I would like to say a few words. I refer to Theodore Miniati. In our city for the last half century or thereabouts he was a bright, active, moving spirit in the ebb and flow of the Levant trade, sharing its prosperity and its misfortunes. Although in his palmiest days he did not rank in the amount of his turnover with the largest shippers to the Mediterranean markets, still he was head of a well-established business, and whatever hard work and energy could command he could claim. Like nearly all his countrymen he was a keen, clear-headed man of business, and there were very few men with whom I was acquainted who more dearly loved a bargain for the bargain's sake than Theodore Miniati. He delighted in ferreting round the market in search of some place where he could get hold of a cheap line in anything. And to his credit it must be said that when he had satisfied his own wants he was always ready to put some friend on to the scent, that he also might profit. He was a most unselfish man in the amount of trouble he would take to benefit others; and he was without doubt a willing pioneer and guide to many a young countryman of his who, starting business, was in want of just the assistance he could render him. I am sure there are those in Manchester today who would gladly acknowledge his thorough unselfishness in this respect.

Perhaps this extreme love of bargaining was in his particular instance a weakness as well as a strength. I am inclined to think that the temptation of threehalfpence or threepence per piece was an inducement to exceed his absolute requirements in making a purchase, and that he sometimes found himself in the position of having to dispose of two commercial dinners (as it were) where the appetite only existed for one. This love of bargaining manifested itself in his domestic as well as in his business life. There was hardly a shop that he passed where his capabilities in this direction did not find an opportunity for exercise, and in Shudehill Market his was a well-known face. He had a keen eye for the best joint of meat, the most tempting fish, and the freshest fruit and vegetables. But it is quite possible to overstock a larder as well as a warehouse, and this, I fear, was just one of Mr. Miniati's weaknesses. But as he came to you fresh from his latest triumph you had not the courage to question his wisdom.

A warm, excitable temperament is the characteristic of most Greeks, and he was no exception to the rule. If he felt strongly, his words were a very clear echo of his thoughts. As an illustration, I remember on one occasion when walking to town with him he became so excited about something he was relating to me that he suddenly stopped in the middle of the pathway, and, throwing up his arms wildly to give point to what he was saying, knocked off his hat to the no small amusement of the street urchins who were hovering about. For some years his health had been declining, and you could see that his physical forces were slowly but steadily giving way. The last time that I saw him in town I was shocked at the rapid change which had taken place: I saw that the bolt had been shot and that his days were numbered.

And now that I have been speaking about a few of

the Greeks, let me say a word or two about a Turk. The diminutive figure of Abdullah Ydlibi with his Turkish fez was at one time almost as well known as that of the Chelsea Bun Man. He was the Manchester Consul for the Ottoman Empire when it was not altogether in its present moribund condition. His duties were not then a comparative sinecure, and if you had any business with him you found him to be a pleasant man with much of the European and even a little of the Englishman in his ways and ideas. He had been so long in this country that he had lost many of his Turkish ideas and habits. He and his son were both fond of horse exercise, and it was no uncommon thing to see them riding through the streets mounted on their chargers. The consul did business abroad on his own account, and I am afraid his fees as consul did not represent a very large income. Eventually he had to go back to Constantinople on account of some dispute with the Turkish Government, which was always a misfortune, as, in such a case, one had everything to lose but nothing to gain. If you won your cause, life would certainly be too short to include a settlement; and if you lost it meant ruin; and this was, I think, poor Mr. Ydlibi's position. At the time I was in Constantinople he used to haunt the office of Mr. Ede, the solicitor who was acting for him, and trying to get his case through the Turkish Tidgaret. Our Chancery Courts, at their very worst, were abodes of bliss as compared with the Tidgaret. If in the former hearts were broken and fortunes lost, the results arising from contact with the latter were fearful to contemplate. I saw what sort of a place it was when I was there, and anyone drawn within its fatal portals may exclaim, in the words of Othello: –

"*O, now for ever Farewell the tranquil mind;*
farewell content."

When I last saw Abdullah Ydlibi he had almost arrived at the stage of hopeless despair; he haunted the courts like a restless spirit longing and hoping for the verdict in his favour, which was never to be given. His money all spent, like a drowning man he clutched at each straw as it floated past him, to sink at last never to rise again. In my last interview with him, I realised what a contrast he was to the bright, energetic little being who in former days went in and out amongst us; who took life so easily, and who always apparently managed to get on to the sunny side of life's pathway.

I must not forget to mention the brothers Cababe, Paul and Peter, who for many years had almost a monopoly of the Syrian trade with Aleppo, until the Jews, at first by twos and threes and then in shoals, settled here, and by competition forced the trade out of their hands. Now there is, I fear, very little margin of profit left for anybody, but in those good old times I am sure either Paul or Peter would have disdained any thing less than 20 per cent. return on their shipments, and they looked with horror on the inroads made upon profits by the new-comers. Peter Cababe was a thin, spare, melancholy-looking man, pleasant when he liked and when things went smoothly; but with a truly Eastern temper when he was roused. When he lost his temper there was no possibility of a mistake about it, his face darkened and a fierce look came into his eyes which spoke of hidden fires beneath. His brother Paul was a man of good and gracious presence, robust in form, he was at the same time handsome, and always arrayed in the most spotless attire. He used to wear large frilled shirts, of the finest texture and faultlessly got up, with voluminous white waistcoats to match. He had a weakness for handsome jewellery, which he was not shy about wearing. He was perhaps a little pompous in manner, and when he entered an omnibus and deposited himself in a seat you always realised that he was there. I used to have the impression that, if not exactly vain, he was not averse to a little notice or admiration, and more especially on the part of the ladies. He was very polite and gentlemanly, but like his brother he had an excitable temperament, and those who had transactions with him had to be careful not to offend his dignity.

Talking of the Levant trade, if there existed a man who seemed more than another especially cut out to do business successfully with all Greeks, Armenians, Turks, and Syrians, that man was John B. Lee. He was a splendid salesman, and he was a clever man who left his place or got away from the persuasive eloquence of his tongue on the Exchange without having been landed into his capacious net. John B. Lee always weighed up his man, and knew exactly the sort of fly with which to bait his hook; but if all else failed he had an order book which, on being produced, could effect wonders, and was, in an emergency hardly ever known to fail. He was just a man who seeemed to fit into the time and occasion; hardworking and energetic all his life, he took a great pleasure in his business, and I certainly think he had no greater happiness than the landing of a good big fish in the shape of a large order, and more especially if, to secure it, all his clever tactics were called into play.

When the Liverpool Cotton Market was excited and prices advancing, that was the time when our worthy friend made the best display of his talents, and when his capabilities as a past-master salesman shone out most brilliantly. Perhaps some Levant merchant, having heard early of the Liverpool position, would quietly and modestly slip into John B. Lee's place in the hopes of getting some lines through at old prices. If he expected to catch our friend asleep he would be woefully mistaken. You might take it for granted that dear John was fully alive to the position; he was always one of the early birds looking out for his morning worm. He would very likely commence the engagement by point blank refusing to take orders at any price, or he would frighten his foreign friend nearly out of his wits by asking him some prohibitive price. Then the gentleman from the Levant would probably offer some small advance which would be almost indignantly refused. After some skirmishing in attack and defence, accompanied by a number of "bless my souls" on the part of J. B, he would suddenly assume a friendly, confidential manner, and hurrying his friend into a corner for fear even the office boy might hear, he would address him in something like the following style: "Now, my dear friend, you know I would do anything to oblige you, and if you will promise me that you will never let a soul know, I will book your order at so and so," naming a price; "but mind, only for this once. I wouldn't do it for another creature in Manchester." Perhaps this Levant friend still struggled, and offered some intermediate price, at which the master salesman would turn away grieved and offended, and tell him he had better try elsewhere. At this point the fish would probably come to the fly and be quietly and gracefully landed. Then he would see him to the door, and once more beseeching him not to breathe to a soul what he had done for him, give him an affectionate pat on the shoulder, and send him on his way rejoicing.

VI.

IT is now nearly a quarter of a century since the familiar face and form of James Hurst passed away from us, and it is considerably more since he formed a part of active Manchester business life. Gifted originally with a strong and powerful frame, he coupled with it a clear brain, a strong will, and excellent business capabilities. He was a man who, so long as he was fit and well, could not be idle either physically or mentally. His desire was to be always up and doing; but even the strongest frame can only stand a certain amount of strain, and eventually his health broke down through allowing an exceptionally vigorous and powerful frame to work at too high a pressure. When he was in his prime his was a busy life, and when the battle of the mineral oil trade had to be fought he threw himself into it, and championed its cause with such energy and dogged determination that it was, I think, greatly owing to his exertions that the revolution in the oil trade, brought about by the introduction of Young's mineral oil[27], was so quickly developed throughout the country.

He was an indefatigable traveller, and wherever he went he was a favourite, his mind being stored, and his conversation embellished with an inexhaustible fund of wit and anecdote. On a railway station, if he appeared hurrying for a train, the occupants of the carriages would bid eagerly for his company, a seat would always be found for him, and his humorous remarks and quick repartees were sure to keep the company in a merry mood. On the Exchange when he entered, he was surrounded by numerous friends, who were always ready to listen to whatever he might have to say on subjects practical, political, religious, or financial, as the case might be. On every one of these topics James Hurst had very clear and decided views, and certainly there was no one who was less afraid of expressing what he thought. These views might not always meet with the approval of his listeners, and they might at times be stated with a directness not always palatable to an opponent; but at the same time there would be a humorous ring about his remarks which mellowed the bluntness of his statements.

I remember an incident at the time of the election of Cawley and Charley for Salford, on whose behalf Mr. Hurst was approached by a youthful canvasser. How any canvasser on the Conservative aide had been commissioned to call upon him for his vote I am sure I do not know, as his strong Liberal principles were almost as well known as the Infirmary clock. Perhaps it had been done for some joke, for the best man in the three kingdoms would have found it impossible to make any impression on his staunch convictions; but when a mild and gentle-looking youth had been marked off for this task the result may be imagined. I happened to be present when this somewhat diffident and nervous representative was ushered into the

---

27. *James Young (1811-1883) served on a committee of the Manchester Literary and Philosophical Society and established the Manchester Examiner newspaper in 1846. He established the first commericial oil refinery in the world in Bathgate, West Lothian in 1850.*

room. Advancing towards Mr. Hurst in a slightly self-conscious way, his hands occupied in the performance called washing with invisible soap, he begged that he might be allowed to solicit his vote on behalf of Messrs. Cawley and Charley. Without any preliminary beating about the bush, and with a suddenness and bluntness which was almost startling, Mr. Hurst exclaimed: "Cawley and Charley? Why, I wouldn't touch them with a pair of tongs." As there could not be the smallest room for doubting the sincerity of this declaration, the youthful politician backed out of the room as quickly as he could. As he retired the merry twinkle in Mr. Hurst's eye told how he enjoyed the whole situation. What the poor young man did or thought I never heard.

Mr. Hurst was a warm-hearted, generous man, and there are some who are still alive who can bear testimony to this. But he often took a pleasure in hiding or disguising what he did, preferring to do an act of kindness in some way peculiarly his own. I remember hearing of an instance of this where a man who had been in his employment fell into needy circumstances and bad health. Being told by Mr. Hurst that he thought he could prescribe a pill for him which he fancied might suit his complaint, he asked him to call at the office, and he would let him try one. This he did, and was handed a small pill-box, which on opening he found a golden pill in the shape of a sovereign. These pills and boxes were made up regularly for him, and I have not the least doubt they completed the work of recovery, whilst at the same time it afforded Mr. Hurst the opportunity of doing a generous deed in his own particular way.

Amongst the many portraits in the painting of the Exchange subscribers there is not one which to my mind more closely resembles the original than that of William Birch, jun. It will be noticed that it is taken with his head uncovered, only one other member being so represented, and I can almost imagine why this is the case. The idea the artist had in taking these likenesses was to present as far as possible not only the individual, but at the same time some characteristic by which he might be recognised; and anyone who looks carefully at the painting and knew the men will have this brought home to him. With regard to William Birch, jun, there was, perhaps, no one who went upon the boards who was more particular about his personal appearance. His hair was brushed and parted with such scrupulous care that it would have been a matter of difficulty to find an individual hair out of place, and his moustache was tended in the same way. His linen was pure and spotless, and his small black tie exact and neat to a degree. His frock coat fitted him with the accuracy of a glove, and did credit to his tailor. His gloves were guiltless of a wrinkle, and in his hand he usually carried a dainty little cane. In fact, as you looked at him you could not avoid the impression that the looking-glass played no unimportant part in the arrangement of his whole turnout.

When doing business on the Exchange he would take out a little gem of a notebook and a pencil to match, which struck you as hardly large enough to record the numerous and important transactions which passed through his hands. In addition to being an Indian commission merchant with an extensive business, he devoted himself to philanthropic work, and was also a well-known local preacher. For many years he held Sunday evening services in the Free Trade Hall, which were largely attended by all classes of the community. He was a self-appointed minister, and, although not what might be termed a brilliant speaker, he had the gift of interesting and drawing the people to his services. The Cornbrook Orphanage was his origination, and he worked hard in its interests for a number of years. Some time after he left Manchester and had settled in Australia, this building was handed over by the trustees to the Boys' and Girls' Refuges and Homes Committee, who dealt with the property.

There is another man who was called away on the 2nd of January, 1898, but for many years before he died his once familiar, genial face, was rarely seen on the boards of the Manchester Exchange. I speak of John Ferguson, than whom a more modest or gentle man of business it would have been difficult to find. Although one of the recognised authorities, at one period of his life, in the yarn trade, he was wholly unobtrusive and retiring in his nature. He could not bear to do business at high pressure, and his soul abhorred fussiness and undue excitement. His face was one which inspired confidence from its frank, self-evident truthfulness. You could not look in his face and doubt a word he said; in fact, he was one to whom you could honestly apply the motto that "his word was as good as his bond" John Ferguson was truly a very pleasant, unmistakable type of the plain, straightforward, unassuming Lancashire worthy. Short of stature, and almost nervous in manner, he had a quiet, thoughtful reserve about him which made you respect his judgment in any matter of business, whilst his hand-shake and smile were things to be remembered as indicative of the good man and true.

One of his peculiarities was that he had an apparent objection to being in the streets alone. Wherever you came across John Ferguson you would invariably find him linked arm-in-arm with some friend, and I think any other form of progression (at least, in the city) would have been uncomfortable. Thirty or forty years ago it was quite the ordinary practice for gentlemen to walk arm-in-arm; now such a thing would almost be regarded with ridicule. But John Ferguson clung to the old style in this particular; he felt more easy when he had a friend to whom he could "buckle to," and to see him coming along in this fashion reminded you of the old Lancashire poem:

"*Coom, Mary, link thee arm i' moine.*"

In the days of tricks in trade, short reelings in yarns, and other abominations, men of the truly manly type of John Ferguson acted as a healthy leaven in a commercial community such as ours.

CHAPTER LIV

The Manchester Chess Club. March 12th, 1897.

HOW comes it to pass that in a large centre like Manchester and Salford the Manchester Chess Club is so indifferently supported? There are, I think, very few even of those who are not players of the game who are not prepared to extend to it a benevolent sympathy, and who consider it ought in some form or another to have the general good wishes of the community. I think it is a thousand pities that such a noble and intellectual pastime should not receive more adequate assistance, at least from those who in a cold-blooded, platonic sort of way give it their blessing, and which, by the way, is all they do give it.

With the additional funds that a largely-extended subscription would place at the disposal of the committee, they would be enabled to initiate more tournaments and matches, and develop a more general interest in the game. It is not necessary that every member of the club should be a player; numbers of those who are at present subscribers are quite content to belong to the "gallery" – in other words, to be onlookers of the game. There is no pleasanter way of spending a spare half-hour than by running into the Chess Club and witnessing a wellfought game of chess.

And the "gallery" man is in the happy position that he can select his own battlefield and watch the style of game which interests him most. He has ample choice; from the game that is designated as "skittles" to the lengthy, hard-fought encounter of the "1st class" men. But before giving a description of the Manchester Chess Club and some of its present-day members, I would like to revert for a few minutes to the time, now many years ago, when an upper room of Bakewell's, the confectioner's in St.

Mary's Gate, was the home of the M.C.C.

It was there I first witnessed Blackburne perform the feat of playing twenty games blindfold, and I can remember him so well sitting quietly at the fireplace, and as the moves at each board were brought to him he seemed to call back mentally as you looked at him the whole situation of the game, and would very quickly give his reply to his opponent's move.

At the time of which I speak, M. Bateson Wood and S. Cohen were both regular visitors at the club; and there was C. A. Duval, the President, and Mr. Potter, of Potter and Wood. Then there was J. S. Kipping, with his negligé, very much auburn hair. Yes, that old-fashioned upper room was a very pleasant place to pass a quiet, enjoyable evening. After all, I think there is much in chess to bring out the good qualities of a man. It is a game at which one is bound to exercise self-control, and to learn how to be beaten with a good grace. It is a game which, I think, without doubt develops the reasoning faculties, and teaches one not to take life too much in a hurry. It induces to quiet companionship, and I think there are very few real earnest chess players who are mean minded. There is one special feature which denotes the chess player, and that is that he is almost without exception a smoker, and not only so, but he is, as a rule, a never-ending smoker; it seems to be a part of his life, and I really believe there are very few who could play their best without a pipe or a cigar in their mouths to help them along. To a non-smoker, therefore, it is perhaps a little choky on first entering a room where a number of chess boards are occupied. You try to look as if you rather liked it, and after you have coughed your throat into a quiescent state, you have to be content to go in for an unlimited supply of second-hand smoking, by taking into your lungs as much as you can inhale of what is floating about.

It is pleasant to recall the old times and the well-remembered faces of those who gathered round the tables in the St. Mary's Gate quarters, fighting their mimic battles and interchanging friendly badinage. Most of those whom I call to mind have passed over to the great majority. Bateson Wood, with his subdued peculiar tone of voice and a half sort of lisp; S. Cohen, with his quiet, genial manner, and whom, by the way, I first remember dating back some fifty years, clothed in a jacket of Lincoln green with a large bow and a sheaf of arrows, a la Robin Hood, shooting over the field of the Athenæum Cricket Club. So must it be; we come and go, and the place that we knew, it knows us no more.

One of the most regular, and, at the same time, entertaining habitues of the present room is the doctor, who has his French class-rooms on the same floor, and is, therefore, always on the spot, ready at all times and under all circumstances to give his advice on any game that may be proceeding. The doctor is very fond of his little joke, and is the acknowledged freelance of the M.C.C. He does not play so much himself, although he has immortalised some opening in chess, which goes by the name of the "Callithumpian." There are those who profess to despise the opening, but at times the doctor, when in the mood for playing, triumphs with it over his foes, and, like a hen after laying an egg, he enjoys a chuckle at the expense of its detractors. The doctor is blessed with an abundance of good humour, and during the whole time I have known him I have never seen him ruffled in temper. Whoever else may be offended he never is, and when he is beaten in a game, he takes his beating like a true philosopher. The doctor does not encourage reading in the room, and when a member overcome with the fatigues of the day dozes over his paper, a sly twinkle comes into his eye and the attention of the other members is called to the delinquent, who somehow feels that the doctor's eye in upon him, and, suddenly rousing himself, reads with a sort of fierce determination, to show how terribly awake he is.

Then there is the member who goes by the name of "The German Band." The reason for this cognomen is not far to seek, as nearly all the time he is playing a game of chess he gives utterance to the most dismal and unearthly sounds, which, when you are first introduced to them, are apt to disturb you, but it is astonishing how a human being can, by degrees, get accustomed to almost anything. When he is not playing the German band, or mewing like a cat, he is talking some incomprehensible kind of gibberish, which has no sort of meaning either to himself or anybody else, but it appears to amuse him, so the rest of those present have to be content. One afternoon we made a collection of fourpence, I think, if he would desist, but he was at it again in a few minutes. Still, in spite of his little ways, "The German Band" is a kind-hearted, amiable creature, and he can play an excellent game of chess, and has beaten Blackburne several times in match encounters.

Then there is the professor, quiet and pleasant, who plays a very good average game of chess, a man who moves out his pieces in a mild, inoffensive sort of way, as if he were not doing anything in particular, a man who lays the suspicions of his opponent to rest, until all at once he finds himself in a hopeless condition and unable to do anything but resign. When he has arrived at this point the professor's face will light up with a quaint, innocent smile, as much as to say, "Yes, my dear fellow, I see it is so, but I really do not know how it came about." At the time he is playing his game, he has the faculty of enjoying a joke that is, perhaps, taking place at the other end of the room, and where the laugh comes in his will be heard mingling with the rest, although at the time he appeared to be absorbed in his game.

Then there is the President, with his bright, good-humoured face, with a pleasant, genial word for one and all. A man who always seems able to take a cheery view of things, and has the knack of infusing his cheerfulness into others. He plays chess at a railroad speed, making his moves in reply almost before his opponent's hand is off his piece. And all the time he is playing he keeps up a rattling fire of pleasantry, making as many puns in half an hour as the rest of the room would do in a month. He usually plays with an old friend, and to listen to their give-and-take during the progress of play is good fun for the onlookers.

There are two gentlemen who always appear to be playing back games, showing each other what they would have done had the other done so and so. There is nothing the gallery objects to more than having to watch these stale encounters. There seems to be a want of interest and satisfaction in them as compared with looking at a brand new game, even though played by men of the second or third class. Life to me seems to be too short to fight our battles over again.

There is also the gentleman, one of the "gallery," who always likes to get to one corner of the room where he can read the paper, overlook a chess board, and smoke his pipe contentedly. He says he is an old man, but he does not look it; he is vigorous of speech and action, and takes in all that is going on about him with watchful eyes and ears. He has a splendid memory, and for almost everything that is said or related he has an anecdote to illustrate the point in question. He can talk genuine Lancashire when he likes; and as I write I am reminded of a couple of Lancashire anecdotes he told us one day, which he said were old, but perhaps some of my readers may not have heard them, so I give them as well as I can remember them. Of course, to have heard them given in the Lancashire dialect added greatly to their point.

It appears there used to be at one time a minister, who was Rector of Harpurhey Church. He was a man who was not too well liked in his parish, nor was he greatly noted for the amount of spiritual work he did amongst the people. For convenience we will call him Marshall. He had amongst his parishioners an old Lancashire fellow, who had been in bad health for some time, and the minister eventually went to call upon him and see how he was getting on.

The minister entered the room where the invalid was

lying, when the following dialogue took place: –

"Well, John," said the minister, "how are you getting on? I hope you are feeling better."

"No, I connot say as oi do, Maister Marshall," answered John. "I dout as oi've pretty nearly finished wi' this world, and I mun be looking out for'th next."

"I'm sorry you are so low about yourself, John. What is your particular ailment?" asked the minister.

"Oi connot sleep at noights," replied John; "and when I do get sleeping oi'm troubled wi' bad dreams; they freeten me."

"And what is it you dream about?" said Mr. Marshall. "Tell me all about your dreams, it may help to relieve you."

"Thank you kindly, Maister Marshall, perhaps it will," said the old man. "Well'th last bad dream as oi had, I thought I wur dead, and wurse thon that, that I wur taken down below. Th' place wur awfu' hot and I wur very uncomfortable. It seems down theer there ain't no sitting accommodation for ordinary folk, and I had to walk about, hot as it wur until I wur loike to drop. There was one arm cheer as I seed, but it were red hot, so I didn't loike to sit in it. And I went on walking about until my feet fair ached again. At last I could ston' it no longer, and I wur fain to go and sit in th' cheer hot as it wur. I hadn't been theer above a minute or two, when a chap cum up to see me and sez, ' Here, I say, John, you munnut sit in that cheer.' 'Whoy not,' sez oi. ' Oh,' he says, 'that cheer's not for the loike of you; it's reserved' 'Reserved or not, sez oi, ' I mun sit somewheer, and there's no wheer else to sit as oi can see.' 'I connot help that, John,' said the m.on, 'you mun get out of it as fast as you con. That cheer is being kept ready for Maister Marshall, o' Harpurhey.' "

What Mr. Marshall said I do not know, but John did not see him again for some time. However, John continued to be very poorly, and eventually he paid him another visit in order to comfort and condole with him.

"Well, John," said the minister, "I hope you are feeling

a little easier."

"Well," said John, "perhaps oi om a bit better nor oi wur, but oi'm still troubled wi' me dreams, oi connot get off em."

"Indeed," said Mr. Marshall, "and what were you dreaming about this time?"

"Oh, same old thing, I thought as oi wur dead," replied John.

"What again," said his minister.

"Aye, but this time I thought oi wur taken up instead o' down, which were an improvement onth' last deeing. When oi geet op to'th gate, oi knocked to get in, but they wouldn't open th' dur. They told me as they didn't know me, and that thee'd bin no arrangement made for me. Oi said as I mun geet in, and I kept on knocking. At length Peter himself came to'th dur and asked me who I wur. Oi tould him as my name wur John Waggett, and that oi wur one of Maister Marshall's congregation. 'What,' he sez, ' Marshall O' Harpurhey.' 'The very mon,' sez oi. When he heard that he tould them to open th' dur at once. 'Come in, John,' sez he. 'We havna had a mon from Marshall's o' Harpurhey for mony a yurr.' "

The same member was talking one day about some subscription and the inadequate response that had been made to it. He said it reminded him of the American gentleman who was lecturing somewhere, and when at the close he sent round his hat for the usual collection, it was eventually returned to him – empty. "Gentlemen," said the lecturer, "in such an audience as this I am thankful to get even my hat back."

It is a great gift to be always ready with some anecdote that fits in appropriately with the topic of conversation. The member of the M.C.C. to whom I refer is especially gifted in that direction, and when he is in the mood his flow of conversation and anecdote helps to make half-an-hour pass very rapidly.

Another member of the club who, when he is there, is not easily overlooked, is the Alderman – an Alderman par excellence. Robust of form, gracious of manner, eloquent of speech, he is withal a true lover and very fair exponent of the game of chess. He loves a pipe, and you realise, as you look at him sitting at the chessboard with the fragrant fumes of his choice tobacco, impressing themselves upon your senses, you realise that you see before you a man who knows how to enjoy his "otium cum dignitate."

Then I must not forget to mention the Club Cat. At once when you cast your eyes on Mr. Thomas Cat, you realise that he is no ordinary creature of his kind. He has none of the soft, sidling, purring ways about him noticeable in most cats. He is a regular little Englishman, a John Bull of a fellow. If you are on his visiting list, he comes forward to you in a downright straightforward sort of style, looks up in your face, opens his mouth, and speaks to you. Most cats whine, but he speaks out plainly what he has on his mind. He almost says in so many words, "Well, here you are again, old fellow, and I am very glad to see you; give us a wag of your paw." Yes, he is quite ready to shake hands; and if you are one of his particular friends, if you make a hoop with your arms he will jump through it. But he does it in a sort of way, as much as to say, "Well there, if you wish I'll jump for you, but really you know this kind of thing is rather childish." There is nothing of the sneak about our Thomas Cat; he says what he means, and means what he does. I am sure if at any time he has any disagreement with another of his tribe, he will express himself very clearly; he will let that other cat know and feel what he thinks of him.

The Manchester Chess Club.

To the Editor of the "Manchester Weekly Times.

"SIR,– It is now some four years ago since I ventured to lay before you my impressions and conclusions with regard to the Club and some of its members, not forgetting even the cat. It is very probable I should not, for many reasons, have broken silence again, were it not for the impression made upon me by the lamented death of our worthy ex-President (John Whittaker, of Nelson). And this it is which has induced me to say a few words respecting the changes which have come over the Club and its members during that period of time. And first of all as to the Club itself, which, thanks, I consider, in a large measure to the energy, devotion, and supervision of our genial President, has developed lately into a comfortable and attractive clubroom, and one which certainly ought to induce those who profess to have a love for the great game to enroll themselves as members. For it is a place where even those who may not be active exponents of the game may pass many very pleasant hours in social intercourse, and it is an astonishment to me that, situated as the rooms are, in such close proximity to the Manchester Exchange, people do not more readily avail themselves of the advantages which are offered them. And now to speak of some of its members. As I glance back through the last few years I recognise the stern fact that death has been busy amongst us, but more especially has the Club felt the impress of his cold hand in the person of our kindly ex-President, John Whittaker. Until bad health overtook him, his very entrance into the clubroom was like a sunbeam, for he was so merry and bright that his presence did us all good, and it is sad to think that he will never again gallop through the moves of a game of chess to a running accompaniment of puns and pleasantries with those around him. It was always a pleasure to sit at the table where he might be playing, and I never heard a harsh or unkind word fall from his mouth; he was too full of the milk of human kindness to do or say anything with a sting in it. But although he and others have passed away, and we mourn their loss, there are still many of the old faces left to cheer us with their presence. Our chatty friend is there, as of old, ready to entertain the gallery with his humorous remarks and suggestions on the various games, or anything else that may come into his mind. And although the 'Inspector-general' may have to call him to order from time to time, we feel that his enforced silence would be a distinct loss to the Club in general, and to the gallery in particular. Then the members who delight themselves in playing back games are still in evidence, and continue with wonderful self-satisfaction the working out of their ghost-like problems. We have the member who still charms with his pessimistic utterances about the position of his game, and how his opponent is making matters uncomfortable for him, but these jeremiads are usually followed by his enemy's downfall, whilst a smile of almost child-like innocence is seen escaping over his countenance. There are many of whom I would like to say a word or two, but time and space are precious. I can only say that as 'One of the Gallery' I have made many friendships in the rooms of the Manchester Chess Club which I shall always prize. By the way, I must not forget Mr. Thomas Cat; he is still with us, and as genuine a fellow as he ever was.

"Yours truly, ONE OF THE GALLERY." November 29th, 1901.

CHAPTER LV

Some of the Churches and Chapels of Manchester and Salford and their past Ministers – St. Simon's and the Rev. Ephraim Harper – St. Alban's and the Rev. J. E. Sedgwick.

ANY critical retrospect on my part of the ministers of the various denominations who during the last fifty years have helped to form and develop the religious life of our community, would be a task altogether beyond my capabilities; and yet it seems to me that having, during that period of time, been brought into, more or less, personal contact with a large number of our local divines, some slight account of those who helped to mould our spiritual life, and of their good work in our midst, may not be altogether without interest at the present time. Such a record must partake very much of gleanings here and there, a collection of what might be termed shreds and patches, which have been jotted down from time to time in the note-book of my memory. My excuse for making these remarks is, that in my younger days, with regard to preachers I was somewhat of a cosmopolitan in my nature. That is to say, I took a real pleasure in listening to able preachers of various denominations, trying to discover how many points there were amongst them on which there was agreement rather than the reverse, and endeavouring to avoid being unduly biassed by sectarianism. For this reason I have found myself from time to time in Churches many and various, and have thus been enabled and privileged to form a fair judgment of the capabilities of some of the ministers, who in the days that are gone have helped so materially to elevate and direct the energies and wealth of the people into high, worthy and noble channels. For I think it will be conceded that, on the whole, the people of Manchester and Salford are kindly, warm-hearted and generous, and, being so, it was fortunate that their impulses were guided, stimulated and encouraged by the various ministers who had been placed here, and acted as spiritual guardians to their numerous flocks.

Manchester, and indeed Lancashire, was at that time jumping, as it might be said, to prosperity in every direction, and it was therefore most important that the increasing wealth of the community should be directed into wisely and well-considered schemes of philanthropy and charity. The ministers of the various denominations had, therefore, the opportunity and responsibility given them of, to a certain extent, guiding the outflow, and I think as one looks back it must be allowed that they acted with wisdom and discretion, when one considers the many noble institutions which have sprung up amongst us during the last 50 years.

In this catalogue of the ministers of religion who have materially helped in building up these numerous institutions for good, I would mention Hugh Stowell, Maclaren, Bardsley, MacFadyen, Parker, McKerrow, McCaw, and Fraser – the late Bishop of Manchester. There were, of course, many others who, although perhaps not such shining lights, did good and strenuous work in our midst, and to whom the thanks of the community are also due.

It was in 1845 that we went as a family to live in Broughton, and soon after doing so we joined St. Simon's Church in Springfield Lane, Salford, which was consecrated in the year 1849, by Bishop Lee[28], the first Bishop of Manchester. It was the first time that I had witnessed such a ceremony, and it impressed me greatly. The Reverend Ephraim Harper was the first Rector appointed to this living, and, although he was not by any means a brilliant preacher, he was thoughtful, earnest and conscientious in the discharge of his duties, and we sat under him for many years.

It might be mentioned here that before the bridge

was built in Sherbourne Street over the Irwell we had to go to St. Simon's along Great Clowes Street and across Broughton Bridge, over which there was a toll charge of one halfpenny from Salford to Broughton, but those living in Broughton passed over free. This charge was disputed by the people of Salford, and the feeling raised against it was so strong that a fund was started to oppose the toll, and a ferry boat plied free of charge from Salford, to the Broughton side of the river. Eventually it was considered best to abolish the small charge, which did more harm than good.

The Rector of St. Simon's was evangelical in his views; in fact I think I might say that there was not at this time any High Church party, at least as we now understand the term, in either Manchester or Salford. The Rector preached in the black Geneva gown, only some very few of the clergy then preaching in the white surplice; in fact I think that the only two points which might be looked upon as at all ritualistic in those days consisted in the wearing of the white surplice when preaching, and turning towards the East when repeating the Belief. The evangelical party looked upon even these two small innovations with dread and suspicion, and as very Romish in their tendency, but they had not to wait long before these matters were mere trifles to the innovations which followed.

What might be termed the religious gala day of the year for young people was the Whit-Sunday gathering of the school children connected with the various churches. On these occasions the whole of the front portion of the centre aisle of the church was reserved for the children. The girls, from the smallest mites upwards, were dressed in pure white, with close-fitting white muslin caps on their heads. It was a pretty sight to see all these bright-looking little ones, grouped in the centre of the church, and singing the hymns especially appointed and printed for the occasion, with their pure, sweet, treble voices. This was always a red-letter day at St. Simon's, and for weeks before the mothers would be getting their girls' dresses ready, so that they might look their very best. Probably vanity had a certain share in what they did, but after all it was a very pardonable weakness. Another impressive service was the admission of young men and maidens to their first Communion. The arrangements were the same as they are at the present time, the Bishop appointing a certain Sunday and church in some district where all those going forward for Confirmation were assembled. The young girls on this occasion would be all dressed in pure white, with simple muslin veils, and it was a solemn and a beautiful sight to see one side of the church filled with these bride-like maidens. Such a fair scene, and such an impressive dedication of young life, could not but have a beneficial effect on those engaged in it.

Of course there was at St. Simon's the usual Sunday School connected with the church, where a band of active young workers, headed by the curate, the Rev. J. E. Sedgwick, reaped the success of their self-denying labours. Amongst those who were most prominent in this work were T. W. Freston, Arthur Bates and Roderick Anderson, supplemented by a number of zealous young ladies. It was during his curacy at St. Simon's that the Rev. J. E. Sedgwick developed his very High Church tendencies, which eventually caused him to resign his position as curate. After he left he took a small place in Moulton Street, closely adjoining Lockett's engraving works, and it was here that he laid the foundation of St. Alban's Church and congregation. Mr. Sedgwick, who was a man full of youthful earnestness and quiet determination, as well as being a strong religious devotee, soon gathered round him a large body of enthusiastic workers, over whom he exercised a wonderful influence. He was gifted with great zeal and self-sacrifice, and he soon succeeded in building up a church and congregation which have long been noted in Manchester for their extremely high ritualistic practices, but at the same time for their devotion and

28. *First Bishop of Manchester 1848-1870*

work. As may be supposed, outside those who were his whole-hearted supporters he was not regarded with much favour on account of his extreme views; but he fought on in spite of determined opposition, living practically the life of a monk. He established a Guild of Sisters of Mercy, who visited and worked the parish as it had never been done before. The poor and the distressed of the district were looked after and cared for in a way which soon won them over to his cause; and so, when the Church of St. Alban's, in Waterloo Road, was sufficiently advanced to allow of services being held in it, it was soon filled with worshippers. Of course it made a serious difference to St. Simon's Church when Mr. Sedgwick and his devoted auxiliaries seceded from it, and so there was more to do for those who were left behind.

Some of my sisters taught in the Sunday School, and on one occasion an amusing incident happened in connection therewith, in which I figured somewhat uncomfortably. There was one young lady, a friend of my sisters, who used to call for them before breakfast on the Sunday mornings, so that they might walk down together to the school. At the time to which I refer a cousin of mine was staying with us on a visit, and he happened to be a notedly good hand at a practical joke. On the morning in question, having just risen, we saw from our bedroom window that the young lady had just come to the door. My relative dared me to go down to the dining-room, where she was waiting, and put my head inside the door. I at once accepted the challenge, without pausing to consider the fitness of things, for in my boyish days for me to be dared, was in most cases, to do. Our attire was somewhat primitive, and might have passed muster amongst the Indian chiefs barring the lack of tomahawks and scalps, but, however picturesque from this point of view, blankets, though voluminous, and dishevelled locks are hardly full dress. Well, down the stairs we rushed, and I had no sooner popped my head inside the door with "Good morning" on my lips, than I felt myself pushed suddenly and violently from behind, and landed into the room. At the same time the door was shut and held behind me to prevent any retreat. My feelings may be imagined, and dragging open the door I escaped upstairs as quickly as my legs would carry me, whilst the derisive laughter of my relative was heard in the distance. Moral, never be dared!

CHAPTER LVI

Canon McGrath – Canon Bardsley – Canon Hugh Stowell – Doctor Parker.

PRIOR to St. Paul's Church, Kersal, being built, Canon McGrath was Rector of St. Ann's Church in the City, where he had a large body of worshippers, by whom he was greatly beloved. He was succeeded at St. Ann's by the Reverend James Bardsley, between whom, except that both were able, earnest Christian ministers, a greater contrast could hardly be imagined. In appearance, Canon McGrath was an exceptionally handsome, refined-looking man, whereas the Reverend James Bardsley was perhaps one of the plainest men to be found in the streets of Manchester, a fact of which he was himself quite aware. But although this was so, the real goodness of the man shone out in his face, making his otherwise plain features even attractive. He was a taller man than Mr. McGrath and more robust, but without his grace of manner or carriage, being heavy of foot and ungainly in walk. But James Bardsley was such an honest, true and good man that his little gaucheries almost helped to endear him the more to all who knew him. The differences noticeable between these two men physically were quite as apparent in their discourses. Mr. McGrath preached with studied finish, every sentence and thought being expressed clearly, logically and in the most carefully-considered language. Mr. Bardsley, on the other hand, had a direct, blunt manner and address, giving utterance to his thoughts in the simplest of language, but at the same time forcibly, carrying conviction to the listener with every sentence that he spoke. With Mr. McGrath you felt that the ideas of the preacher on his subject had reached their end and climax with the close of his sermon; but with the other when his time expired and he had to close, you felt that he had only, as it were, begun to warm to his subject – that ideas so crowded in upon him that the difficulty was to give them time for utterance. Both these ministers filled their appointed places in the busy round of our Manchester life, and did so in the highest and worthiest sense, leaving a felt blank when they had each in their appointed time passed away.

Mr. McGrath was succeeded at St. Paul's Church, Kersal, by the Reverend Charles Dallas Marston, a remarkably gifted preacher, and full as this Church had been in Mr. McGrath's time, it was often impossible to obtain sittings whilst Mr. Marston occupied its pulpit. It was quite a pleasant sight to see the worshippers trooping into Kersal Church at this period of its existence, the road being crowded with the people who attended there. Mr. Marston afterwards left for London, but subsequently fell into bad health and had to retire from ministerial work. I sat under him for some years, and it was a privilege to do so, as he was a most eloquent preacher, as well as a very good man. In those days the Church itself was very full, whilst the Churchyard was comparatively empty. But death has been busy since Kersal Church was erected in the year 1851, and now the Churchyard is crowded with its memorials to those who have passed away.

Canon, or, as he was more familiarly and affectionately designated, Hugh Stowell, occupied a very important position amongst us for many years, and he formed what might be termed at one period of his life, the pivot on which the religious life of Manchester and Salford turned both in the pulpit and on the platform, he stood forth pre-eminent as preacher and speaker. He was a man of strong feelings and strong convictions, and was capable on account of his eloquence and personality of deeply impressing his listeners and awakening them to a sense of their duties and responsibilities. The cause which had managed to enlist Hugh Stowell as its advocate was sure of an able supporter, as his intense earnestness carried conviction with all he said. Christ Church, Salford, of which he was the Rector (after leaving St. Stephen's, where he had been curate), was filled to overflowing, and it was a difficult matter for visitors, of whom there was an abundance, to find accommodation, in spite of the noted courtesy of the regular seat-holders, who were always ready to put themselves to much inconvenience in order to oblige the numbers who came to listen to the great preacher from far and near. When it became known, too, that Hugh Stowell was to be one of the speakers at any public meeting crowds of people always flocked to hear him; and when money was required for any worthy object, an appeal from Hugh Stowell always met with a ready response. An amusing incident came to my knowledge in connection with some fund in which he was interested, and for which he was raising some £1,200. As usual in such cases, he went first to a staunch supporter of his, Robert Gardiner, who was both wealthy and generous, but somewhat peculiar at times. In this instance he complained that Mr. Stowell always came to him to head the list of subscribers, and declined to make the start. He told him to go to another supporter of his whom he named, but told him that whatever this man gave he would give five times as much. The other man, although well off, was not noted for being over generous, and Robert (familiarly known as Bobby) Gardiner, thought he had mentally gauged the giving limit of his friend. With this handle Hugh Stowell induced his other friend to head the list with £100, being especially moved to do so, when he knew the condition which attached to his donation.

When Hugh Stowell returned and told Robert Gardiner what he had done, the latter winced a bit, no doubt, but he gave his £500 like a man. Those, in Manchester, were the days of big givings, that is to say, taking into account the then size and wealth of the community.

In appearance Hugh Stowell was a tall, massive man, with a commanding presence, yet his face was not strong-looking in repose. When, however, he became fired with the subject he had in hand, he seemed to become inspired, his whole face lighted up, and the words flowed from him in an unbroken stream of eloquence, and with a wealth of power and energy of which at a first glance he seemed incapable. When in the pulpit he would take hold of the large Bible which lay before him, with a nervous, twitching action, his first words were halting and almost disconnected, and to anyone listening to him for the first time, they did not give promise of great things. But then, as he warmed to his subject, his eye brightened, his form became erect, his lip hardened, all hesitancy disappeared, and you listened in rapt attention.

I often visited his Church, crossing over from Broughton along the Suspension Bridge, which is now a thing of the past. I shall always remember one particular Sunday evening when we walked over in the usual way. It happened to be just after the trial of a doctor of the name of Palmer, who had been condemned for the murder of a man named Cook. The case created a great sensation at the time, as the murder had been committed in a slow, calculating, deliberate manner by poison, and the public mind was very much exercised about it. This was the topic on this evening which he chose for his discourse, taking as his text the words from the book of **ii. Kings, ch. 8, v. 13:** *"Is thy servant a dog that he should do this great thing."* Hazael's words were in answer to Elisha when he told him of all the evil he would do; and the sincerity of Hazael's reply denying the bare possibility of his committing the wickedness prophesied by the Man of God.

It was, I think, one of the most powerful appeals to man's better nature to which I ever listened, pointing us, as he did, to the fact that the crime which would horrify at first, continued sin will enable the wicked to contemplate and carry out at length without remorse; that in the pathway of sin there is absolutely no limit to man's depravity, but that there is an education in crime as there is in everything else. The premises of the sermon were probably neither very original nor even uncommon, but the eloquence and earnestness with which his conclusions were brought home to the minds of his listeners were powerful in the extreme.

It is astonishing how the comicalities of life cling even to the most serious things, as an incident which comes to my mind will serve to illustrate. I have the impression that it happened at Christ Church, but it is so long ago that I may be wrong as to where it occurred. My sister at one time when leaving the house for church, took up as she supposed her Prayer Book and hurried away. When seated in the pew at church she as usual placed her book before her, well in the sight of all the worshippers about her. As she rose to take part in the service and was about to take her Prayer Book into her hand, to her horror she saw staring her in the face, and in bold letters, somebody's – I forget who's – "Book of Comic Songs." Her shame and confusion may be imagined.

So many years have come and gone since Dr. Parker was the Pastor of Cavendish Street Chapel that to some it may come as a surprise to be told that he ever had a ministerial charge in Manchester. But this was so, and he occupied for years a very important position in the Church life of our City, for he was a man of exceptional capabilities, and of great originality of mind. He might by some be considered somewhat dramatic in his style, and this appearance lent itself to this style of preaching, as although not large of stature he had very mobile features and long flowing locks which he threw back from his forehead, thus lending particular emphasis to what he was saying. I have heard from him some most excellent discourses, powerfully and effectively delivered. I remember that at one time he was delivering a series of addresses on Moses, and so remarkable were they that whilst they continued I willingly journeyed each Sunday evening from Broughton all the way to Stretford Road on foot to hear him.

He had some peculiarities which were quite his own. For instance, after some special effort, which had perhaps told upon him, I have seen him sit down in the middle of his discourse and take a rest, and then continue his subject where he had left off. His was perhaps more the American style of preaching, and he reminded me greatly of Talmage whom I heard when he was at the zenith of his fame in America, and with whom I must say I was greatly impressed, both with his originality and also with his strong, practical, commonsense Christianity. But he, too, had his peculiarities; for example, when he entered the platform from which he preached, he came in with hat, coat and umbrella as if he were entering a private house, actions which to the ordinary English mind, gave at first an impression almost of irreverence, but this soon wore off when he entered fully into the subject matter of his discourse.

Similarly, Dr. Parker had certain eccentricities of manner and speech, at which at times one was disposed to smile, but this was but the shell, and when he presented you with the kernel you felt satisfied. When he migrated to London he soon had a large congregation of worshippers, and his services and addresses at the Temple became quite noted. He was a man of very independent views on questions social, political and religious, and on all of them he spoke out freely and fearlessly. He has now passed away honoured and respected after a long life, crowded with work.

CHAPTER LVII

Trinity Presbyterian Church and the Rev. William McCaw – Chorlton Road Chapel and the Rev. J. L. Macfadyen – Union Chapel and the Rev. Alexander MacLaren – The Rev. Arthur Mursell – St. Alban's and the Rev. Knox-Little.

OF the ministers who were connected with the English Presbyterian Church in Manchester there is none more worthy of notice than the Rev. William McCaw, afterwards Doctor McCaw. He was the first minister of Trinity Presbyterian Church, in New Bridge Street, now converted into the Young Women's Christian Association. Trinity Church has lately been rebuilt on Cheetham Hill Road, at the top of Waterloo Road. The foundation-stone of the original Church was laid on the 13th of August, 1845. Mr. McCaw, a North of Ireland man, soon proved himself a most acceptable pastor to the large congregation which quickly gathered round him, and although he was not perhaps what might be considered exactly a brilliant preacher, yet on occasions even this title might have been fairly applied to him, and under all circumstances his discourses were both interesting and instructive. On certain topics he could wax very eloquent, and he was also a minister who most thoroughly and conscientiously prepared himself for his pulpit ministrations. As a visitor, too, amongst his flock he could not have been excelled, and high and low, rich and poor, always found in Mr. McCaw a kindly adviser and a true, reliable friend. In the sick room he was always a welcome guest, bright, cheery, sympathetic and warm-hearted.

He was a hard worker both in his Church and out of it, at all times ready to take his full share of the labours and responsibilities which must devolve upon any minister who wishes to do his duty to the community in which he is placed. Whatever he undertook you might be sure it would be done thoroughly, courageously, and to the best of his ability, and he always impressed those with whom he came in contact and who had to work with him with his earnestness of purpose and his purity of motive.

Even on matters in which you found you were not able to agree with him, you could not but be satisfied of the transparent honesty of his convictions. There was no sting in anything he said, his nature was too kindly for that, and he was a man who was ready to believe in the integrity of your motives as well as his own. We should take no harm if a little more of this disposition existed amongst us, and more especially so in matters political, where it is far too much the custom to hint doubts at the bona fides of those from whom we differ.

He retired many years ago from the pastorate of Trinity Church, the work being too heavy for him, and he accepted a call to Jersey, where he remained for some years, and where he was much appreciated until lately he occupied the post of Clerk of Synod, which he filled with much ability for some time, and where his matured knowledge of Church law and discipline helped the ecclesiastical wheels of the Presbyterian Synod to revolve easily and smoothly. In this position he was always noted for his genial manner and kindly, courteous bearing, which were at all times appreciated by those with whom he came in contact. Eventually old age compelled him to give up all ministerial work, and he went to live in the North of Ireland, where he recently died, leaving behind him a very sweet and pleasant memory.

The Rev. J. A. Macfadyen, the Congregational minister of Chorlton Road Chapel, was a sound and able preacher, and a most zealous worker. In fact, so much so that it is thought that his death was in some measure accelerated by the strain which he put upon an over-taxed brain. I had many opportunities of hearing him in his own pulpit years ago, and was greatly struck with his quiet, thoughtful power as a preacher. He was a man whom, having once heard, you were anxious to hear again. However, it was more particularly as a systematic worker and organiser that he was such a pillar of strength, and lent such material aid to the Congregational cause. Wherever and whenever he was wanted he was ready to go, but working at such high pressure must tell its tale even on the strongest physique, and so in spite of his determination to still struggle on, he had to succumb at the last, and so he passed away worn out with work rather than with years.

It will be thirty-six years on the 15th of November next since Union Chapel, in Oxford Street, was opened for worship, and the Rev. Alexander MacLaren was appointed minister. Very fortunate it was for Manchester that the steps of such an exceptionally able man were directed to us, for he was a minister endowed with intellectual gifts of a very high order. He was a man of original mind, keen, logical and full of resource, whilst he was, moreover, a faithful ambassador of the Word, and a remarkably powerful preacher. With such characteristics Alexander MacLaren soon made a name for himself and gathered round him a large body of worshippers who were devoted to him. Never apparently very robust, he during the last thirty years took upon himself an amount of work of which many a stronger man might well have been proud. He has a style of preaching peculiarly his own, and owing to the almost painfully intense earnestness of his delivery one hearing him for the first time might not perhaps be favourably impressed. But when once you have become accustomed to his highly-strung nervous diction, you are then fully able to realise and appreciate as you listen to him, the exceptional ability of the man who is addressing you. The infirmities of years have at length compelled him to resign his ministerial charge at Union Chapel, but he is still with us, and his wonderful capabilities as a preacher and leader of religious thought, together with his many Christian activities, will long be remembered and gratefully acknowledged by the people of Manchester.

For many years the Reverend Arthur Mursell was a very well-known preacher in Manchester, and for some time large crowds attended his services which he held in the Free Trade Hall every Sunday evening. Some of those who flocked to hear him did so probably on account of the sensational character of his discourses, when often he would startle his hearers by the extraordinary things he said. He did good in his way, but I must confess that I never felt drawn towards him or his services, and did not personally attend his meetings. It was enough for me to see every Monday morning the walls and hoardings placarded with the title of his previous evening's address, which, as a rule, was more forcible than refined. His object no doubt was to arrest people's attention, and in this he was certainly successful; but as to whether it was wisely or judiciously done was a matter about which there was considerable difference of opinion. The titles of his lectures usually consisted of some slang expression or expletive, or perhaps some familiar joke of the day. With these, however, he was able to attract large crowds to listen to him; but at length he became stale, and so, unable perhaps to provide his audiences with fresh "tit-bits," his followers dwindled away, his lectures were discontinued, and eventually he left Manchester.

St. Alban's Church, Cheetwood, although built in 1864, was not consecrated by Bishop Fraser until 1874, the reason for this being that the ritualistic practices carried on at this church were disapproved of by both Bishops Lee and Fraser, and even at the last there was great difficulty in getting the latter to consent to its consecration. Of the various ministers who succeeded the Rev. J. E. Sedgwick at the Church of St. Albans there was no one who could compare with the Rev. Knox-Little, for, whatever his ritualistic practices or convictions were, there was no doubt as to the zeal and devotion which characterised his labour amongst the people of Cheetwood and its surroundings, nor as to the love and

THE REVEREND WILLIAM McCAW,
First Minister of Trinity Presbyterian Church.

esteem in which he was held by all who really knew him. Although physically anything but a strong man, yet the amount of personal work which he took upon himself was astonishing. I think it might fairly be said of him that he was never idle; whenever and wherever you saw him you felt that he was absorbed in his work. Even if he entered a tram he would endeavour to get into some quiet corner where he would become engrossed in some book, and appeared oblivious of all around him. But it was as a preacher that Knox-Little was more particularly gifted, and he had a soft persuasive eloquence which had a wonderful effect upon his listeners. When he rose in the pulpit you felt instinctively, as you looked at him and he commenced to speak, that his whole being was saturated with the subject matter of his discourse, that the man was speaking to you from his very heart, and that the only limit to his convincing eloquence was his physical endurance. However long he might preach the interest was sustained, and, feeling deeply the truths he was preaching, he seemed to have the power of transmitting to others what he himself felt and believed. His ideas came to him rapidly, and they were as quickly expressed in a natural flow of well-chosen language.

Whatever his teaching may have been as to religious form and doctrine, his sermons, so far as I have listened to them, were models for the furtherance of real practical Christianity. The vital part of his preaching appeared to be to make us all truer, better men and women, and, although I do not agree with him in some things, believe him to be an earnest, true-hearted, devoted Christian minister.

CHAPTER LVIII

The Wesleyan Body and H. B. Harrison – Dr. McKerrow and Lloyd St. Chapel – Dr. Guthrie, of Edinburgh – The late Bishop Fraser.

I FEAR it may be thought that in dealing with the subject of Ministers and Churches, that I may seem to be ignoring many able men of various denominations, other than those of whom I have been hitherto writing. This is certainly not my wish or desire; but I am in this matter narrowed down to mention only those with whom in some form or another I have come into direct and frequent contact. Of course I am fully aware of the great work done in Manchester and Salford by the Wesleyan body during the period of time to which I am referring; but one reason why their ministers do not come so prominently before the public is, that owing to the Circuit system, and the changing of their ministers periodically, they do not become so identified with the continuous life of a city or town, as if they had been permanently placed in a certain locality. I am sure their plan has many advantages, but after all there is a great deal in personality, and I have a strong conviction that where a minister is "the right man in the right place," the longer the connection continues, the better for the work as a whole. In such a case the man is able to do and say things, and to call forth the efforts of his people, in a way that it seems to me, a changing ministry is not so well able to do.

Of course, in the Wesleyan body more labour and responsibility devolves upon the lay members of their congregations, and an instance of such a member comes before me in the person of H. B. Harrison, than whom a more hard-working, energetic, cheery Christian layman it would be difficult to meet with. Whatever this man did he put his whole soul into it. Christianity with him was all that was bright, attractive and encouraging; and he not only thought and felt this himself, but he had the happy knack of imbuing those with whom he came into contact with the same spirit. His was a hearty, healthy, robust Christianity, which carried conviction with it wherever he went. He was for some years a member of the Committee of the Boys' Refuges and Homes, and in other ways was a most active, thorough worker. He was taken away very suddenly, and his death was not only a serious loss to the Wesleyan body itself, but also to all Christian work in this part of the country.

It seems very difficult to realise that in Lloyd Street, opposite to where the Manchester Town Hall stands, there stood in my young days the Presbyterian Chapel, where for thirty years the Rev. William McKerrow ministered to his flock prior to the removal of the chapel to Brunswick Street in the year 1858. In those days business and religion were often very closely associated as regards locality. For instance, it seems strange to be told that the Sunday Schools of Lloyd Street Chapel, were in the upper part of a warehouse, then occupied by a Greek shipping firm, Tamvaco, Micrulachi and Mavrogordato; so that in the wareroom below goods were being prepared for shipment to clothe the bodies of the heathen, whilst in the room above children of the neighbourhood were being spiritually cared for. Only those who know what Lloyd Street and its surroundings were like fifty years ago are able to form any conception of or appreciate the changes which have taken place in that locality. The improvements are so widespread that it is a difficult matter to bring back to one's mind what the place was like in the old days. A little below where Dr. McKerrow's chapel stood, there were numbers of dilapidated tenements and dens of every kind, with inhabitants to match them. Even to this day there are a few of the old buildings left, which can serve as a sample of what this spot resembled when these harmonised with the whole.

On one side of Brazennose Street a number of the old private houses are still to be seen; but they are now turned into offices and warehouses. About thirty years ago I had offices in this street in one of these old private houses, and I was informed by an elderly lady friend, and a relative of Dr. McKerrow's, that she occupied the house where my offices were, and that my private office had formerly been her kitchen, and the general office and wareroom had been manufactured out of the back-yard. This same lady also pointed out to me, what I had not previously observed, namely, that the cupboards and drawers, and the door leading into the hall were all made of good old mahogany. In those days ladies were permitted to go into their own kitchens, and even to indulge in a little fancy cooking, without-being ordered out by the cook; so they bestowed a little more care and expense on kitchens then when building private houses.

Close round the spot to which I am alluding there was an admixture of churches and chapels, respectability and poverty, elbowing each other in a most incongruous fashion.

My personal knowledge of Dr. McKerrow commenced after he had migrated to Brunswick Street. Like the Rev. James Bardsley, he could not have been designated a handsome man, but "handsome is that handsome does," for he was an able, earnest preacher, and a capital worker. As there are some Irishmen who somehow never lose their brogue, so there are Scotchmen who also never lose their native accent. Dr. McKerrow was one of these, and although he had lived in Manchester for over fifty years, he was, I think, as essentially Scotch in his utterance as if he had never quitted the land of his birth. The Doctor was a man who had very strong political convictions, and he was not one to hide them under a bushel. He was a frequent contributor to the columns of the *Examiner and Times*, which was in his time a very powerful and widely-read organ of the Liberal party in this district. He was, too, a large shareholder in the paper, and it was,

I think, often his mouthpiece on many of the religious, political and social questions of the day.

The last time I heard him speak in public was at the funeral of John Stuart, the banker, but he was on this occasion very infirm, and he evidently felt that it would not be long before he, too, would be laid in his last resting place. He fully realised that he had finished his course, and that the time of his departure was at hand. As I have already said, I cannot pretend to mention a tithe of the men who ministered amongst us, nor yet of those who came from near and far to stir us up to a more active Spiritual life. But, I believe, it was a pleasure for such men to fill our pulpits and to be found on our platforms, to share in the throb of our busy City life, and to further the various Christian causes for which they pleaded.

Amongst these visitors there is one whom I would like to single out, and that for a special reason. I allude to Dr. Guthrie, of Edinburgh, and my reason for making an exception in his case is that I would like very much to refer to a sermon which I heard him preach about forty years ago in the Free Trade Hall. It was a discourse which I shall never forget, and the impression it made upon me was so great that perhaps I may be excused if I shortly epitomise its heads. The text was, "Thy calf, oh Samaria, hath cast thee off." The words as he uttered them hardly seemed to present themselves as being capable of any exceptionally powerful treatment, but if anyone who reads these pages happened to be present on the occasion to which I refer, they will, I am sure, confirm me in saying that this sermon of Dr. Guthrie's was one of the most dramatic and heart-searching appeals to which they ever listened. Crowded as the hall was to its fullest capacity, the preacher seemed to hold his audience spellbound. Except for the one full, clear ringing voice which filled that huge hall, there was otherwise a stillness that made itself felt. Of course in any case it must be mentioned that at the time of which I write Dr. Guthrie was considered to be perhaps the finest orator of his day, but I imagine he even excelled himself on that particular evening. There are times in the lives of such men when they appear to be inspired, and this was what he seemed to be on that occasion, for every point of his sermon struck home with startling and true dramatic effect.

He spoke first of the curse the Golden Calf had been to the children of Israel, and how its worship had brought upon them God's judgments again and again, and how, whatever they did and wherever they went, the consequences of their idolatry pursued them. Then he proceeded to make a personal application of the text, pointing out how every sin which we fall down to and worship becomes our golden calf, bringing with it its inevitable punishment. Selfishness, ambition, worldliness, impurity, intemperance, each with its own special attractions and with it its own special judgment. And so as each sin was vividly pictured with its climax and final punishment, he would stretch forth his arm at the imaginary sinner and, as it were, single him out, giving sentence against him, as the words of the text rang through the hall, "Thy Calf, oh Samaria, hath cast thee off."

And now, before bringing these clerical reminiscences to a close, there is just one other man respecting whom I must say a few words, for he was one who filled a large place in the affections, not only of the people of Manchester and Salford, but of Lancashire as a whole. I allude to the Rev. James Fraser, who succeeded the Rev. James Prince Lee as Bishop of Manchester in 1870. Bishop Fraser was a man who endeared himself to everyone with whom he came into contact, and so much so that he went by the affectionate soubriquet, of "The Bishop of all denominations." He was, and could be, loyal to his own Church, and yet have full sympathy with those outside its pale. The effect of this was that there was more active co-operation amongst the various Christian Churches, an object very dear to his heart. He was certainly one of the most lovable, simple-minded ministers of the Gospel, with whom it was possible to come into contact; and he was always ready, in spite of the very heavy official duties which devolved upon him, to go anywhere or do anything if he could be of service to a good cause. It was a real pleasure to see his bright, fresh, genial countenance wherever you met it, and to listen to the tones of his voice so expressive of kindly sympathy. I have never seen what might be termed a hard look upon his face, although at times. I have seen it troubled, and this more especially during the later years of his life, when exceptional ecclesiastical anxieties pressed so heavily upon him, and when the ever-increasing burden of work had broken down to a certain extent his otherwise natural elasticity of mind and body. More particularly I call to mind the last occasion on which he attended the annual meeting of the Boys' and Girls' Refuges. When speaking on the report dealing with all the misery, distress and neglect with which these institutions have to deal, a sadly troubled look came into his face as he spoke of all these human problems of our earthly existence which were crying aloud for solution, and which, in spite of Christian effort, were so difficult to surmount and grapple with in any adequate manner.

The late Bishop Fraser and his wife, the latter of whom died some years ago, were always true and fast friends of the Refuge, ready at all times to take their share in the work. It was delightful to see the Bishop going in and out amongst the boys and girls with a bright, cheery word for each and all, which won the hearts not only of the boys and girls themselves, but also of those who witnessed the kindliness of heart which prompted all he said and did.

If he could not be called a powerful preacher, he always at least spoke from the depths of a wellspring of deep Christian love. If the cause for which he was speaking had his full knowledge and sympathy, he pleaded for it with simple, but impressive earnestness. To hear him preach on a Christmas morning did anybody good to

THE LATE BISHOP FRASER

*Elected to the current Diocese of
Manchester, January 21st 1870*

listen to him, for you realised what this season meant to him, and what he wished it to be to all who heard him, a day of goodwill, a time of innocent rejoicing and gladness. The dear, good Bishop passed away very suddenly at the last, and very few had even heard that he was ill. When therefore the midday papers flashed the news of his death through the City there was real sorrow and sinking of heart. For we realised as a community that we had lost one near and dear to us all, a good and true man, and a faithful ambassador of his Lord and Master.

INDEX

15 puzzle 230

Abdullah Ydlibi (Manchester Consul for the Ottoman Empire) 309
Agecroft 78
Agecroft Bridge 79
Albert Park 57
Albert Square 156
Albion Club, The 166
Alderman Ivie Mackie 161
Alderman Willert 84
All Saint's, Oxford Rd 182
Ardwick 187
Ardwick Green 184,185
Ardwick Hall 187
Art Gallery, Mosley St 138
Assize Courts 105
Athenæum Cricket Club 107,319

Bancroft Street 144
Bank of Manchester 172
Bank Street 162
Barge, Thomas 84
Belle Vue 76
Benani (Egyptian trader) 213
Bengelun (Moor businessman) 212
Ben Lang's 116
Birch, Tom 298
Birch jnr., William 315
Bishop Fraser 291
Bishop Lee, first Bishop of Manchester 328
Black Bridge 208
Blackburne 318
Blackfield Lane 77,79
Blackstake Farm 191,192
Blagomeno, A. D. 304

Bleackley's Farm 52
Bles, S D (shipping merchant) 293
Bond Street (now Princess St) 141,145
Bonfire Night - descriptions of 223
Booth Street 166,183
Borough Court 171
Brazennose Street 126, 143,347
Bridge Street 129,130,132,133
Bright, John (MP) 157,160
Brooks, G. V. (actor) 260
Broom Lane 76
Broughton 53
Broughton Bridge (Great Clowes St.) 329
Broughton Cricket Club 54
Broughton Lane 50,54,73,205,206,294
Broughton Priory (Harrop's Folly) 60
Broughton Town Hall 54
Brown's Chop House 153
Brown Street 166, 167, 169,171
Brunswick Street 346
Burlington Street 194
Bury New Road 50,51,52,73,76, 83,84,90,96,303
Buses 181,183

"Cheap John" 43
Cababe, Paul & Peter 310
Callender, William Romaine (MP) 145,157
Calvert, Charles (actor) 263,269,270
Campfield 39
Cannon Street 34

Canon McGrath 333
Carol singers 66
Cateaton Street 118
Cavendish Street Chapel 337
Chancery Lane 166
Cheetham Hill 76,187
Cheetham Hill Road 80
Cheetwood Lane 94,99
chimney sweeps 9,184
Chorlton-on-Medlock 7,189
Chorlton Road Chapel 340
Chorlton Street 149
City News, The 192
Clarence Street 141,143
Clarendon Club,
Mosley St 86, 166
Cliff, The (Salford) 63,74,205
Coach travel 169
Cobden Liberal Club 54
Comber, Dr 24
Congregational Chapel 89
Conservative Party, The 157
Constantinople 301,304
Cooper Street 20,141,143,145
Corporation Street 84,153
Cotton Famine Relief Fund 146
County Prison
(Strangeways) 105
cricket 54,57
croquet 232
Cross Street 131,141,150,162,167
Crown Court 105
Cruikshank, George (artist) 200
Curtis, Matthew 190
cycling 233

Dalton, Dr. John 8,138
Davenport Brothers, The
229,250
David Street 141
Dean Maclure 85
Deansgate
39,118,121,126,128,138
Dickens, Charles 5,29,143
Disraeli, Benjamin 29
Dr. Beard's School 73
Dr. McKerrow 347

Dr. Radford 77
Drinkwater's Park 79
Ducie Street 160,162
Duke of Wellington 218

Earl of Ellesmere 218
Elections 159
Exchange 150
Exchange Street 150,151

Fairfield Street 184
Faucit, Helen (actress) 271
Faulkner Street 8,17,36,141
Fawkes, Guy 115
Ferguson, John 316
fires 17
Fitzgerald's Castle 61,62,63,208
Fountain Street 166
Franconi's Hippodrome 30
Free Trade Hall
29,258,283,315,342,348
Frith, William Powell 200

gas, use of 34
General Post Office 171
George Street 17
Gilbert and Sullivan 281
Gladstone, Murray 290,291
Gladstone, William
Ewart (PM) 239
golf 233,234
Goodier, Krauss and
Company 101
Granby Row 184
Great Cheetham Street 73
Great Clowes Street
51,67,88,207,329
Great Ducie Street 101
Great Exhibition (1851)
- account of 219,220
Greenheys Abbey 195
Greenheys Lane 194,195
Grosvenor Hotel 115
Guardian Insurance
Company 145,146

Hallé, Sir Charles (conductor)

278,282,284,287
Hanging Ditch 118
Hanover Square 76
Hardman Street 126
Harpurhey Church 321
Hart Street 149
Hayes, Catherine (singer) 283
Haymarket Company 266
Herr Formes (opera singer) 277
Heywood, Abel 187,188
Heywood, John (stationer
& bookseller) 126
Heywood, Oliver 156
Heywood, Sir Benjamin 156
Heywood's Bank 154
Higgins, George (spinner) 297
High Street, Chorlton-
on-Medlock 191
Hilton Street 73
Holker, John Q.C. 107
Hooke, Richard (artist) 80
Horton, Miss P (actress) 257
Houldsworth, Henry 187
Houldsworth, William Henry 69
Howard (jewellers) 151
Hunt and Roskell's
(jewellers) 150
Hurdy-gurdy men 11
Hurst, James 312,313,314

Ionides, Constantine 134
Irving, Henry (actor) 257

James, Edward Q..C. 106,188
Jewish Colony, The
(Strangeways) 102
John Dalton Street 138,139
John Rylands and
Sons, High St 19
Julien, Mons. (performer) 286

Kendal, Milne and Co 134,190
Kendal, Thomas 190
Kersal 76
Kersal Bar 93
Kersal Bus Office 82
Kersal Church 78,144

Kersal Cricket Ground 78
Kersal Edge 63
Kersal Hotel 78
Kersal Moor 78,209,210,233
Kersal Moor Races 77
Kew Bridge Street 101
King Street 160,164,166
Knott Mill Fair 39,47

Langworthy, Edward Riley 193
Langworthy, George 192
lawn tennis 233
Lawson, Sir Wilfrid 240
Leach, John 200
Lee, John B. 311
Liebert, Bernard 292,293
Lime Grove 192,193
Liverpool Cotton Market 311
Lloyd Street 346
Loder, E. J. (conductor) 278
Lodge's Nursery Gardens 50
London, account of first
visit to 220,221
London Road 184
London Road Station (now
Piccadilly station) 174, 184, 219
Lord Brougham 105
Lord Palmerston 197
Lord Roberts 219
Lord Shaftesbury 105
Lower Broughton 207
Lower Broughton Road 73
Lower King Street
134,136,137,183

MacEwen (omnibus
operator) 182
Mackie, Ivie (Mayor of
Manchester) 161,190
Maclure, Sir John William
(1st Baronet) 145,146
Madame Caradori's
Opera Troupe 277
Magnetic Telegraph
Company, The 164
Major Street 149
Manchester Arcade 159

Manchester Art Treasures
Exhibition, 1857 196,198
Manchester Athenaeum
29,54,258
Manchester Carriage
Company 182
Manchester Cathedral 93,113
Manchester Chess Club 142,317
Manchester Courier 157,158
Manchester Cricket Club 186
*Manchester Daily Examiner
and Times* 162,283,347
*Manchester Evening
Mail* 157,158
Manchester Fire Brigade 21
Manchester Free Reference
Library 165,167
Manchester Moors 209
Manchester music 282
Manchester racecourse 61
Manchester Streets, the
navigation of 33
Market Street
122,150,162,169,174
Marx 93
Mather, William 71
Mathews, Charles 254
May Day processions 184
Mechanic's Institution,
Cooper St 27
Meecoe 214,215
Mendel, Sam 292
mesmerism 229
milkcarts 92
Miniati, Theodore
(Merchant) 307
Miss Woolgar 263
Montgomery, Walter (actor) 249
Moor Road, Kersal 78
Moors (Moroccan)
description of 210,212,216
Morocco 212
Morris Dancers 65
Mosley Street 138,166
Mr. Dixon's School 74
Mr. Figgins School 74
Mr. Jackson's School 67

Mr. Makinson's School 73
Mr Sale (solicitor) 85,166
Murray, William
(horse-dealer) 64
Murray Street 88
Murray Street, Higher
Broughton 157

Neill, Robert 294
Newall's Buildings, St
Ann's Square 150, 160
New Bailey Prison, Salford 132
New Bridge Street 73
Norfolk Street 211
Northumberland Street 76

Old Trafford 197
Old Trafford Hotel 51
Oliver, George (merchant) 298
Ollivant's 151
Owens College, Quay St 73,74
Oxford Street 192,194

Park Lane 84
Peacock, H. B. 283
Peel Park 88,100,207,218
Peter Street 128
Piccadilly 122,174,178
Plymouth Grove 189,190,191
Pomona Gardens 116
Pope, Sam K.C. 107
popular songs 230
Portland Place, Piccadilly 187
Portland Street 145,147,149
Postal services (changes in) 171
Presbyterian Chapel,
Lloyd St 346
Prestwich 53
Prestwich Church 76
Prestwich Clough 76,79
Prestwich reservoir 79
Prince's Theatre 258,269
Prince Albert 218
Prince Consort 197
Princess Street
141,142,143,144,150,292
Priory Inn 61

Punch 200
Punch and Judy 11
Pyne-Harrison Opera
Company 280

Quack Doctors 47
Quaker's Chapel, Mount St 24
Quakers 25
Quay Street 73
Queen's Theatre 129,259
Queen Victoria 197,218,219

Racecourse Company 208
railway travel 175
Red Lion Street (now
Barton Square) 157
Reeves, Sims
(actor/singer) 245, 283
Reform Club, The 167
Reuss, Ernest 190
Rev. James Fraser (Bishop
of Manchester) 349
Rev. William McCaw 339
Reverend Arthur Mursell 342
Reverend James Bardsley 333
Reverend Knox-Little 99
Richard and Edward
Broadhurst (agents) 297
Richmond Grove, C-on-M 191
Richter, Dr Hans 288
Ridgefield 139
River Medlock 184
Robert Neill and Sons,
Sherbourne St, Strangeways 20
Rose, Thomas 21,23
Rose, William 21
Royal Exchange
150,159,289,291,325
Royal Italian Opera 278
Rusholme Road 192
Russell, Henry (singer) 284,285
Russell, Lord Chief Justice 109
Rylands, John 186
Rylands Library 186

Satterfield's 154
Sedgwick, Amy

(actress) 248,250
Sewell, James 193
Shakespeare, William 238
Sherbourne Street
50,90,93,131,182,329
Ship Canal Company 208
Shudehill Market 308
Sichel, A. S. (noted
gourmand) 190
Singleton Rd 80
Sir Joseph Heron 198
Slade's School,
Broughton Lane 51
Slater, Mr (solicitor) 143
Smith, Junius (Strangeways
Hall) 100
Sofiano, Mr (trader) 295,296
Sothern (playright) 272
Sounding Alley 138
Southall Street 100
Souvazoglu, Theodore
(merchant) 300
Sowler, Thomas 157
spiritual mediums 229
Spring Gardens 129,166,259
St. Alban's Church,
Waterloo Rd 330,331, 342
St. Alban's Rectory 99
St. Ann's Church 333
St. Ann's Square 34,39,1
22,150,153,154,159,216
St. George's, Hulme 36
St. James's Church 38
St. James's Church,
Broughton 87
St. Jude's 36
St. Mary's Gate
121,122,142,317,318
St. Paul's Church,
Kersal 233,333,334
St. Simon's Church,
Springfield Lane 93,328,329
St. Thomas's Church,
Ardwick Green 185
St. Valentine's Day 226
Statue of Oliver Cromwell 115
Stellfox, George 299

Stony Knolls 88
Stowell, Hugh (preacher) 335
Strangeways 94,100,103,206
Strangeways Hall 100,105
Strangeways Tollbar 93
street hawking 9
Street Vendors 15
Stretford Road 337
Stuart 71
Stuart, John (banker) 84, 348

Table turning 228
Tambaci, Paul 303,304
Tasle Alley 138
Tasle Street 138
taxi cabs 178
Temple Street 6
Teneriffe Street, Broughton, 50
Theatre Royal 18,225,2
45,248,251,269,282
Theatrical recollections 236
The Beehive, Portland St 148
The Circus Tavern, corner
Princess/Portland St 148
The Cornbrook Orphanage 315
The Crescent, Salford 205
The Free Lance (newspaper) 85
The Great Flood of 1866 205
The Grey Horse, Portland St 148
The Grove Inn 88,90
The Irwell 62
The Monkey Inn,
Portland St 148
The Old Boar's Head 137
The Queen's Arms,
Portland St 148
The Star Hotel 134
The Times (London) 161
Thirlmere 79
Thomas Forshaw 211
thought reading 229
Tib Street 178
tollbars 93
Toole, J. L. (actor) 272
Town's Yard 21,144
Town Hall 141,144,167
Trams 181

Trinity Presbyterian Church,
New Bridge Street, 339
Turner, James Aspinall MP 55
Turner, William (son of J A
Turner (MP)) 225,248,299

Uncle Tom's Cabin (play) 273
Union Bank of Manchester 194
Union Chapel, Oxford
Street 341
Unitarian Chapel,
New Bridge St 73
Upper Camp Street 207

Van Amburgh's Circus 30
Victoria Hotel 121
Victoria Market 121,122,124
Victoria Park 193
Victoria Street 118,151
Vine Street 78

Wagner 279
Wallett, "The Queen's Jester" 32
water 92
Waterhouse, Alfred 167
Waterloo Road 94
Whaite's Art Repository 130
Wheeler's (newsagents) 160
Whit-Sunday Walk 329
Whitworth Park 191
Whitworth Street 184
Withy Grove 83,169
Woodland Terrace 51
Woolsack Hotel 101
Worsley Hall 218
Wray, Reverend Cecil 185

York Street 17,166,259

SULLY

THE INSIDE STORY OF MANCHESTER CITY'S NOTORIOUS MAYNE LINE SERVICE CREW

ISBN: 1901746534

£8.95 - Softback - 224 pp

SPECIAL OFFER - MENTION THIS ADVERT AND GET THE BOOK FOR JUST £6 - POST FREE - CALL 0161 872 3319

FOR ALMOST 25 YEARS, Tony Sullivan has been a member of some of the most violent gangs following Manchester City. He has also toured Britain and Europe as a professional 'grafter'. Sullivan ran with the Mayne Line Motorway Service Crew in the early 80s. Here he details how they gained a fearsome reputation nationwide. From St James' Park to Upton Park, the Mayne Line ruled British football, the most fearsome football mob during, hooliganism's 'Golden Age'.

Now, with his hooligan career at a close, 'Sully' looks back on this violent era and relives the good hidings handed out and the kickings received. He also details some of the stunts he and his mates pulled - using the cover of his fellow fans to 'earn' a living in an era before extensive CCTV surveillance, often with unexpected results.

Along the way he contrasts the exploits of the various supporters groups he encountered - the scouser's well known propensity for using a blade, the United supporter's unwillingness to take part in a fight unless they were certain to win it and the craziness of a typical away day in Newcastle city centre in the early eighties.

Later, as police cracked down on hoolganism, many left the scene and the Mayne Line disbanded. Still Sully carried on regardless, the violence and buzz still a 'drug'. Unfortunately, several custodial sentences curtailed his career including, in 1991, an incidental involvement in the Strangeways Riot and its aftermath.

The 1990s also saw a slew of hooligan memoirs hit the nation's bookshelves, often written by people with tenuous connections to the incidents described. Others sought to celebrate hooligan culture as somekind of weekly fashion parade. Sully has little time for either as he explains:

> *"Over the years I have been beaten, stabbed, had bottles cracked on my head and had lads threatening to come round my gaff - but you wont hear me complain. This book is a true account of those years, devoid of sensational bullshit."*

'SULLY'

MORRISSEY'S MANCHESTER

THE ESSENTIAL SMITHS TOUR

PHILL GATENBY

£8.95 - SOFTBACK - 224 PP

SPECIAL OFFER - MENTION THIS ADVERT AND GET THE BOOK FOR JUST £6 - POST FREE - CALL 0161 872 3319

'If you're a Smiths fanatic your memorabilia will hardly be complete without this.'
MANCHESTER EVENING NEWS

"Don't get on the plane without it.'
MORRISSEY-TOUR.COM

---

yrically unique, Morrissey saw post-industrial Manchester differently. Where most recognised the derelict remains of a Victorian powerhouse, he saw humour, where others saw post-industrial squalor, he felt frisson of romance. As a result Manchester became as much a part of e Smiths output as the guitars, drums and vocals. As their fame grew, ingers in far away lands wondered about the location of the 'Cemetry tes' or the setting of 'Vicar in a Tutu'. Unusually, these places still exist l provide the devotee with places of pilgramage - could Manchester offer thing else?

In the first edition of this guidebook, Phill Gatenby set out three tours ering 20 or more sites that either featured in The Smiths music or were damental to their development as a band - from early rehearsal spaces the scene of their most memorable gigs. Now updated, Morrissey's nchester has added new places to visit, more lyrical references and more kground information on one of the world's most influential bands.

However the most fundamental change any reader/visitor will notice are continual changes to Manchester itself - a city in perpetual flux. Since first edition venues have either been demolished, refurbished or shorn heir identity - hence the need for an update. Now containing 40 new ges, an improved layout, a revised map of the city centre, Morrissey's nchester has been fully updated.

COMPLETIST'S DELIGHT
THE FULL EMPIRE BACK LIST

ISBN	TITLE	AUTHOR	PRICE
1901746003	SF Barnes: His Life and Times	A Searle	£14.95
1901746011	Chasing Glory	R Grillo	£7.95
190174602X	Three Curries and a Shish Kebab	R Bott	£7.99
1901746038	Seasons to Remember	D Kirkley	£6.95
1901746046	Cups For Cock-Ups+	A Shaw	£8.99
1901746054	Glory Denied	R Grillo	£8.95
1901746062	Standing the Test of Time	B Alley	£16.95
1901746070	The Encyclopaedia of Scottish Cricket	D Potter	£9.99
1901746089	The Silent Cry	J MacPhee	£7.99
1901746097	The Amazing Sports Quiz Book	F Brockett	£6.99
1901746100	I'm Not God, I'm Just a Referee	R Entwistle	£7.99
1901746119	The League Cricket Annual Review 2000	ed. S. Fish	£6.99
1901746143	Roger Byrne - Captain of the Busby Babes	I McCartney	£16.95
1901746151	The IT Manager's Handbook	D Miller	£24.99
190174616X	Blue Tomorrow	M Meehan	£9.99
1901746178	Atkinson for England	G James	£5.99
1901746186	Think Cricket	C Bazalgette	£6.00
1901746194	The League Cricket Annual Review 2001	ed. S. Fish	£7.99
1901746208	Jock McAvoy - Fighting Legend *	B Hughes	£9.95
1901746216	The Tommy Taylor Story*	B Hughes	£8.99
1901746224	Willie Pep*+	B Hughes	£9.95
1901746232	For King & Country*+	B Hughes	£8.95
1901746240	Three In A Row	P Windridge	£7.99
1901746259	Violet - Life of a legendary goalscorer+PB	R Cavanagh	£16.95
1901746267	Starmaker	B Hughes	£16.95
1901746283	Morrissey's Manchester	P Gatenby	£5.99
1901746305	The IT Manager's Handbook (e-book)	D Miller	£17.99
1901746313	Sir Alex, United & Me	A Pacino	£8.99
1901746321	Bobby Murdoch, Different Class	D Potter	£10.99
190174633X	Goodison Maestros	D Hayes	£5.99
1901746348	Anfield Maestros	D Hayes	£5.99
1901746364	Out of the Void	B Yates	£9.99
1901746356	The King - Denis Law, hero of the...	B Hughes	£17.95
1901746372	The Two Faces of Lee Harvey Oswald	G B Fleming	£8.99
1901746380	My Blue Heaven	D Friend	£10.99
1901746399	Violet - life of a legendary goalscorer	B Hughes	£11.99
1901746402	Quiz Setting Made Easy	J Dawson	£7.99
1901746410	The Insider's Guide to Manchester United	J Doherty	£20
1901746437	Catch a Falling Star	N Young	£17.95
1901746453	Birth of the Babes	T Whelan	£12.95
190174647X	Back from the Brink	J Blundell	£10.95
1901746488	The Real Jason Robinson	D Swanton	£17.95

1901746496	This Simple Game	K Barnes	£14.95
1901746518	The Complete George Best	D Phillips	£10.95
1901746526	From Goalline to Touch line	J Crompton	£16.95
1901746534	Sully	A Sullivan	£8.95
1901746542	Memories...	P Hince	£10.95
1901746550	Reminiscences of Manchester	L Hayes	£11.95
1901746569	Morrissey's Manchester (2nd Ed.)	P Gatenby	£8.95

* Originally published by Collyhurst & Moston Lads Club
+ Out of print PB Superceded by Paperback edition
To order any of these books email: enquiries@empire-uk.com or call 0161 872 3319